Pierson Guides

COLORADO

SKI ATLAS
& WINTER RECREATION GUIDE

TABLE OF CONTENTS

Published by

Pierson Graphics Corp.

800 Lincoln St. • Denver, Colorado • 80203
(303) 623-4299 • (800) 456-8703

www.coloradomaps.com

Base cartographic rendering compiled and prepared by ISSI. Topography, hydrography, transportation, locales, airports, and summits adapted from USGS digital data sources. Federal land boundaries from the Bureau of Land Management. Projection - UTM, NAD27, Zone 13.

ISSI Consulting Group, Inc.
999 18th Street, Suite 1450, South Tower
Denver, CO 80202
(303) 292-4142
www.issiinc.com

ISSI is a multi-disciplinary firm offering services in: GIS - Large Format Scanning -
Document Conversion - Regulatory Compliance - Information Technology - Policy, Science, and Engineering

Pierson Graphics Corp.
Quality mapping of Colorado and the world since 1979.

LEE RITCHIE
President
PAUL G. GIBBS
Vice President & C.O.O. &
General Manager

---**SALES AND MARKETING DIVISION**---
BRUCE FULLER
Senior Vice President
Sales & Marketing
MYRA ARMON KEEBLE
BRAD WIERSCHKE
Sales Coordinators-Special Accounts

---**PUBLICATIONS DIVISION**---
CHRIS PAPPAS
Vice President & Division Manager
VANESSA REEVES
Assistant Manager of Cartography &
Director of GIS Development
ERIN TENORIO
Director of Data Acquisition
CHARLOTTE SHISKA • ELLEN ARTHURS
Geographic Research Analyst
STEFFANI McCHESNEY
Editor / Writer
KEVIN KULUVAR • DOUG RULISON
GIS Development
LAURIE QUERQUES
AARON RHODES • ROBERT JACOBUS
Cartographers

---**CUSTOM MAPS/**
DESIGN & PUBLISHING---
ANNA SCHMIDT
Production Manager
REVA RICH
Publishing Designer
PATRICIO GARCIA
Manager of Photography

---**RETAIL DIVISION**---
JEFF SHIFFER
Vice President &
Manager of Retail Operations
JOE WOODWARD
Purchasing Manager
DAVID SUNDBY
Retail Store Manager (Hampden)
ROBERTA TOWER
Telemarketing
NICK ZARLENGO II
Web Site Administrator
PETER ZUNIGA • SOLVEIG KJESETH
ROLAND HOLTZ • SEAN HLOUSEK
KURT SCHUELKE • BRIAN CHANECKA
JOHN GIRVAN • VIRGINIA LIND
MORGAN BROWNING
Retail Sales Associates
PATRICK GRIEGO
Retail Production Manager
JASON BOYER
Shipping and Receiving
ANDREW ALEXANDER
Transportation

---**ADMINISTRATION**---
JOANNA FORD
Manager of Human Resources &
Administration
JEROME ROGERS
Manager of Inventory Control
TERRY CRANE
Receiving Clerk
ANJI TECHMEYER
Accounting Clerk

PRINTED IN CANADA

LEGEND

167	Freeways Interchange with Exit Number	
	U.S. Highways	
15	State Highways Mileage Between Points	
	County Road	
	Forest Road	
	Residential Road	
— · — · —	State Boundaries	
	County Boundaries	
• • • •	Continental Divide	
T 79 W	Township and Range	
Mt. Elbert 14,433 ×	Mountain Peaks & Elevations	
Tennessee Pass 10,404	Mountain Passes & Elevations	

♿	Wheelchair Accessible (ADA)
⚑	Public Campground
⚡	Trailheads
🎿	Downhill Skiing
🎿	Cross-Country Skiing
▲	Point of Interest
✈	General Aviation Airport
✈	Passenger Airports
✈	Military Airports
⭐	Scenic Byways
★	State Capital

Tribal Lands
BLM
BLM - Wilderness Designation
Bureau of Reclamation
Department of Defense
National Forest Service
National Forest Service - Wilderness Designation
Fish and Wildlife Service
National Park Service
Municipalities with Populations Greater than 25,000
Other Federal Lands

○	0 - 1,000	◯	County Seat 0 - 1,000
◎	1,000 - 5,000	◎	County Seat 1,000 - 5,000
◉	5,000 - 10,000	◉	County Seat 5,000 - 10,000
○	10,000 - 25,000	◯	County Seat 10,000 - 25,000
◎	25,000 - 50,000	◎	County Seat 25,000 - 50,000
◉	50,000 & over	◉	County Seat 50,000 & over
•	Unincorporated Area	•	Unincorporated Area

USING THIS ATLAS

The Colorado Recreation Atlas has many features to assist you in planning trips and traveling around the state. The book is divided into four major sections for easy use. Study the legend to become familiar with the symbols, which locate campsites, trailheads and ski areas. Scenic Byways and select ADA accessible areas are also marked.

Safety is always the most important consideration when planning a trip in winter. Always check the weather reports and be sure that you have the proper equipment for the trip you are planning. Do not try to drive a family sedan on a four-wheel drive road. For statewide road conditions call (303) 639-1111. See the General Information page for more contact information.

SKIERS CODE OF RESPONSIBILITY

- Always stay in control and be able to stop or avoid other people or objects.
- People ahead of you have the right of way. It is your responsibility to avoid them.
- You must not stop where you obstruct a trail or are not visible from above.
- Whenever starting downhill or merging into a trail, look uphill and yield to others.
- Always use devices to help prevent runaway equipment.
- Observe all posted signs and warning. Keep off closed trails and out of closed areas.
- Prior to using any lift, you must have the knowledge and ability to load, ride, and unload safely.
- Know the code. It's your responsibility. This is a partial list. Be safety conscious.

WINTER SAFETY

Colorado is beautiful in winter. And dangerous. Take the weather seriously. Conditions can change rapidly. Altitude is another factor to be aware of. Thirty percent of visitors to the state suffer from some form of altitude sickness. Use proper precautions to make your outdoor experience safe and enjoyable.

Driving: Heed all road condition warnings. Radio stations around the state provide current weather and road information. The radio frequencies for the area you are traveling in are posted on signs along the highways. Have your car winterized. Be sure the vehicle you are traveling in is in good working order and can handle the driving conditions you will be facing. Several telephone numbers and web sites with current weather information are listed in the General Information section on page 103. Check before you go.

Weather Conditions: Dress for the occasion. You don't want to have to walk through a blizzard in a windbreaker and sneakers if you have a breakdown. Wear sunscreen even if the day is overcast. Stock your car with safety equipment including a small shovel, flares, and jumper cables. A blanket, nonperishable food items and a candle and matches will help if you get stuck in your car for any length of time.

Avalanches: Safety is even more important in the backcountry in winter. Take an avalanche safety course to be prepared for the risks involved in traveling away from groomed and patrolled areas. Consider carrying an avalanche beacon. Several organizations offering courses and current avalanche conditions are listed in the General Information section. Ignorance can kill you.

SCENIC BYWAYS

www.dot.state.co.us/public/recreationtourism/coloradobyways/
Contact the local BLM office or Ranger District for additional byway information.
Note: Portions of byways may have seasonal closings and may be accessible only by high-clearance 4-wheel drive vehicles.

ALPINE LOOP - Length: 63 miles Driving time: 4 to 6 hours
Contact: BLM-Gunnison Resource Area, (970) 641-0471 • p. 28 ❄ ▲

CACHE LA POUDRE-NORTH PARK - Length: 101 miles Driving time: 3 hours
Contact: Arapaho/ Roosevelt NF, Estes-Poudre Ranger District
(970) 498-2719 • p. 5, 7

COLORADO RIVER HEADWATERS - Length: 80 miles Driving Time: 2 hours
Contact: Grand County Historical Society (970) 725-3939 • p. 9

FLAT TOPS TRAIL - Length: 82 miles Driving time: 2 hours
Contact: USFS - Yampa Ranger District (970) 638-4516 • p. 2

FRONTIER PATHWAYS - Length: 103 miles Driving time: 2 hours
Contact: Greenhorn Valley Chamber of Commerce (719) 676-3000 • p. 30

GOLD BELT TOUR - Length: 131 miles Driving time: 5 hours
Contact: BLM-Royal Gorge Resource Area (719) 275-0631 • p. 24 ❄ ▲

GRAND MESA - Length: 63 miles Driving time: 2 hours
Contact: Grand Mesa Byway Association (800) 436-3041 • p. 3, 21 ❄

GUANELLA PASS - Length: 22 miles Driving time: 1 hour
Contact: Clear Creek County Tourism Board (303) 567-0607 • p. 14

HIGHWAY OF LEGENDS - Length: 82 miles Driving Time: 2 hours
Contact: Scenic Highway of Legends Corp (719) 742-3822 • p. 30

LOS CAMINOS ANTIGUOS - Length: 129 miles Driving time: 3 hours
Contact: BLM-San Luis Resource Area (719) 589-4975 • p. 30

MOUNT EVANS - Length: 28 miles (one way) Driving time: 1 hour (one way)
Contact: USFS - Clear Creek Ranger District (303) 567-2901 • p. 14 ❄

PAWNEE PIONEER TRAILS - Length: 125 miles Driving time: 2 hours
Contact: USFS - Pawnee National Grasslands (970) 353-5004 • p. 8, 17

PEAK TO PEAK - Length: 55 miles Driving time: 80 minutes
Contact: Boulder Convention & Visitor's Bureau (303) 442-2911 • p. 10

SAN JUAN SKYWAY - Length: 236 Driving time: 6 hours
Contact: Community Services, Fort Lewis College (970) 247-7310 • p. 27

SANTA FE TRAIL - Length: 188 miles Driving time: 4 hours
Contact: Trinidad/Las Animas Economic Development Inc
(719) 846-9412 • p. 31

SILVER THREAD - Length: 75 miles Driving time: 2 hours
Contact: Creede Chamber of Commerce (719) 658-2374 • p. 28

SOUTH PLATTE RIVER TRAIL - Length: 19 miles Driving time: 30 minutes
Contact: Sedgwick County Economic Development (970) 474-3504 • p. 18

TOP OF THE ROCKIES - Length: 82 miles Driving time: 2 hours
Contact: Greater Leadville Area Chamber of Commerce (719) 486-3900 / (800) 933-3901 • p. 13

TRAIL OF THE ANCIENTS - Length: 114 miles Driving time: 3 hours
Contact: Anasazi Heritage Center (970) 882-4811 • p. 27

UNAWEEP/TABEGUACHE - Length: 133 miles Driving time: 3 hours
Contact: Bureau of Land Management, Montrose District Office
(970) 249-6047 • p. 21

WEST ELK LOOP - Length: 205 miles Driving time: 6 to 8 hours
Contact: U.S. Forest Service, Carbondale (970) 963-2266 • p. 22 ❄

❄ Portions of Scenic Byway closed in winter.

▲ 4-wheel drive needed in some areas.

Mileage Between COLORADO Cities

	Alamosa	Aspen	Boulder	Breckenridge	Brighton	Buena Vista	Burlington	Canon City	Central City	Colorado Springs	Cortez	Craig	Denver	Durango	Eagle	Estes Park	Fort Collins	Fort Morgan	Glenwood Springs	Grand Junction	Greeley	Gunnison	Julesburg	La Junta	Lamar	Leadville	Limon	Longmont	Loveland	Montrose	Pueblo	Salida	Springfield	Steamboat Springs	Sterling	Trinidad	Vail	Walsenburg
Aspen	163																																					
Boulder	227	168																																				
Breckenridge	154	100	87																																			
Brighton	231	179	26	98																																		
Buena Vista	100	63	132	59	136																																	
Burlington	296	308	188	245	180	245																																
Canon City	139	145	142	96	134	82	195																															
Central City	217	144	36	63	52	119	199	146																														
Colorado Springs	163	157	97	105	89	94	150	45	102																													
Cortez	194	277	392	319	396	264	490	302	382	347																												
Craig	296	157	219	146	226	197	373	242	191	251	349																											
Denver	212	162	30	81	22	117	163	115	34	70	377	208																										
Durango	149	249	347	274	350	219	445	257	336	302	45	321	332																									
Eagle	192	72	134	66	146	92	292	163	110	172	290	125	128	262																								
Estes Park	280	204	36	123	59	185	230	183	63	138	445	182	71	399	165																							
Fort Collins	274	223	46	141	53	179	224	177	82	132	439	202	65	394	189	42																						
Fort Morgan	290	238	87	157	61	195	141	193	111	148	455	285	81	409	204	102	81																					
Glenwood Springs	204	41	165	97	177	104	324	187	141	198	259	116	159	231	31	196	220	236																				
Grand Junction	249	130	254	186	265	193	412	248	230	287	197	152	248	169	120	285	308	324	89																			
Greeley	264	212	51	131	33	169	193	166	86	122	428	233	54	383	178	50	30	51	209	298																		
Gunnison	122	146	211	138	214	83	316	121	201	166	201	278	196	173	176	265	258	273	162	126	247																	
Julesburg	393	339	190	260	164	298	123	285	214	240	558	364	182	512	308	205	162	103	339	427	154	376																
La Junta	147	247	202	199	194	184	159	102	207	105	341	345	175	296	265	243	237	181	290	350	227	224	265															
Lamar	202	302	229	254	220	239	107	158	239	159	397	400	203	351	320	270	264	198	345	405	251	279	230	56														
Leadville	134	59	109	41	120	34	267	117	85	129	299	162	103	254	54	145	164	179	89	170	153	118	282	220	275													
Limon	228	230	111	168	103	168	77	118	122	73	421	296	86	375	215	153	147	83	246	335	135	239	167	98	117	190												
Longmont	247	196	15	115	26	152	197	150	51	105	412	215	38	367	150	33	19	73	193	282	35	211	182	210	287	137	120											
Loveland	261	210	34	129	41	167	212	165	69	120	427	212	53	381	177	30	13	72	208	296	21	245	175	225	252	151	135	18										
Montrose	187	141	276	203	280	149	382	186	265	231	136	213	261	108	154	319	323	339	123	61	312	65	442	289	344	183	305	296	311									
Pueblo	122	184	189	136	131	121	191	39	144	42	316	282	112	271	202	180	174	190	227	287	164	161	280	64	119	155	114	147	162	226								
Salida	83	88	153	80	157	26	253	57	143	102	248	222	138	202	118	207	200	216	193	189	66	319	160	215	60	176	173	188	132	97								
Springfield	233	348	274	300	266	285	153	204	285	205	427	446	249	382	366	315	310	244	391	451	296	325	276	101	46	319	163	283	297	390	165	261						
Steamboat Springs	254	155	177	104	184	154	331	200	148	209	373	42	166	345	83	140	160	243	114	194	238	322	303	371	120	254	173	170	237	240	180	416						
Sterling	335	281	132	202	106	204	141	227	156	182	499	304	121	454	249	147	102	45	280	379	96	318	59	206	224	224	108	123	117	383	221	260	270	262				
Trinidad	109	242	242	221	216	179	237	125	229	127	304	367	197	259	272	265	259	252	283	349	249	217	336	81	136	214	169	232	247	283	86	154	123	325	277			
Vail	172	102	104	36	116	62	262	133	80	142	320	131	98	292	30	140	159	174	61	150	172	201	148	156	278	258	319	38	185	132	147	184	172	98	336	219	310	
Walsenburg	73	205	187	184	179	142	223	88	192	90	267	330	160	222	235	228	222	238	247	307	212	181	327	130	177	156	176	160	289	263	49	117	160	289	263	37	215	
Wray	351	324	173	243	147	281	55	251	197	206	540	330	166	495	290	187	167	86	321	410	137	359	67	217	163	265	133	164	158	424	246	301	209	327	85	292	260	279

Come out and enjoy some of the best snow in the world. Many opportunities are available using specialized training and equipment. With the new adaptive sports equipment, almost anyone can participate, and even compete, in all the winter activities Colorado is famous for.

Photo by John Weiland / National Sports Center for the Disabled

Three organizations of note are the nonprofit National Sports Center for the Disabled (NSCD), the Colorado Ski School for the Blind (CSSB) and the Adaptive Sports Association (ASA). They are all dedicated to creating a sense of self-esteem and athletic achievement in their students.

Fifteen ski areas in the state have special programs offering lessons in downhill and cross-country skiing, snowboarding, and competition ski racing. Several ski schools and associations also offer training for individuals who want to become instructors and guides. Check the ski area listings for telephone numbers and other contact information.

Colorado has several different European-style hut systems in the backcountry. Some huts are built to ADA standards of accessibility. The Tenth Mountain Division Hut Association and the Summit Hut system each have ADA accessible huts. Getting to these huts requires some ingenuity. Two methods used are snowmobiles and ski patrol-type sleds. Four-wheel drive vehicles are possible where permitted. A yurt stay is available through Never Summer Nordic, Inc.

ADAPTIVE SPORTS ASSOCIATION
PO Box 1884
Durango, CO 81302
Phone: (970) 259-0374
Web sites: www.ski-purg.com/adaptive.htm or www.frontier.net/~asa/

COLORADO SKI SCHOOL FOR THE BLIND
Box 558
Avon, CO 81620
Phone: (970) 479-3072 Voice
      (970) 479-3071 TTY/TDD

NATIONAL SPORTS CENTER FOR THE DISABLED
PO Box 1290
Winter Park, CO 80482
Phone: (970) 726-1540
      (303) 316-1504
Web site: www.nscd.org

Photo by Darcy Kiefel / National Sports Center for the Disabled

NEVER SUMMER NORDIC, INC.
Box 1983
Fort Collins, Co 80522
Phone: (970) 482-9411
Web site: www.neversummernordic.com

SUMMIT HUTS ASSOCIATION
P.O. Box 2830
Breckenridge, CO 80424
Phone: (970) 453-8583
Web site: www.huts.org

TENTH MOUNTAIN DIVISION HUT ASSOCIATION
1280 Ute Ave., Suite 12
Aspen, CO 81611
Phone: (970) 925-5775
Web site: www.huts.org

US DEAF SKI & SNOWBOARD ASSOCIATION
Web site: www.usdssa.org

Photo by Darcy Kiefel / National Sports Center for the Disabled

SKI AREAS

NAME OF SKI AREA	INFORMATION	WEB SITE	PAGE	GRID	SKI AREA PAGE
Arapahoe Basin	(888) ARAPHOE / (970) 468-0718	www.arapahoebasin.com	14	A-1	36
Aspen Highlands	(800) 525-6200 / (970) 925-1220	www.skiaspen.com	4	C-3	37
Aspen Mountain	(800) 525-6200 / (970) 925-1220	www.skiaspen.com	4	C-3	38
Beaver Creek	(970) 845-6610	www.snow.com	13	B-1	39-40
Berthoud Pass	(800) 754-2378 / (303) 569-0100	www.berthoudpass.com	10	B-4	41
Breckenridge	(800) 789-SNOW	www.snow.com	14	A-2	41-42
Buttermilk	(800) 525-6200 / (970) 920-1220	www.skiaspen.com	4	C-3	43
Copper Mountain Resort	(800) 458-8386 / (970) 968-2882	www.ski-copper.com	13	C-2	44
Crested Butte	(888) TO-POWDER / (970) 349-2333	www.crestedbutteresort.com	4/22	C-2	45
Cuchara Mountain	(888) 282-4272 / (719) 742-3163	www.cuchara.com	30	A-3	46
Eldora	(888) 2-ELDORA / (303) 440-8700	www.eldora.com	10	C-3	47
Howelsen Hill	970-879-8499	www.ci.steamboat.co.us	2	C-2	48
Keystone	(800) 468-5004 / (970) 496-2316	www.keystone.snow.com	14	A-1	49
Loveland	(800) 736-3SKI / (303) 569-3203	www.skiloveland.com	14	A-1	50
Monarch	(888) 996-7669 / (719) 539-3573	www.skimonarch.com	23	A-3	51
Powderhorn	(970) 268-5700	www.powderhorn.com	21	C-1	52
Purgatory	(970) 247-9000	www.ski-purg.com	27	C-2	53-54
Silver Creek Ski & Golf Ranch	(800) 754-7458 / (970) 887-3384	www.silvercreek-resort.com	10	A-2	55
Ski Cooper	(719) 486-3684	www.skicooper.com	13	B-3	56
Snowmass	(800) 526-6200 / (970) 925-1220	www.skiaspen.com	4	C-3	57-58
Steamboat	(970) 879-6111	www.steamboat-ski.com	2	C-2	59
Sunlight Mountain Resort	(800) 445-7931 / (970) 945-7491	www.sunlightmtn.com	4	B-3	60
Telluride	(800) 801-4832 / (970) 728-6900	www.telski.com	28	A-2	61
Vail	(800) 525-2287 / (970) 476-5601	www.snow.com	13	B-1	64
Winter Park/Mary Jane	(970) 726-5514 / (303) 892-0961	www.skiwinterpark.com	10	B-3	65
Wolf Creek	(970) 264-5639	www.wolfcreekski.com	28	C-3	66

© Jack Affleck / Vail Resorts

© Byron Hetzler / Berthoud Pass Ski Area

Photo by T.R. Youngstrom / Telluride Ski Resort

© Winter Park Resort

Photo courtesy of Steamboat Ski Area

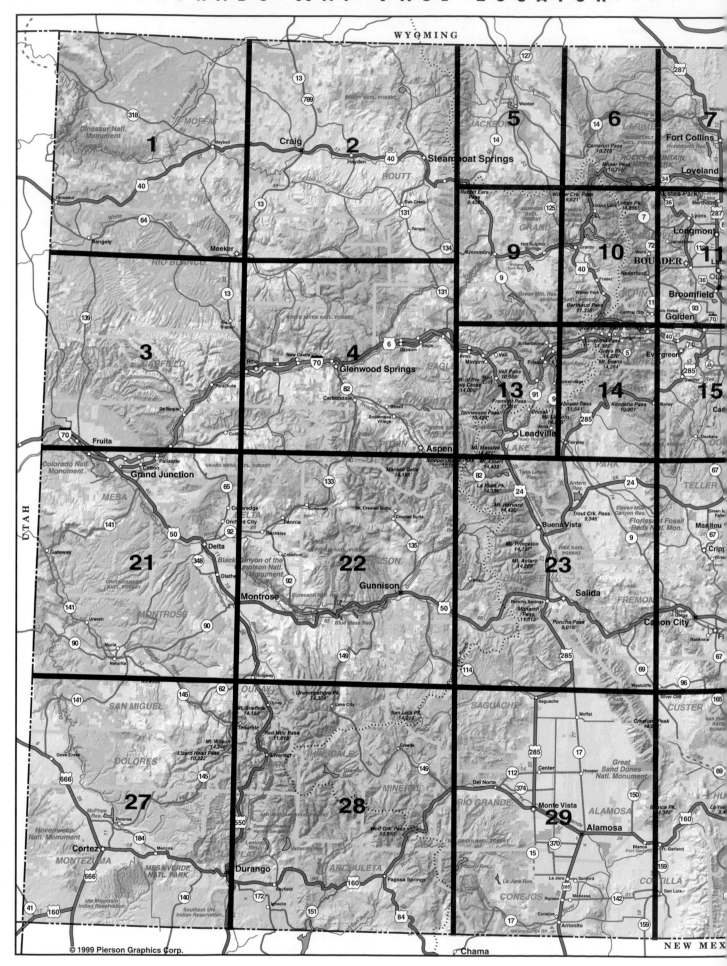

© 1999 Pierson Graphics Corp.

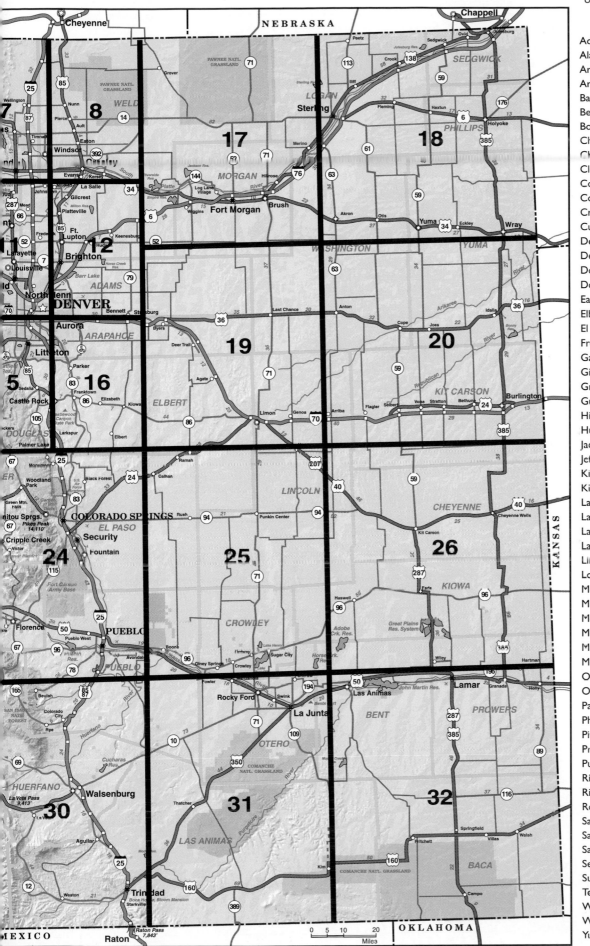

COUNTIES
U.S. CENSUS 1997
POPULATION
ESTIMATE

COUNTIES
U.S. CENSUS 1997
POPULATION
ESTIMATE

County	Population
Adams	316,066
Alamosa	14,374
Arapahoe	463,201
Archuleta	8,515
Baca	4,398
Bent	5,480
Boulder	261,617
Chaffee	15,022
Cheyenne	2,277
Clear Creek	8,917
Conejos	7,826
Costilla	3,643
Crowley	4,265
Custer	3,292
Delta	25,820
Denver	498,985
Dolores	1,706
Douglas	126,248
Eagle	31,950
Elbert	17,527
El Paso	480,041
Fremont	42,956
Garfield	37,627
Gilpin	3,967
Grand	9,843
Gunnison	12,198
Hinsdale	698
Huerfano	6,722
Jackson	1,533
Jefferson	496,656
Kiowa	1,666
Kit Carson	7,174
Lake	6,323
La Plata	40,145
Larimer	226,021
Las Animas	14,488
Lincoln	5,611
Logan	18,102
Mesa	110,681
Mineral	678
Moffat	12,291
Montezuma	22,269
Montrose	30,278
Morgan	25,149
Otero	20,858
Ouray	3,200
Park	12,730
Phillips	4,322
Pitkin	13,577
Prowers	13,652
Pueblo	132,901
Rio Blanco	6,287
Rio Grande	11,403
Routt	17,230
Saguache	5,906
San Juan	557
San Miguel	5,322
Sedgwick	2,604
Summit	18,468
Teller	19,790
Washington	4,627
Weld	155,582
Yuma	9,372

COLORADO RECREATIONAL

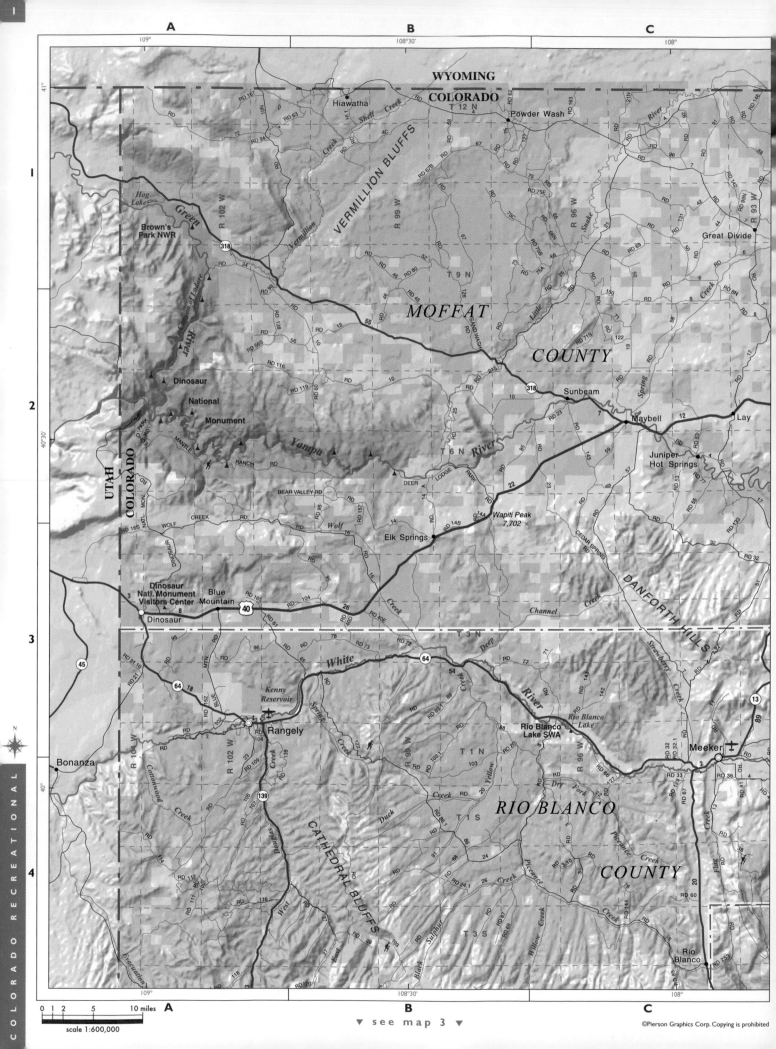

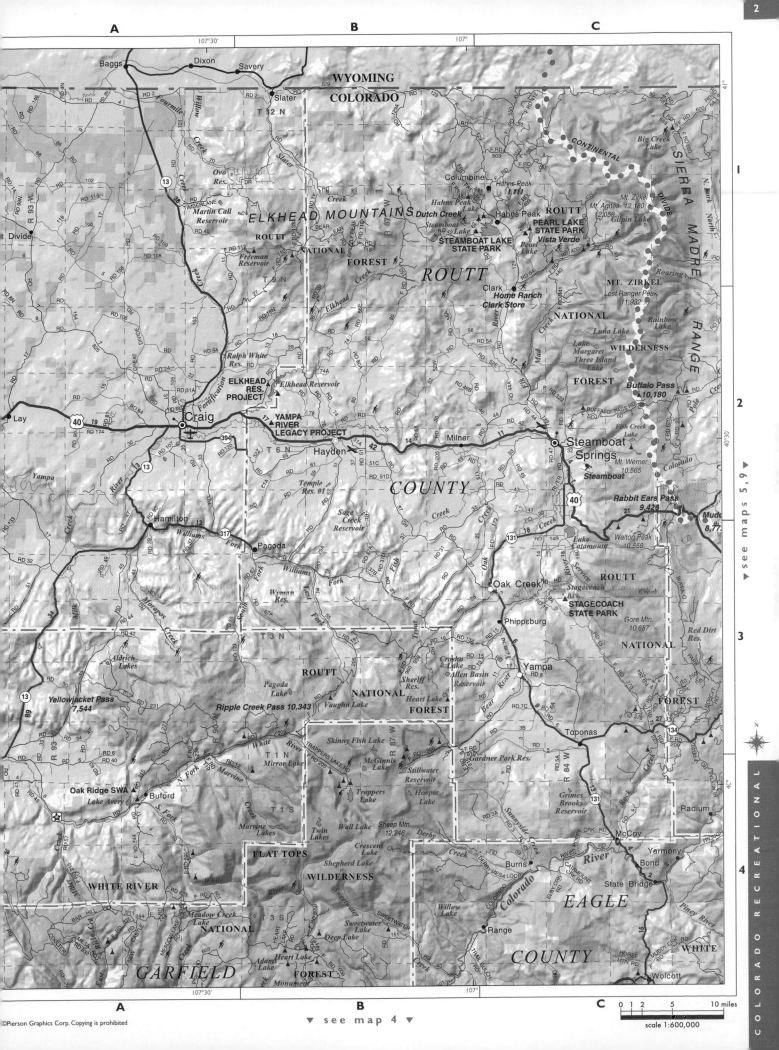

3

COLORADO RECREATIONAL

A — Rangely, 104, 109°, R 104 W, R 102 W

Cottonwood Creek, Douglas Creek, Evacuation Creek, West Creek, East Creek, Salt Creek, Cathedral Bluffs

Douglas Pass 8,266
Baxter Pass 8,422

139

UTAH / COLORADO

RIO BLANCO COUNTY

Rio Blanco Lake SWA
64
Meeker

Dry Fork, Yellow Creek, Piceance Creek, Black Sulphur Creek, Willow Creek, Rio Blanco

13

ROAN PLATEAU
GARFIELD COUNTY

ROAN CLIFFS

Rifle
70   81   Rulison
MORRISANIA
Parachute 75   Battlement Mesa
6   60   13
BATTLEMENT MESA

Mack Mesa Lake
HIGHLINE STATE PARK
Highline Lake

DeBeque 62

GRAND MESA

BOOK CLIFFS
GRAND VALLEY

70   Mack
Loma
6   Fruita
Horse Thief Canyon SWA
RABBIT
Colorado

Colorado River

ISLAND ACRES STATE PARK
Cameo
Palisade
Clifton

De Beque Canyon

330   Collbran
VEGA STATE PARK

65
Molina
Mesa
GRAND

MESA COUNTY

Grand Junction
Redlands
Colorado National Monument
Orchard Mesa
Mesa College
COLORADO RIVER STATE PARK
340

Powderhorn
Skyway
Grand Mesa
Island Lake
Griffith Lake
Bonham Res.
Leon Lake
Bayou Lake
Park Reservoir

MESA
FOR

Thompson Reservoirs
Glade Park
Whitewater
50
Hallenbeck Res.
Juanita Res.
Cheney Reservoir

GRAND

Cedaredge
65

DELTA COUNTY

Schraeder Res.
GRAND MESA NATIONAL FOREST
Fruita Reservoirs
141   44

West Creek, Casto Res., Big Dominguez Creek, Gunnison River

Broughton
Dominguez
Escalante
North Delta
Delta
Austin
92
Orchard City
Fruit Growers Res.

0 1 2 5   10 miles   A
scale 1:600,000

B   C

©Pierson Graphics Corp. Copying is prohibited

A B C

107°30' 107° 134

Oak Ridge SWA
Lake Avery
Buford
N. Fork Marvine

Mirror Lake
White River

Skinny Fish Lake
McGinnis Lake
Stillwater Reservoir
Hooper Lake
Trappers Lake
Wall Lake
Darby Creek
Twin Lakes
Sheep Mtn. 12,246

Toponas
131
Gardner Park Res.
Bear
Grimes Reservoir
Brooks Reservoir
Sunnyside
POPPY CRK RD
McCoy
Radium

FLAT TOPS WILDERNESS

WHITE RIVER

NATIONAL

Meadow Creek Lake

Crescent Lake

Range

EAGLE
Bond
Yarmony
State Bridge
WHITE

1

Heart Lake
Adams Lake
FOREST
Monument Lake
Blue Lake
Haypress Lake
Deep Lake

Sweetwater Lake
Sweetwater

Willow Lake

Wolcott 157
Eagle River

RIFLE FALLS STATE PARK
RIFLE GAP STATE PARK
13
HARVEY GAP STATE PARK
Rifle Gap Res.
325

New Castle
Chacra
West Glenwood
No Name
Glenwood Springs
Historic Area

Dotsero
183 55 140
Gypsum
Eagle 147
BELLYACHE RD
Edwards 163
6 10
COUNTY

GLENWOOD CANYON
70
AMTRAK

WHITE RIVER
SYLVAN LAKE STATE PARK
Mt. Jackson 13,670
HOLY WILDE

2

Rifle
6
Silt
97
Colorado
GARFIELD COUNTY

82
Consolidated Res.
Van Springs Res.
Spring Park Reservoir
Cattle Creek

NATIONAL
Crooked Creek Pass 10,002
Woods Lake
Sylvan Lake

BATTLEMENT MESA

Ski Sunlight
Carbondale
Basalt Christine Unit SWA
Basalt
Fryingpan
Meredith
Biglow
Diamond J Ranch
Nast
39°30'

GRAND MESA
NATIONAL
WHITE RIVER
FOREST

Thompson

Mt. Sopris 12,953
133
Snowmass
Woody Creek
PITKIN
FOREST
Lenado
Crystal River

3

GA STATE PARK
Vega Reservoir
GRAND MESA
NATIONAL
FOREST
Bonham Res.
Leon Lake

NATIONAL
Redstone
Rodstone Inn
MAROON BELLS
Capitol Pk. 14,130
Snowmass Lake
Snowmass Village
Wildcat Res.
Snowmass
SNOWMASS
WILDERNESS
Buttermilk
Aspen
Aspen Highlands
Aspen Mountain
82
HUNTER FRYINGPAN WILDERNESS
Warren Lakes
Grizzly Res.
38

MESA
Overland Reservoir
Bailey Reservoir
Goodenough Reservoir
Marble
McClure Pass 8,755
DIVIDE
Chair Mtn. 12,721
Beaver Lake
Snowmass Mtn. 14,092
N. Maroon Peak 14,014
Maroon Peak 14,156
Maroon Lake
Pyramid Peak 14,018
Ashcroft
Castle Peak 14,265
Ashcroft
Taylor Pass 11,928
Taylor Lake

COUNTY

ELK MOUNTAINS

4

DELTA
Patterson Reservoirs
RAGGEDS
Treasure Mtn. 13,526
Purple Mtn. 12,957
WILDERNESS
Schofield Pass 10,707
Star Peak 13,521
Lily Pond
Spring Creek Res.

Somerset
Paonia Res.
PAONIA STATE PARK
Gothic
Mt. Crested Butte
Crested Butte
Taylor Park Res.
Matchless Mtn. 12,383

Bowie
Paonia
133
187
Minnesota Res.
Mt. Gunnison 12,719
Lost Lake
GUNNISON
Ohio Pass 10,074
Kebler Pass 9,980
Lake Irwin
Irwin
Peanut Lake
Crested Butte
Whetstone Mtn. 12,595
135

92 13
Hotchkiss
Lazear
Beaver Reservoir
MOUNTAINS
NATIONAL
Baldwin
Mt. Guero

COUNTY

A B C

107°30' 107°

0 1 2 5 10 miles

scale 1:600,000

▼ see maps 13,23 ▶

COLORADO RECREATIONAL

COLORADO

ROUTT NATIONAL FOREST

Davis Pk. 11,422

Big Creek Lakes

Seven Lakes

Red Elephant Mtn. ×11,569

Little Agnes Mtn. 11,233

Big Agnes Mtn. × 12,059

Mt. Zirkel × 12,180

Blue Lake / Blue Hill

Twin Lake / Ute Lake

Gilpin Lake

Three Island Lake

Beaver Lake

Bear Mtn. 11,601

Bighorn Lakes

Lake Katherine

Pine Creek

Red Canyon Res.

SIERRA MADRE RANGE

MT. ZIRKEL WILDERNESS

Wolverine Lake

Ptarmigan Lake

Pristine Lake

The Dome × 11,739

Lost Ranger Pk. × 11,932

Roxy Ann Lake

Slide Lake

Luna Lake

Lake Elbert

Aqua Fria Lake

Rainbow Lake

Rasberry

Delaney Lakes

Delaney Butte Lakes SWA

Lake John **SWA**

Lake John

Boettcher Lake

NORTH PARK

Cowdrey Cowdrey Lake El. 7,910

Walden El. 8,099

Walden Res.

Arapaho National Wildlife Refuge

Case Reservoirs

JACKSON

COUNTY

Johnny Moore Mtn. 9,050 ×

Kings Canyon

Pinkham

CONTINENTAL DIVIDE

R 83 W R 82 W R 81 W R 80 W R 79 W R 78 W

Soda Mtn. 10,804 ×

Newcomb

Lake Albert / Whale Lake

Jonah Lake

Buffalo Pass 10,180

Sawmill Lake

Doran Creek

Pole Mtn. Lake

Coalmont

Pole Mtn. 9,234 ×

McFarlane Res.

Buffalo Creek

Grizzly Lakes

Hidden Lakes

Mexican Res.

Addison Res.

Ridings Res.

Clayton Res.

Shawver Res.

Lake Dinosaur

Fish Creek Lake

Long Lake

Round Lake

Colorado Creek

Mexican Creek

Spicer

Seymour Lake

Hecla Res.

Buffalo Pk. 9,433

Rand

Mt. Werner 10,565

Lost Lake

Rabbit Ears Pk. 10,654

Rabbit Ears Pass 9,426

White Slide 9,531

W. Arapaho Res.

Ironclad Mtn.

Spice Pk. 8,664

Slackweiss Res.

Two Ledge Res.

Flat Lake

Red Hill ×11,454

Beaver Lake

Little Haystack Mtn. 10,681

ROUTT NATIONAL FOREST

Dumont Lake

Walton Peak 10,559 ×

Muddy Pass 8,772

Lily Lake

Lake Agnes

Diamond Mtn. × 9,442

PARK RANGE

Diamond Creek

Whiteley Peak Res.

Red Slide Mtn. 10,871

Hyannis Pk. 11,602

Sheep Mtn. 11,819

RABBIT EARS

Willow Creek Pass 9,621

Parkview Mtn.

◄ see map 2 ◄

▼ see map 9 ▼

0 1 2 5 miles

scale 1:300,000

WYOMING
COLORADO

LARIMER

COUNTY

LARAMIE MOUNTAINS

Honholz Lake
Stuck Creek
Grace Creek
Laramie Creek
Shell Creek
Sand Creek

Black Mtn. 9,949
Eaton Res.
Sheep Creek
Panhandle Res.
Beaver Meadows
Creedmore Lakes

Glendevey
McIntyre
Deadman
Deadwood

ROOSEVELT

Red Feather Lakes El. 8,200
Hiawatha Lake
West L.
Letitia Lake
Dowdy Lake
Parvin Lake
Bellaire Lake

Log Cabin

Trails End

MEDICINE BOW

RAWAH

Elk Mtn. ×8,818
McIntyre Lake
Upper Camp Lake
Rawah Lakes
Clear Creek
Clear Lake
Twin Crater Lakes
Island Lake
Kelly Lake
Ruby Jewel Lake

WILDERNESS

State Forest
State Park

Michigan Reservoir
Gould
Owl Mtn. 10,957

ROUTT

NATL

FOREST

RANGE

Radial Mtn. 11,241

Nunn Creek

Twin Lakes Laramie Lake
Chambers Lake
Barnes Meadow Res.

Joe Wright Res.
Trap Lake

Cameron Pass 10,276

NEOTA
WILDERNESS
DIVIDE

Snow Lake
Lake Agnes
Mt. Richtofen 12,940

GRAND

Lake of the Clouds
Howard Mtn. 12,910
Mt. Nimbus 12,706

Milner Pass 10,758

CONTINENTAL

Idylwilde
Rustic El. 7,522
Eggers

14

Cache la Poudre River

NATIONAL

Sevenmile

CROWN POINT

COMANCHE PEAK
WILDERNESS

Peterson Lake

ROOSEVELT

Browns Lake
Comanche Res.
Comanche Pk. 12,702
Hourglass Res.

FOREST

Box Prairie

Twin Lakes Res.

Signal Mtn. 11,262

NATIONAL

CACHE la POUDRE
WILDERNESS

Mirror Lake

ROCKY MOUNTAIN
Hague Creek

NATIONAL PARK

Hagues Pk. 13,560
Crystal Lake
Mummy Mtn. 13,425

COMANCHE
PEAK
WILDERNESS

Glen Haven

Ypsilon Mtn. 13,514×
Fall River Pass 11,796
Spectacle Lakes

Trail Ridge Rd. High Pt. 12,183 (Seasonal)

Iceberg Pass 11,827

Arrowhead Lake

Inkwell Lake
Mt. Julian 12,928

34

34

34

Estes Park El. 7,522

36

Rocky Mountain National Park Headquarters

7

Marys Lake
Lake Estes

36

COUNTY

▼ see map 10 ▼

see map 7

COLORADO RECREATIONAL

0 1 2 5 miles
scale 1:300,000

A B C
1 2 3 4

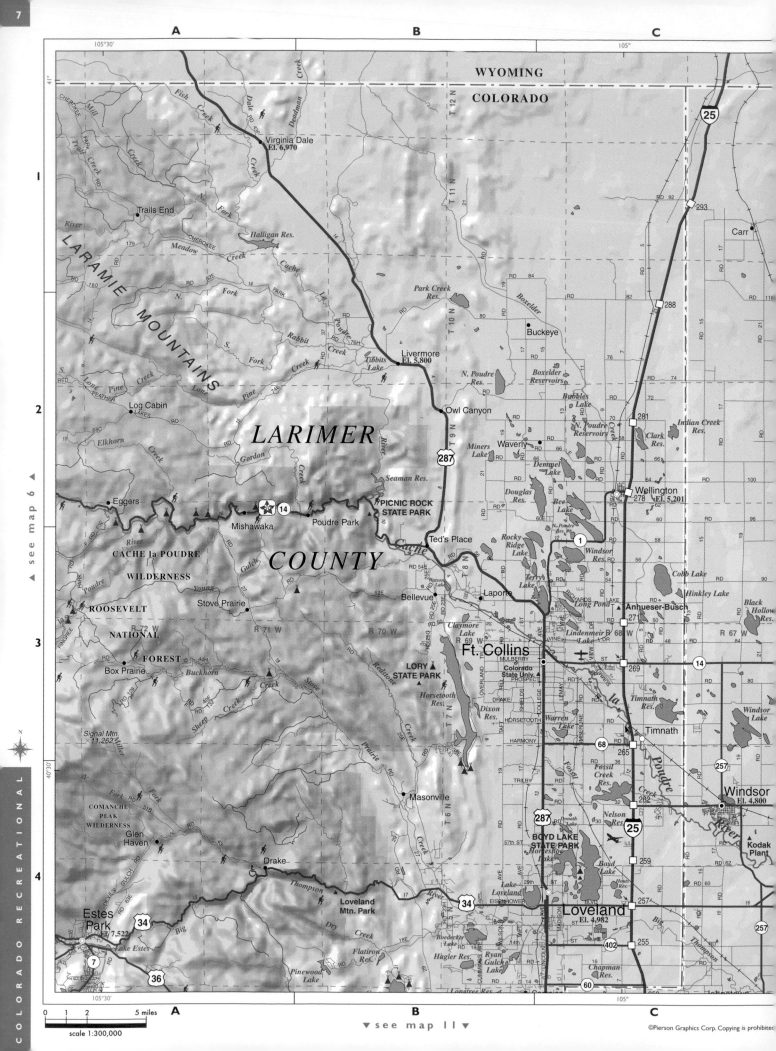

A   **B**   **C**

105°30'

41°

WYOMING

COLORADO

25

T 12 N

RD 92

293

1

Trails End

Virginia Dale
El. 6,970

Halligan Res.

Park Creek Res.

Buckeye

288

Carr

T 11 N

14

LARAMIE

RD 180

Log Cabin

LARIMER

Livermore
El. 5,800

Tibbits Lake

N. Poudre Res.

Boxelder Reservoirs

Bubbles Lake

281

Indian Creek Res.

Clark Res.

2

MOUNTAINS

Elkhorn

Gordon

Owl Canyon

287

Miners Lake

Waverly

N. Poudre Reservoirs

Denimel Lake

278   Wellington
El. 5,201

Eggers

Seaman Res.

PICNIC ROCK STATE PARK

Douglas Res.

Bee Lake

1

Rocky Ridge Lake

Windsor Res.

Cobb Lake

Hinkley Lake

Black Hollow Res.

14

Mishawaka

Poudre Park

COUNTY

Ted's Place

Cache

Bellevue

Laporte

Terry Lake

Long Pond

Anhueser-Busch

271

CACHE la POUDRE

WILDERNESS

Stove Prairie

Claymore Lake

Ft. Collins

Lindenmeir Lake

269

3

ROOSEVELT

NATIONAL

R 72 W   R 71 W   R 70 W   R 69 W

LORY STATE PARK

Colorado State Univ.

14

Box Prairie

Buckhorn

Horsetooth Res.

Dixon Res.

Timnath Res.

Windsor Lake

Signal Mtn. 11,262

Warren Lake

Timnath

257

Windsor
El. 4,800

68

265

Masonville

Fossil Creek Res.

25

282

Kodak Plant

4

COMANCHE PEAK WILDERNESS

Glen Haven

Drake

287

Nelson Res.

259

Loveland Mtn. Park

34

BOYD LAKE STATE PARK

Boyd Lake

Estes Park
El. 7,522

34

Thompson

Lake Loveland

Loveland
El. 4,982

257

255

7

36

Pinewood Lake

Flatiron Res.

Hugler Res.

Ryan Gulch Lake

Chapman Res.

402

60

105°30'

A   **B**   **C**

0   1   2   5 miles

scale 1:300,000

▲ see map 6 ▲

▼ see map 11 ▼

COLORADO Recreational

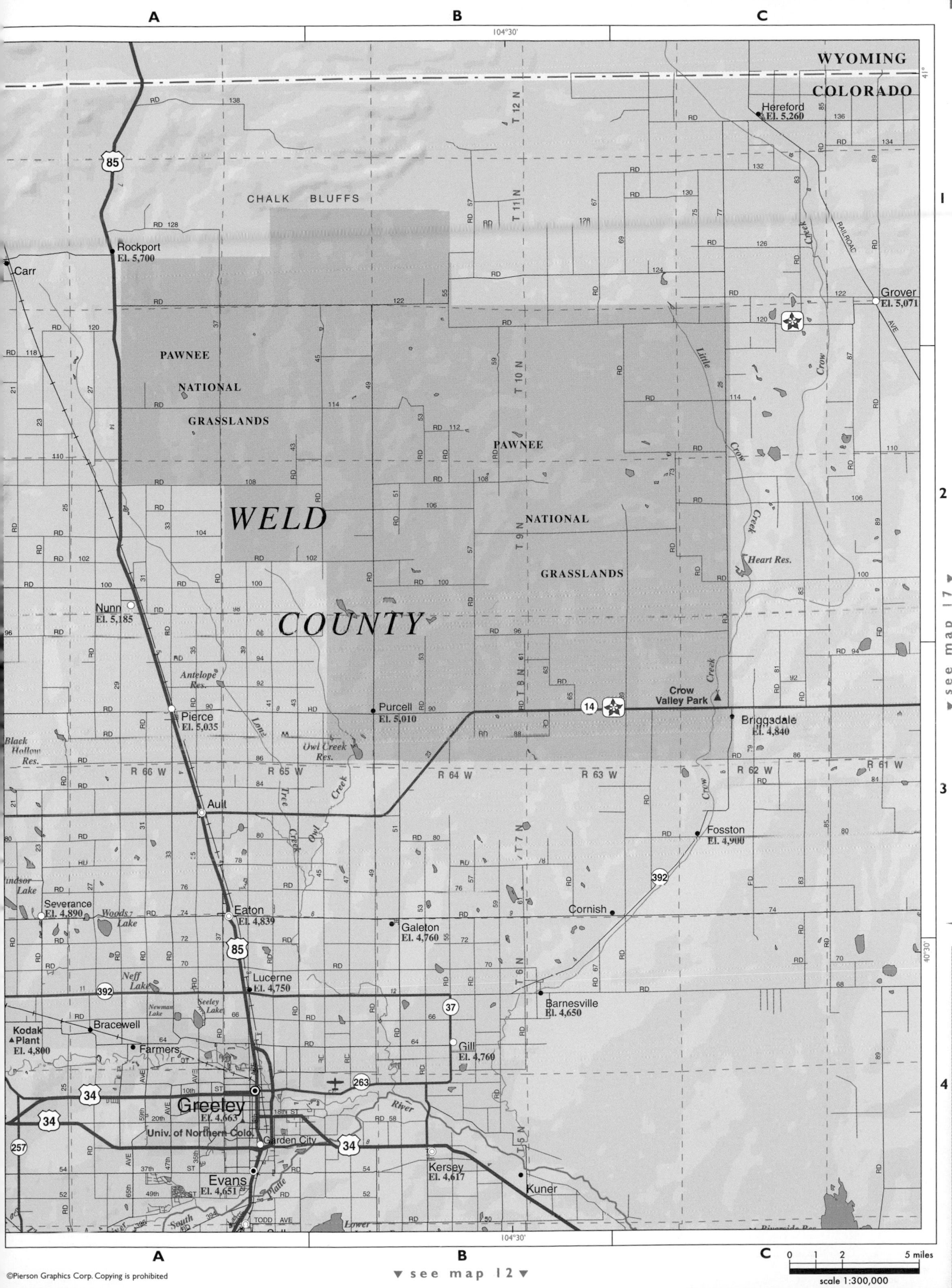

WYOMING
COLORADO

A 104°30' **B** **C**

Hereford
El. 5,260

CHALK BLUFFS

Rockport
El. 5,700

Carr

Grover
El. 5,071

PAWNEE

NATIONAL

GRASSLANDS

WELD

Nunn
El. 5,185

COUNTY

PAWNEE

NATIONAL

GRASSLANDS

Heart Res.

Antelope
Res.

Crow
Valley Park

Purcell
El. 5,010

14

Briggsdale
El. 4,840

Pierce
El. 5,035

Black
Hollow
Res.

Owl Creek
Res.

R 66 W   R 65 W   R 64 W   R 63 W   R 62 W   R 61 W

Ault

Fosston
El. 4,900

392

Severance
El. 4,890

Woods
Lake

Eaton
El. 4,839

Cornish

Galeton
El. 4,760

Neff
Lake

Lucerne
El. 4,750

Barnesville
El. 4,650

392

Newman
Lake

Seeley
Lake

37

Kodak
Plant
El. 4,800

Bracewell

Gill
El. 4,760

Farmers

263

34

Greeley
El. 4,663

34

257

Univ. of Northern Colo.

Garden City

34

Evans
El. 4,651

Kersey
El. 4,617

Kuner

South Platte River

Lower

104°30'

A ▼ see map 12 ▼ **B** **C**

0 1 2 5 miles

scale 1:300,000

▼ see map 17 ▼

COLORADO RECREATIONAL

1

2

3

4

41°

40°30'

A   B   C

106°30'

ROUTT COUNTY

GRAND COUNTY

EAGLE COUNTY

SUMMIT COUNTY

Harrison 10,559

Lake Agnes

Whiteley Peak Res.

Whiteley Peak 10,115

Red Slide Mtn. 10,871

9,621

Troublesome Pass 10,027

Parkview Mtn. 12,296

ROUTT

NATIONAL

Gore Mtn. × 10,687

FOREST

Basin Res.

Binco Res.

Albert Res.

Sheep Mtn. × 11,361
Matheson Res.

Middle Carter Mtn. 8,958

Coal Mtn. 9,543

Silver Creek

Little Rock Creek

Pinto Tyler Mtn. 9,375

Red Dirt Res.

Deer Creek

Dirt Creek

Hinman Res.

Wolford Mtn. Res.

Wolford Mtn. 9,170

Slide Mtn. 9,931

Elk Mtn. 11,419

40

Hot Sulphur Springs

El. 7,670

134

Sheep Creek

MOONEY RD.

Kremmling El. 7,670

Parshall

AMTRAK

Junction Butte 8,700

Williams Fork Res.

Black Mtn. 10,454

Sylvan Res.

Radium El. 6,910

© Pierson Graphics Corp.

Beaver Creek

Battle Mtn. ×

Conger Mesa × 8,731

Colorado River

Blue River

Mc Coy

Yarmony Mtn. 9,516

Yarmony

Sheep Mtn.

Haystack Mtn. 9,111

9

Green Mtn. 9,408

Green Mtn. Reservoir

Williams Pk. 11,619

Bond

State Bridge El. 6,740

Heeney El. 7,870

Flat Top 9,811

Ute Pass 9,524

131

Cottonwood Peak 11,477

Walters Lake

Piney Peak 11,563

Hoagland Res.

Lower Cataract Lake

Upper Cataract Lake

Blue Lake

Black Lake

Palmer Knob 8,870

WHITE RIVER

NATIONAL

FOREST

Slough Grass Res.

Slate Mtn. 11,104

Eagles Nest 13,091 ×

Mt. Powell 13,575

Bubble Lake

Upper Slate Lake

Slate Lake

GORE RANGE

Mama Lake

EAGLES NEST

WILDERNESS

Piney Lake

Lost Lake

Pitkin Lake

Boulder Lake

Keller Mtn. 13,085

Wolcott El. 6,960

157

0 1 2   5 miles

scale 1:300,000

A   B   C

◄ see map 2 ►

COLORADO RECREATIONAL

A   B   C

106°   105°30'

NEVER SUMMER
WILDERNESS

Bowen Lake

ARAPAHO

NATL.

FOREST

CONTINENTAL DIVIDE

Ptarmigan Lake

Hallett Peak 12,713

ROCKY MOUNTAIN

Taylor Peak 13,153

Lake Nokoni

Bear Lake

Mills Lake

Sky Pond

Chasm Lake

ROOSEVELT

NATIONAL

Twin Sisters Peaks 11,428

Grand Lake Touring Center

Grand Lake

NATIONAL PARK

Mt. Meeker 13,911

14,256

Meeker Park

FOREST

125

Shadow Mtn. Res.

Soda Springs

ARAPAHO NATL.
REC. AREA

Isolation Peak 13,118

Spirit Lake

Sandbeach Lake

BOULDER

Allenspark

7

C Lazy U Ranch

Willow Creek Res.

Lake Granby

Columbine

Paradise

Pipit Lake

Bluebird Lake

Copeland Mtn. 13,176

Pear Res.

COUNTY

Lazy H Ranch

River

Raymond

Hiamovi Mtn. 12,395

Island Lake

Red Deer Lake

Peaceful Valley

Peaceful Valley

40

Colorado

34

Granby El. 7,935

Windy Gap Reservoir

INDIAN PEAKS

Roaring Fork

Monarch Lake

Strawberry Lake

Buchanan

Coney

ROOSEVELT

NATIONAL

Mt.Audubon 13,223

Beaver Res.

Brainard Lake

Ward El. 9,253

Gold Lake

MIDDLE

Meadow Creek Res.

Crater Lake

WILDERNESS

Blue Lake

Long Lake

Left Hand Park Res.

Silver Lake

Glacier Lake

Navajo Peak 13,409

PARK

Silvercreek

N. Arapaho Peak 13,502

Triple Lake

72

R 74 W

R 73 W

R 72 W

Mt. Neva 12,814

Caribou

Boulder Creek

ARAPAHO

Tabernash

Y.M.C.A. Snow Mountain Ranch

Devil's Thumb

Jasper Lake

Eldora

Skyscraper

Nederland El. 8,236

Barker Res.

Fraser

Peterson Lake

Univ. of Colo. Observatory

Pine

NATIONAL

Rollins Pass 11,671

Eldora

Ski Idlewild

Winter Park El. 9,110

Moffat Tunnel

Forest Lake

Manchester Lake

Rollinsville

Byers Peak 12,804

East Portal

Heart Lake

Tolland

GILPIN

Gilpin

Starr Peak 10,493

Winter Park

Mary Jane

AMTRAK

James Peak Lake

ROOSEVELT

Snowline Lake

Thorn Lake

FRASER

40

James Peak 13,294

NATIONAL

COUNTY

Braecher Lake

Golden State Park

EXPERIMENTAL

Parry Peak 13,391

St. Mary's Glacier

FOREST

St. Mary's

46

NATIONAL

Mt. Nystrom 12,652

Vasquez Peak 12,947

Alice

Missouri Lake

Central City

FOREST

Berthoud Pass Ski Area

DIVIDE

Moore Lake

Central City Opera

Glory Hole

Black Hawk El. 8,042

119

Jones Pass 12,151

Berthoud Pass 11,315

Empire

Historic Mining District

Urad Mine

Englemann Peak 13,362

Dumont

233

Lawson

236

Idaho Springs El. 7,540

70

Hassell Lake

Empire

238

240

243 244

Pettingell Peak 13,553

Bard Peak 13,641

228

CLEAR

241

103

Ptarmigan Peak 12,498

Eisenhower Mem. Tunnel

216

70

Bakerville

221

Silver Plume

226

Georgetown Loop

Georgetown El. 8,519

CREEK

Squaw Pass 9,807

Mt. Sniktau

McClellan House

COUNTY

106°   105°30'

A   B   C

I

2

3

4

0 1 2 5 miles

scale 1:300,000

LARIMER

COUNTY

ROOSEVELT

NATIONAL

FOREST

Twin Sisters Peaks 11,413

Meeker Park

Allenspark

Lazy H Ranch

Raymond El. 7,800

Peaceful Valley

Beaver Res.

Jamestown El. 6,920

Ward El. 9,253

Gold Hill

Sugarloaf

Glacier Lake

Fourmile

Tungsten

Barker Res.

Univ. of Colo. Observatory

Gross Res.

Pinecliffe

Rollinsville El. 8,420

Gilpin

Snowline Lake

Thorn Lake

Braecher Lake

Missouri Lake

Central City El. 8,496

Black Hawk El. 8,042

Historic Mining District

Idaho Springs El. 7,540

Squaw Pass 9,807

Bergen Park

El Rancho

Genesee

Pinewood Lake

Pinewood Springs El. 6,500

Carter Lake

Hertha Res.

Loveland Res.

Lyons El. 5,374

Button Rock Res.

Riverside

Left Hand Valley Res.

Boulder Res.

Allens Lake

Foothills Res.

Lagerman Res.

Hygiene El. 5,090

Longmont El. 4,979

Niwot El. 5,090

IBM

Boulder El. 5,363

Colo. Univ.

U.S. Dept. of Commerce

National Center For Atmospheric Research

Boulder Mtn. Park

Kossler Lake

ELDORADO CANYON STATE PARK

Marshall El. 5,480

Eldorado Springs El. 5,750

Marshall Lake

Superior El. 5,512

Valmont Res.

Canfield

Louisville El. 5,350

Lafayette El. 5,237

Erie El. 5,038

BOULDER

COUNTY

Base Line Res.

Broomfield El. 5,420

Great Western Res.

Rocky Flats Environmental Tech. Site D.O.E.

Jefferson County Airport

N. Jeffco Open Space Park

GOLDEN GATE CANYON STATE PARK

White Ranch Open Space Park

Ralston Res.

Tucker Lake

Leyden

Upper Long Lake

Standley Lake

Westminster

Federal Heights

JEFFERSON

COUNTY

Hyatt Lake

Arvada

Regis Univ.

Wheat Ridge

Mtn. View

Edgewater

Golden El. 5,675

Colorado School of Mines

Lookout Mtn. Park

Colo. RR Museum

Coors

Lakewood

Campion

Berthoud El. 5,050

Mead El. 5,140

Firestone El. 4,970

Frederick El. 4,982

Dacono El. 5,017

Johnstown El. 4,820

Milliker El. 4,760

Ft. St. Vrain Plant

BARBOUR PONDS STATE PARK

McIntosh Lake

Union Res.

Foster Res.

Lake Thomas

Mulligan Res.

Welch Res.

Lonetree Res.

Chapman Res.

DeFrance Res.

Johnstown Res.

Hillsboro Res.

Eastlake

Northglenn

Thornton

Henderson

Commerce City

DENVER El. 5,280

Museum of Natural History

Glendale

Lowry

◄ see map 10 ▲

◄ see map 10 ▲

COLORADO RECREATIONAL

0 1 2 5 miles

scale 1:300,000

©Pierson Graphics Corp. Copying is prohibited.

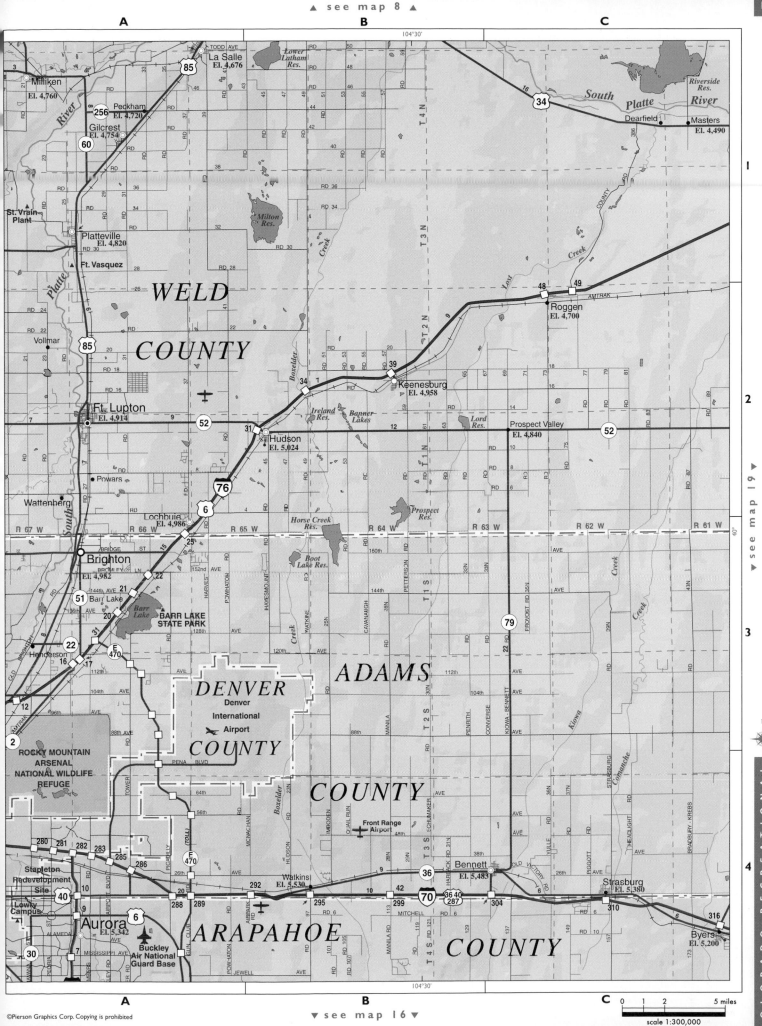

A B C

WELD

COUNTY

Milliken
El. 4,760

La Salle
El. 4,676

Peckham
El. 4,720

Gilcrest
El. 4,754

St. Vrain
Plant

Platteville
El. 4,820

Ft. Vasquez

Vollmar

Lower Latham Res.

Milton Res.

South Platte River

Riverside Res.

Dearfield

Masters
El. 4,490

Roggen
El. 4,700

AMTRAK

Boxelder Creek

Ireland Res.

Banner Lakes

Lord Res.

Keenesburg
El. 4,958

Prospect Valley
El. 4,840

Ft. Lupton
El. 4,914

Hudson
El. 5,024

Powars

Wattenberg

Lochbuie
El. 4,986

Prospect Res.

Horse Creek Res.

Boot Lake Res.

Brighton
El. 4,982

Barr Lake

BARR LAKE
STATE PARK

Henderson

DENVER

COUNTY

Denver
International
Airport

ADAMS

COUNTY

ROCKY MOUNTAIN
ARSENAL
NATIONAL WILDLIFE
REFUGE

PENA BLVD

Front Range
Airport

Stapleton
Redevelopment
Site

Lowry
Campus

Aurora
El. 5,342

Buckley
Air National
Guard Base

Watkins
El. 5,530

Bennett
El. 5,483

Strasburg
El. 5,380

Byers
El. 5,200

ARAPAHOE

COUNTY

A B C

0 1 2   5 miles

scale 1:300,000

COLORADO RECREATIONAL

◄ see map 19 ►

1

2

3

4

A   B   C

106°30'

131
Wolcott El. 6,960
157
70
Edwards
6
163
167
Avon
Dowd
171
Beaver Creek
Minturn
Mama Lake
Piney Lake
WHITE RIVER NATIONAL FOREST
EAGLES NEST WILDERNESS
Lost Lake
Mt. Powell 13,575
Bubble Lake
Upper Slate Lake
Slate Lake
Keller Mtn. 13,085
Boulder Lake

Vail El. 8,150
176 180
Vail
173
EAGLE

Vail Mtn. ×11,250

9
Silverthorne
Buffalo × Mtn. 12,777
Chief × Mtn. 11,377
203
201
Frisco
198
Frisco Exp Trails

COUNTY

WHITE RIVER

Gilman
Red Cliff El. 8,750
NATIONAL

Shrine Pass 11,089
Vail Pass 10,666
190
70
195
Copper Mountain

SYLVAN LAKE STATE PARK
Sylvan Lake
39°30'

Middle Lake
New York Mtn. 12,550
New York Lake
Turquoise Lakes
Mt. Jackson ×13,670
Big Spruce Lake
Big Lake

HOLY CROSS
Mt. of the Holy Cross 14,005
Bowl of Tears
Lake Constantine
Tuhare Lakes
Whitney Peak 13,271
Cleveland Lake

24
Camp Hale
Mitchell
Mt. Powell 13,534

Jacque Peak × 13,205
Breckenridge × Peak 8 12,987
Peak 10 13,633
Crystal Peak 13,852
Spruce Mohawk Lake
Quandary Peak 14,265
Blue Lake
91

Fools Peak × 12,947
Mystic Island Lake
Eagle Lake
Fairview Lake
Harvey Lake
Blodgett Lake
WILDERNESS
Holy Cross City
Gold Park
Missouri Lakes
Savage Peak 13,139
Burnt × Mtn. 11,178

Homestake Peak 13,209
Slide Lake
Tennessee Pass 10,404
Fremont Pass 11,318
Climax El. 11,320
Amax Mine
Mt. Lincoln 14,286
Mt. Cameron × 14,238
Mt. Democrat × 14,148
Mt. Bross × 14,172
Montgomery Res.

Biglow
Diamond J Ranch
North Deimer Lake
Sellar Lake
Cunningham Creek
Coke Oven State Wildlife Area
Mormon Lake
Lyle Lake
DIVIDE
Upper Homestake Lake
Deckers Lake
Tennessee Lakes
Sylvan Lake
Morton Lake
Ski Cooper
SAN ISABEL NATIONAL FOREST

Nast
Chapman Lake
WHITE RIVER
Timberline Lake
Bear Lake
Turquoise Lake

LAKE
Mosquito Pass 13,188
Pennsylvania × Mtn. 13,006
Mt. Sherman 14,036

NATIONAL
Mt. Nast 12,467
Woody Creek
PITKIN
HUNTER
FRYINGPAN
Hagerman Pass 11,980
Windsor Lake
Leadville Jct.
Leadville North
Leadville El. 10,152
Malta
Colorado Mtn. College
COUNTY
Diamond Lake
Gemini Peak 13,951
Mt. Sheridan 13,748
Leavick
Sheep Mtn. × 12,818
Horseshoe Mtn. 13,898

Midway Lake
WILDERNESS
Lost Man Lake
Independence Lake
Linkins Lake
82
Independence
Independence Pass 12,095 (Seasonal)
Deer Mtn. 13,761
Mt. Champion
Blue Lake
SAWATCH RANGE
CONTINENTAL
MT. MASSIVE WILDERNESS
Mt. Massive 14,421
Halfmoon
SAN ISABEL
Mt. Elbert 14,433 Highest Peak in Colorado
Twin Lakes
24
Ptarmigan Peak 13,739
MOSQUITO RANGE
SAN ISABEL NATIONAL FOREST
Weston Pass 11,900 (Seasonal)

0 1 2 5 miles
scale 1:300,000

©Pierson Graphics Corp. Copying is prohibited

106°

105°30'

CLEAR CREEK COUNTY

Urad Mine

Engelman Pk. ×13,362

Lawson 236

238 Idaho Springs

240 El. 7,540

243

244

11,809

Hassell Lake

Bard Pk. ×13,641

Georgetown Lake

Pettingell Pk. 13,553

Mt. Bethel 12,705 ×

Bakerville

Silver Plume

Georgetown El. 8,519

McClellan House

Squaw Pass 9,807

Ptarmigan Peak 12,498

Eisenhower Mem. Tunnel

Mt. Sniktau 13,234 ×

Georgetown Loop

103

Chief Mtn. 11,709 ×

Mt. Judge 10,301

ARAPAHO

216

Loveland Ski Area

Loveland Pass 11,990

Echo L.

ECHO LAKE PARK

ARAPAHO

Brook

NATIONAL

Torreys Peak 14,267

Grey Wolf Mtn. 13,602 ×

5

NATIONAL

Dillon El. 9,156

6

FOREST

Arapahoe Basin

Grays Peak 14,270

Argentine Pk. ×13,738

Guanella Pass 11,669

14 (Seasonal)

Mt. Evans 14,264

FOREST

Dillon Res.

Keystone

Keystone

Montezuma

Santa Fe Peak 13,180

Silver Dollar Lake

Mt. Bierstadt 14,060

Abyss Lake

Beartrack Lakes

SUMMIT

Independence Mtn. 12,614

Geneva Peak 13,266

MT. EVANS

COUNTY

Geneva Mtn. 12,335

WILDERNESS

Harris Park

Webster Pass 12,096

Mt. Logan × 12,871

PIKE

Pine Junction

Lincoln Ghost Town

Whale Peak 13,078

R 74 W

R 73 W

R 72 W

Breckenridge El. 9,603

Georgia Pass 11,585

Jefferson Lake

Webster

285 Grant

NATIONAL

Mt. Guyot 13,370

Linger Lake

El. 8,580

FOREST

Boreas Pass 11,481 (Seasonal)

Baker Lake

South Twin Cone Peak × 12,323

Shawnee

12

Bailey El. 7,750

Blue River

Boreas Mtn. 13,082

Kenosha Pass 10,001

Glenisle

9

PARK

Jefferson El. 9,500

PIKE

Hoosier Pass 11,541

Colorado

PIKE

NATIONAL

Little Baldy Mtn. ×12,142

Como

NATIONAL

Windy Peak 11,970

FOREST

Alma El. 10,355

Como Lake

FOREST

Red Hill Pass 10,051

COUNTY

Bison Peak × 12,431

Fairplay El. 9,953

Tarryall Res. SWA

Tarryall Reservoir

LOST CREEK WILDERNESS

SOUTH PARK

ANTELOPE

9

285

Garo

▼ see map 15 ▼

A   B   C

Idaho Springs
El. 7,540
40
241 243 244
70
103
248
6
40
251 253 254 32
252
El Rancho
El. 7,670
Bergen Park
Lookout Mtn. Park
Genesee
256
259
261
262
264
58
Coors
Golden
El. 5,675
Colorado School of Mines
70
Wheat Ridge
32nd
Edgewater
14
95
264
212 213
210
209
DENVER
El. 5,280
70
Museum of Natural History
40
Lowry
30
83
Squaw Pass
9,807
Chief Mtn.
11,709
Mt. Judge
10,301

CLEAR

Denver Mountain Parks
74
Idledale
Red Rocks Park
470
6
Colfax
Lakewood
26
88
Glendale
25
205
204
203
2
Denver Univ.
201

CREEK

Kittredge
El. 6,810
Brookvale
Mt. Evans State Wildlife Area
Evergreen
El. 7,040
Indian Hills
El. 6,840
Morrison
El. 5,800
8
8
285
Bear Creek Res.
Soda Lake
Hampden
Quincy Ave
Bow Mar
Sheridan
Belleview
Englewood
Cherry Hills Village
199
Cherry Creek Res.
225

COUNTY

Sprucedale
Marshdale
Brook Forest
Tiny Town
Twin Forks
Fenders
Bergen Reservoirs
Marston Lake
Bowles
121
Ken Caryl Ranch
Columbine Valley
Littleton
Greenwood Village
Arapahoe
197
196
195

Aspen Park
S. Turkey
Phillipsburg
El. 7,420
Deermont
Highlands Ranch
470
Lone Tree
194
193

2

Harris Park
Conifer
El. 8,270
Newton Park
Critchell
75
Chatfield Res.
Titan
CHATFIELD STATE PARK
Lockheed Martin
Waterton
El. 5,500
85
Kellytown
Daniels Park
Beverly Hills
191
188

285
Pine Junction
R 72 W
R 71 W
R 70 W
Reynolds Ranch Park
R 69 W
Louviers
El. 5,680
Roxborough
R 68 W
R 67 W
187

JEFFERSON

Foxton
El. 6,460
Aurora Rampart Reservoir
ROXBOROUGH STATE PARK
Sedalia
El. 5,860
184

South Platte
Glenisle
Bailey
El. 7,750
Pine
El. 6,770
105
67
DOUGLAS
183
182

3

Buffalo Creek
El. 6,750
Long Scraggy Peak
8,812
Twin Cedars
South Platte
Pine Nook
Shamballah Ashrama
181

COUNTY

Windy Peak
11,970
Colorado
Wellington Lake
Green Mtn.
10,421
Oxyoke
COUNTY
174
25

Bison Peak
12,431
Buffalo Peak
11,589
Devils Head
9,748
RAMPART
Perry Park
85
87
173

PARK

Deckers
El. 6,400
PIKE
RANGE
Larkspur
El. 6,680
172

LOST
CREEK
WILDERNESS
Cheesman Lake
NATIONAL
163

COUNTY
Westcreek
67
FOREST

TELLER COUNTY

Palmer Lake
105
Elephant Rock

0 1 2   5 miles
scale 1:300,000

ADAMS COUNTY

79

Bennett
El. 5,483

36

Strasburg
El. 5,380

Watkins
El. 5,530

Stapleton Redevelopment Site

COLFAX

40

10

E 470

26th

BROADWAY

AIRPORT BLVD

MONAGHAN RD

HUDSON RD

MANILA RD

IMBODEN RD

HARBACK RD 31N

Old Victory RD

Lyle RD 36N

PIGGOTT RD

HEADLIGHT RD

26th

70

36 40 287

304

310

316

292

295

299

42

6

6th

ALAMEDA

Aurora

30

HAVANA

PEORIA

ILIFF

7

MISSISSIPPI AVE

CHAMBERS

TOWER

GUN CLUB (TOLL) RD

AIRPARK RD

WATKINS RD

MITCHELL RD

BRICK CENTER RD

Byers
El. 5,200

225

4

Buckley Air National Guard Base

30

ARAPAHOE COUNTY

WHPATAN

JEWELL AVE

YALE AVE

AIRLINE RD

LLOYD RD 26

KNUDTSON RD 42

CHERRY CREEK STATE PARK

Cherry Creek Res.

Quincy Res.

PARKER RD

BUCKLEY

SMOKY HILL RD

HIMALAYA

ORCHARD RD

HAMPDEN

QUINCY AVE

Aurora Reservoir

WOLF CREEK

STRASBURG RD 161

BAUGHMAN RD 46

HAWLEY RD 42

KIOWA-BENNETT RD

197

88

196

195

ARAPAHOE RD

JORDAN RD

HILL RD

COUNTY LINE RD

470

194

193

83

E 470

Foxfield

Centennial Airport

LINCOLN AVE

INSPIRATION DR

RILEY LAKE RD

DOUGLAS ELBERT RD

RD 17

RD 186

RD 186

182

65

25

191

W PARKER RD

Parker
El. 5,870

PINE DR

TOMAHAWK

21

Box Elder

29

174

178

188

R 66 W

R 65 W

HILLTOP RD

166

R 64 W

R 63 W

166

R 62 W

R 61 W

28

187

Happy Canyon

The Pinery

HIGH PRAIRIE DR

DEMOCRAT RD

21

ELBERT

154

BAYOU GULCH

158

RD 158

154

184

VALLEY PD

CROWFOOT

17

160

150

183

CASTLE OAKS DR

146

COUNTY

182

MILLER BLVD

Cherry Creek

33

KIOWA CREEK

142

181

Castle Rock
El. 6,202

86

Franktown
El. 6,120

Elizabeth
El. 6,448

7

Kiowa
El. 6,347
RD 134

RD 134

69

CASTLEWOOD CANYON STATE PARK

RD 25

RD 132

17-21

45

RD 128

BIjou

RD 122

174

RUSSELLVILLE RD

TOMICHI RD

RD 52

RD 122

RD 118

9

FREESE RD 69

RD 134

86

RD 54

RD 118

RD 114

5

21

RD 110

RD 110

77

173

UPPER LAKE GULCH RD

SPRING VALLEY RD

CARLBERG RD

13

106

102

RD 102

61

Larkspur Butte

172

83

GREENLAND RD

LUCAS RD

STEELE RD

21

Elbert
El. 6,720

98

167

Greenland

BEST

JONES RD

86 96

53

RD 90

RD 86

163

Monument Hill
7,352'

LORRAINE RD

PALMER DIVIDE

E CHERRY CREEK RD

N ELBERT RD

RAMAH HWY

EL PASO COUNTY

▼ see map 19 ▼

COLORADO RECREATIONAL

0 1 2   5 miles

scale 1:300,000

104°30'

39°30'

◄ see maps 8, 12 ▲

NEBRASKA
COLORADO

Carpenter

Hereford

T 12 N

R 63 W   R 60 W   R 57 W   R 54 W

Grover

PAWNEE

Pawnee
▲ Buttes

NATIONAL

T 9 N

Keota

GRASSLAND   GRASSLAND

Purcell

Briggsdale   Buckingham   Stoneham   Logan

WELD   Raymer   Willard

Fosston   T 6 N   Merino

Cornish

Galeton   Barnesville   Messex

Lucerne   Prewitt Res.

Gill   HH   Prewitt Res. SWA

COUNTY   Cooper

Garden City   Jackson Lake   **MORGAN**   Snyder   Hillrose

Kersey   JACKSON LAKE STATE PARK   Weldona

Evans   Kuner   Goodrich   Log Lane Village

Riverside Res.   Orchard   Village

Milton Res.   Platte   Masters   River   Fort Morgan   Brush

Empire Res.   Wiggins   **COUNTY**

Pinneo

T 3 N

Roggen   AMTRAK   Nine Mile Corner

Keenesburg

Hudson   Prospect Valley   Gary

Prospect Res.   Hoyt   T 1 N

Horse Creek Res.   Woodrow

160th

ADAMS   T 1 S

144th AVE

Denver International Airport   112th   AVE

COUNTY

T 3 S

Watkins   Bennett   Strasburg   Last Chance   Lindon

70   **70**   Byers

scale 1:600,000   **A**   **B**   **C**

▼ see map 19 ▼

0 1 2   5   10 miles

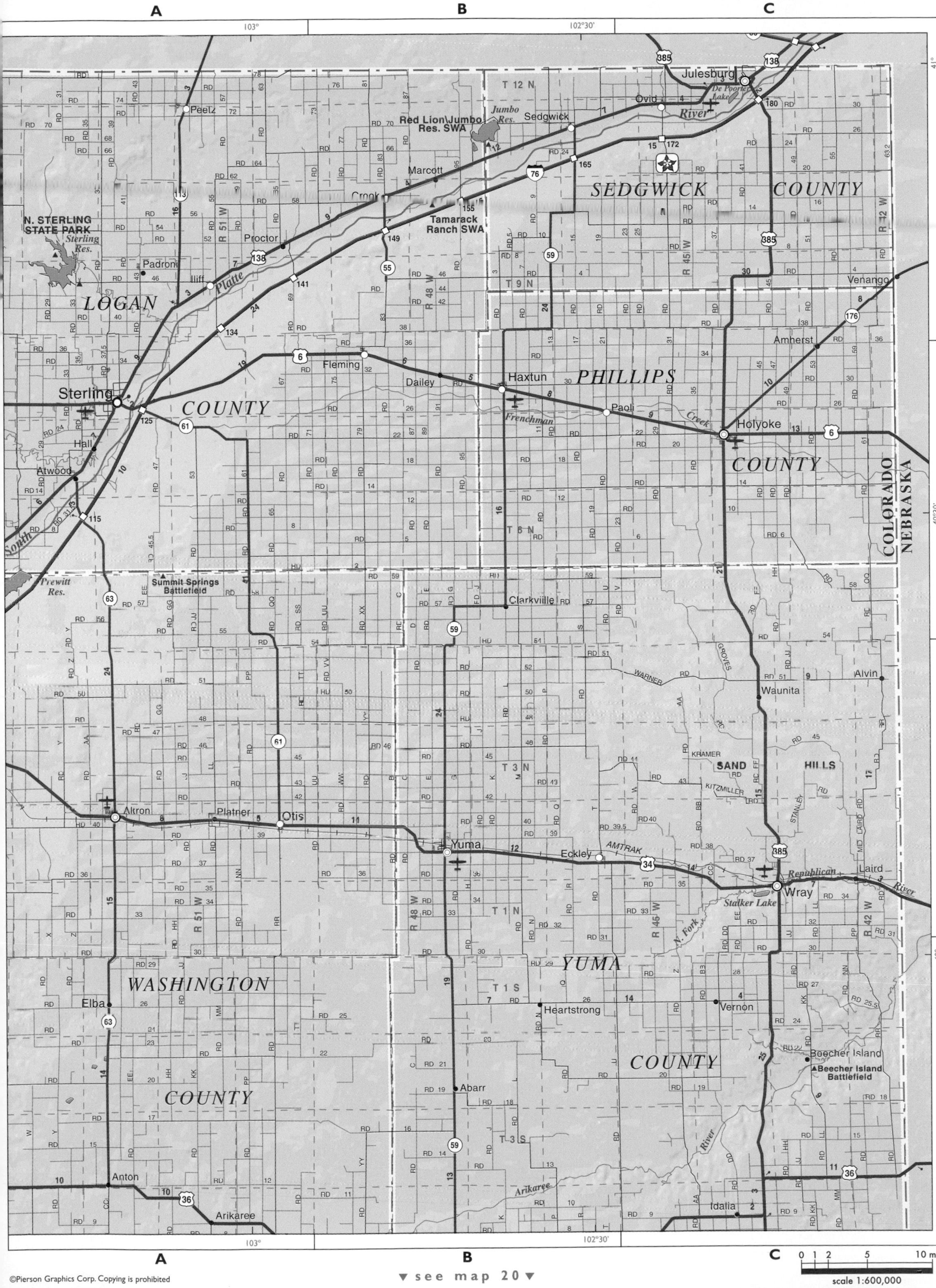

LOGAN COUNTY
PHILLIPS COUNTY
SEDGWICK COUNTY
WASHINGTON COUNTY
YUMA COUNTY

COLORADO
NEBRASKA

Towns and places:
Peetz, Sedgwick, Julesburg, Ovid, Venango, Amherst, Marcott, Crook, Proctor, Padroni, Iliff, Sterling, Hall, Atwood, Fleming, Dailey, Haxtun, Paoli, Holyoke, Clarkville, Alvin, Waunita, Akron, Platner, Otis, Yuma, Eckley, Laird, Wray, Heartstrong, Vernon, Elba, Abarr, Anton, Arikaree, Idalia

N. STERLING STATE PARK
Sterling Res.
Prewitt Res.
Jumbo Res.
Red Lion\Jumbo Res. SWA
Tamarack Ranch SWA
De Poorter Lake
Summit Springs Battlefield
Beecher Island Battlefield
Stalker Lake

SAND HILLS
KRAMER
KITZMILLER

Platte River
South Platte
Frenchman Creek
Warner
Republican River
N. Fork
Arikaree River

Township/Range labels:
T 12 N, T 9 N, T 8 N, T 3 N, T 1 N, T 1 S, T 3 S
R 51 W, R 48 W, R 45 W, R 72 W, R 46 W, R 42 W

Highways: 76, 385, 138, 6, 59, 61, 63, 34, 36, 176, 24, 15, 10, 40

COLORADO RECREATIONAL

0 1 2 5 10 miles
scale 1:600,000

▲ see map 17 ▲

A
B
C
104°30'
104°
103°30'
39°30'
40°
39°
1
2
3
4
WELD COUNTY
MORGAN COUNTY
ADAMS COUNTY
WASHINGTON COUNTY
ARAPAHOE
ELBERT COUNTY
LINCOLN COUNTY
Milton Res.
Empire Res.
Prospect Res.
Horse Creek Res.
Log Lane Village
Fort Morgan
Brush
Pinneo
Wiggins
Roggen
Keenesburg
Hudson
Prospect Valley
Hoyt
Nine Mile Corner
Gary
Woodrow
Watkins
Bennett
Strasburg
Byers
Deer Trail
Last Chance
Lindon
Agate
Bijou
Cedar Point
Elizabeth
Kiowa
Elbert
Matheson
Simla
Ramah
Ramah SWA
Calhan
Eastonville
Peyton
Limon
Genoa
Bovina
Hugo
Clifford
T 3 N
T 1 N
T 3 S
T 6 S
T 9 S
T 12 S
R 63 W
R 60 W
R 57 W
R 54 W
AMTRAK
Boxelder
Kiowa
Bijou
Badger
Big Sandy
N. Fork
Arikaree
0 1 2 5 10 miles
scale 1:600,000

▲ see maps 12, 16 ▲

▼ see map 25 ▼

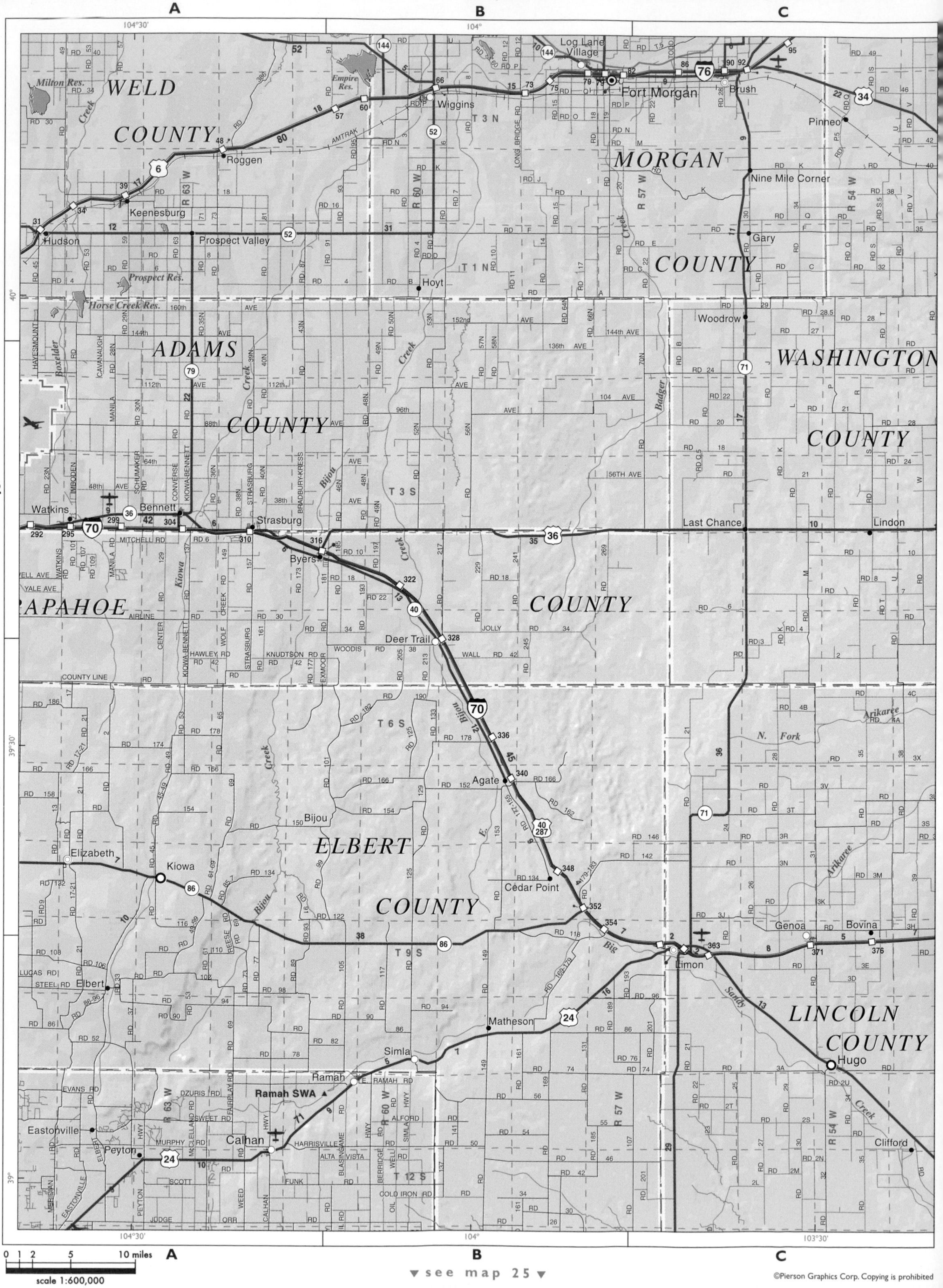

A   B   C

103°   102°30'

Akron Platner Otis Yuma Eckley Laird Wray Waunita

SAND HILLS

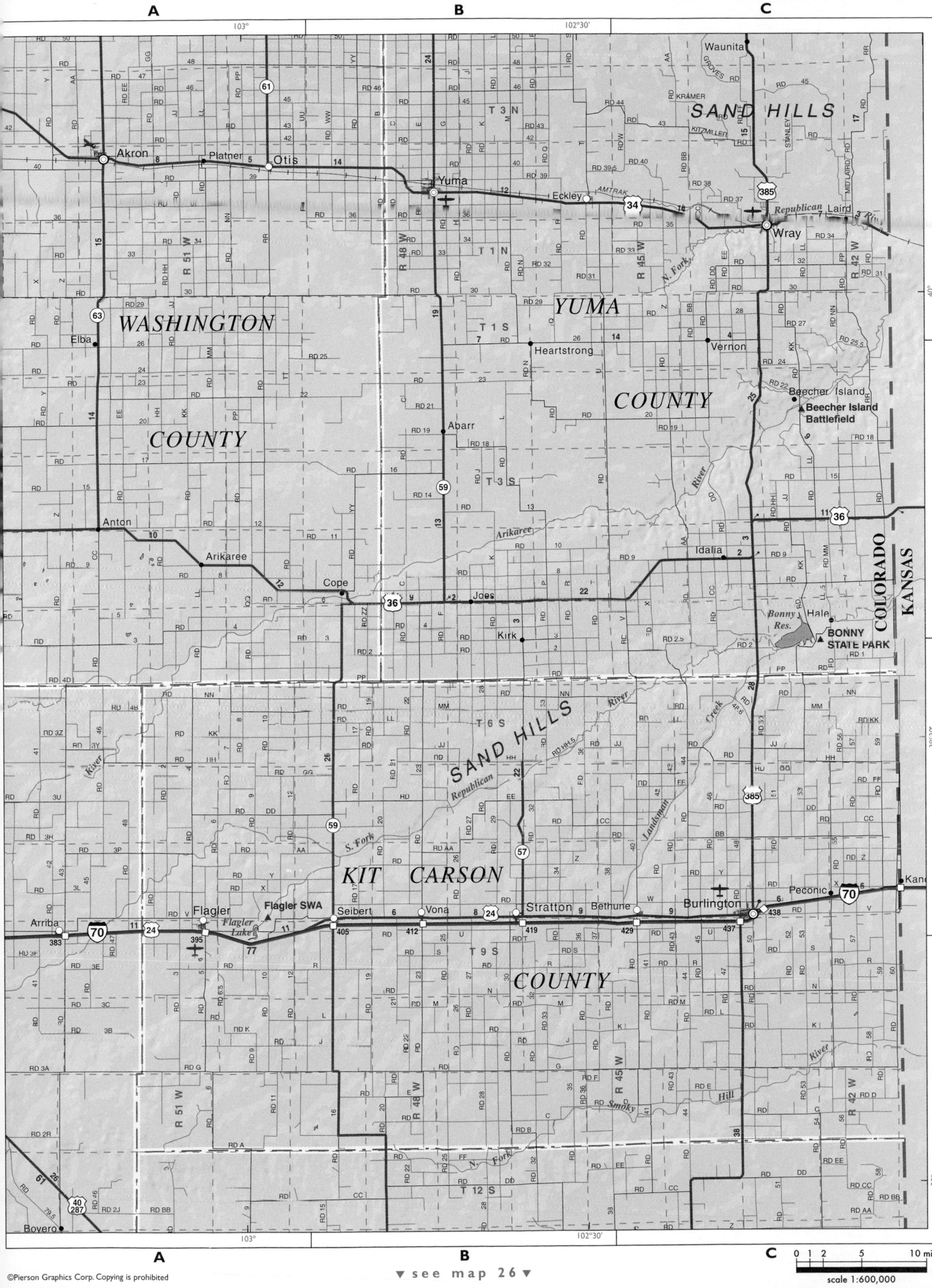

WASHINGTON COUNTY

YUMA COUNTY

Elba Anton Arikaree Cope Joes Kirk

Heartstrong Abarr Vernon

Beecher Island
Beecher Island Battlefield

Idalia Hale

Bonny Res.
BONNY STATE PARK

SAND HILLS

KIT CARSON COUNTY

Arriba Flagler Seibert Vona Stratton Bethune Burlington Peconic Kanorado

Flagler SWA
Flagler Lake

Bovero

COLORADO KANSAS

0 1 2 5 10 miles

scale 1:600,000

A   B   C

21

A   B   C

109°   108°30'   108°

BATTLEMENT

GRAND MESA NATIONAL FOREST

DeBeque

Mack Mesa Lake

HIGHLINE STATE PARK

Highline Lake

VEGA STATE PARK

Castle Peak 8,302

Collbran

BOOK CLIFFS

GRAND VALLEY

Mack

Loma

MESA

Molina

Mesa

GRAND MESA NATIONAL FOREST

330

70

Horse Thief Canyon SWA

RABBIT

Fruita

ISLAND ACRES STATE PARK

Cameo

Clifton

Palisade

De Beque Canyon

Griffith Lake

COUNTY

Colorado River

Redlands

COLORADO NATIONAL MONUMENT

Grand Junction

Mesa College

Colorado River State Park

Horse Mtn. 5,988

Powderhorn

Skyway

Grand Mesa

Leon Lake

Park Res.

UTAH

COLORADO

Thompson Reservoirs

Colorado Monument Mesa

Orchard Mesa

Whitewater

Hallenbeck Res.

Juanita Res.

Island Lake

GRAND MESA

Glade Park

Little

Dolores

Cheney Res.

Cedaredge

Fruita Reservoirs

Schraeder Res.

GRAND MESA NATIONAL FOREST

Broughton

DELTA

Orchard City

Austin

Fruit Growers Res.

92

East Creek

Dominguez

North Delta

Gunnison

River

Escalante

Delta

COUNTY

Gateway

UNCOMPAHGRE

Roubideau

SWEITZER LAKE STATE PARK

PARADOX

Casto Res.

Big Dominguez

Little Dominguez

348

Olathe

50

UNCOMPAHGRE

North Fork

Harry White Reservoir

MONTROSE

Buckeye Res.

Uravan

PLATEAU

Columbine Pass 9,120

Lee Reservoirs

Montrose

Oak Grove

Paradox

VALLEY

Bedrock

San Miguel River

Tabeguache

NATIONAL

COUNTY

Uncompahgre

Chipeta Lake

90

141

Nucla

Vancorum

97

FOREST

OURAY

Naturita

Redvale

COUNTY

145

Norwood

Basin

Dry Creek Basin SWA

Gypsum Gap

Slick Rock

0 1 2   5   10 miles   A

scale 1:600,000

▼ see map 28 ▼

► see map 23 ◄

COLORADO RECREATIONAL

©Pierson Graphics Corp. Copying is prohibited

scale 1:600,000

0 1 2   5   10 miles

▲ see maps 13, 14 ▲

A   106°30'   B   106°   C   105°30'

Top / Lake County area:

Biglow
Nast
NORTH CUNNINGHAM CRK RD
Ski Cooper
Mt. Democrat 14,268
Mt. Bross 14,172
SAN ISABEL NATIONAL FOREST
Como
Climax
Mt. Sherman 14,036
Mosquito Pass 13,188
Alma
TARRYALL
Windy Peak 11,970
LOST CREEK WILDERNESS
Bison Peak 12,431
HAGERMAN
Turquoise Lake
Mosquito Pass
Historic Mining District
Colorado Mtn. College
Leadville
Red Hill Pass 10,051
Fairplay
Tarryall
Tarryall Res. SWA
Tarryall

HUNTER-FRYINGPAN WILDERNESS
Warren Lakes
Malta
LAKE COUNTY
Weston Pass 11,900
PARK
Garo
Antelope Ln
Glentivar
Wilkerson Pass 9,507
24

Mt. Massive 14,421
Independence Pass - 12,095
Mt. Elbert 14,433
Highest Peak in Colorado
Twin Lakes
Balltown
Antero Reservoir
Hartsel
Spinney Mtn. State Park
Spinney Mountain Reservoir

Taylor Lake
MT. MASSIVE WILDERNESS
Grizzly Res.
Twin Lakes Res.
La Plata Peak 14,336
Granite
Clear Creek Res.
SAN ISABEL
Antero Res. SWA
SOUTH PARK
COUNTY
PIKE NATIONAL FOREST
Eleven Mile Canyon Res.

SAWATCH
Lily Pond
Spring Creek Res.
Taylor Park Res.
Vicksburg
Winfield
Mt. Belford 14,197
Mt. Oxford 14,153
Huron Peak 14,005
Missouri Mtn. 14,067
COLLEGIATE PEAKS
Americus
Antero Junction
Trout Creek Pass 9,346
Eleven Mile State Park
Guffey

Matchless Mtn. 12,383
Cottonwood Pass 12,126
Mt. Harvard 14,420
Mt. Columbia 14,073
Mt. Yale 14,196
SAN ISABEL
WILDERNESS
Buena Vista
FOREST
NATIONAL RANGE
Johnson Village
Nathrop

Taylor Park
Tincup
Mirror Lake
Mt. Princeton 14,197
Mt. Princeton Hot Springs
Alpine
Centerville
St. Elmo
Chalk Creek
Mt. Antero 14,269
CHAFFEE COUNTY

GUNNISON
Henry Mtn. 13,254
Tincup Pass 12,121
Cumberland Pass 12,200
FOREST
Tabeguache Peak 14,155
Mt. Shavano 14,229
Arkansas Headwaters State Park
285

Pitkin
Ohio
Parlin
Wauneta Pass 10,280
White Pine
Monarch
Maysville
Salida
FREMONT
291

Waunita Hot Springs
Waunita Hot Springs
Monarch
OLD MONARCH PASS
Monarch Pass 11,312
Poncha Springs

Doyleville
NATIONAL
Mt. Ouray 13,955
Poncha Pass 9,101
Howard
50
COUNTY
Texas Creek

SAGUACHE
Sargents
Marshall Pass 10,842
Coaldale
Cotopaxi

Razor Creek Dome 11,530
Long Branch Baldy 11,974
DIVIDE
Antora Peak 13,266
CONTINENTAL
Bushnell Peak 13,105
Hillside

North Pass - 10,149
Bonanza
Hayden Peak 12,130
SAN ISABEL
SANGRE

HILLS
Cochetopa Pass - 10,032
114
Villa Grove
Rainbow Lake
Brush Creek Lakes
De Weese Reservoir
69

COUNTY
COCHETOPA
Valley View Hot Springs
Electric Peak 13,621
NATIONAL
The Pines
Westcliffe

Saguache
Mineral Hot Springs
285
RIO GRANDE
Gibson Peak 12,861
Rito Alto Peak 13,794
WET MTN
FOREST
VALLEY

Devil's Knob 8,938
Tracy Mtn. 11,017

0 1 2 5   10 miles
scale 1:600,000

◄ see map 22 ►

▼ see map 29 ▼

A   B   C

105°   104°30'

DOUGLAS COUNTY

Twin Cedars
Oxyoke
Shamballah Ashrama
Castle Rock
Elizabeth Kiowa
ELBERT COUNTY
Deckers
Devils Head 9,748
Perry Park
CASTLEWOOD CANYON STATE PARK
176
Larkspur
173
172
Cheesman Reservoir
Westcreek
Greenland
167
163
PIKE
Palmer Lake
161
105
BLACK FOREST
Ramah
NATIONAL
Monument
158
Ramah SWA
FOREST
Baptist Rd.
25
156
Eastonville
Calhan
Woodland Park
U.S. AIR FORCE ACADEMY
Black Forest
Peyton
24
Harrisville
TELLER
Lake George
150
Crystola
149
Green Mtn. Falls
148
Divide
Falcon
Florissant
146
Cascade
Florissant Fossil Beds National Monument
North Catamount Reservoir
Manitou Springs
Colorado Springs
EL PASO
MUELLER RANCH STATE PARK
141
Colorado College
Midland
Historic Area
Ellicott
Yoder
Pikes Peak 14,110
140
24
7
94
Ellicott
COUNTY
Broadmoor
138
83
Gillett
135
Security
Cripple Creek
Cheyenne Mtn. 7,—
132
Widefield
COUNTY
Historic Mining District
Stratton
Cheyenne Mtn. 9,565
Big Johnson Reservoir
Victor
85 87
Hanover
Marigold
Skaguay Reservoir
Fountain
128
Truckton
DOT Test Center
Red Canyon Park
FORT CARSON
Colorado Springs SWA
Hanover
Harkdale
Brush Hollow Reservoir
25
Buckskin Joe
Teller Reservoir
Royal Gorge Park
Canon City
Penrose
Pinon
408
Temple Canyon Park
Williamsburg
Florence
106
SAN
Rockvale
115
120
50
Coal Creek
Wild Horse
Pueblo West
Univ. Southern Colo.
Pueblo Army Depot
Portland
101
67
ISABEL
Pueblo
47
Baxter
Devine Nyburg
North Avondale
Boone
Wetmore
Siloam
Pueblo
50
Vineland
Avondale
209
96
NATIONAL
Adobe Peak 10,188
Pueblo State Park
45
Salt Creek
Lime
Huerfano Lake
Silver Cliff
Querida
McKenzie Junction
98
94
PUEBLO
Nepesta
165
St. Charles Res.
Dotson Reservoir
Rosita
Fairview
91
Stem Beach
Lime
CUSTER COUNTY
Valley View
Burnt Mill
88
83
87
Pueblo Mtn. Park
COUNTY

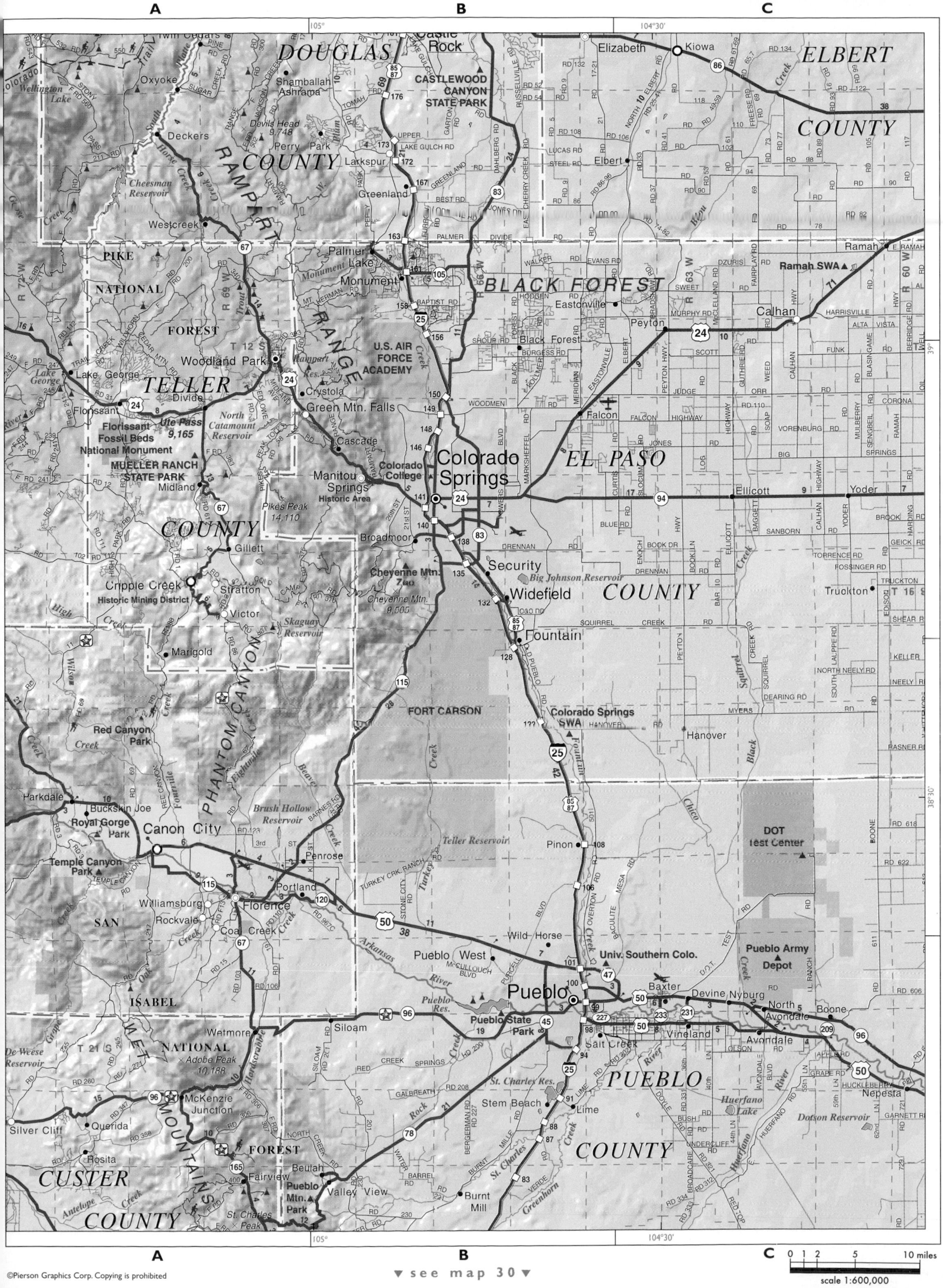

A   B   C

▼ see map 30 ▼

▼ see map 25 ▼

0 1 2 5 10 miles

scale 1:600,000

COLORADO RECREATIONAL

A   B   C

104°30'   104°   103°30'

ELBERT COUNTY

Genoa   Bovina

Limon

Elbert

Matheson

86

Simla

24

Ramah

Ramah SWA

Hugo

Calhan

Peyton

Eastonville

BLACK FOREST

Evans RD

Harrisville

Alta Vista

Clifford

Kinney Lake

Hugo SWA

LINCOLN

Falcon

Vorenburg

Ramah Springs

Kutch

71

94   Ellicott   Yoder   Rush   Punkin Center   94

EL PASO   COUNTY

Truckton

Fossinger

Karval

Karval Lake

Karval SWA

COUNTY

Rush

Kunau

Keller

Neely

Whittemore

Rasner

Colorado Springs SWA

Hanover

DOT Test Center

BOONE

T 18 S

Breckenridge Creek

Arlington

Univ. Southern Colo.

Pueblo Army Depot

CROWLEY

47   Pueblo

Baxter   Devine   Nyburg

North Avondale

Boone

96

COUNTY

Vineland

Avondale

Salt Creek

Lime

50

Huerfano Lake

Nepesta

Dotson Res.

Olney Springs

King Center

Crowley

Ordway

Sugar City

Lake Henry

Lake Meredith

71

Horse Creek Res.

Cheraw

96

PUEBLO

St. Charles River

Fowler

Manzanola

Vroman

Hays

Holbrook Res.

Cheraw Res.

Bent's Old Fort NHS

194

COUNTY

167

Rocky Ford

266

109

Swink

North La Junta

La Junta

OTERO   COUNTY

Hawley

50

VIGIL & ST. VRAIN

10

scale 1:600,000

COLORADO RECREATIONAL

KIT CARSON COUNTY

CHEYENNE COUNTY

KIOWA COUNTY

BENT COUNTY

PROWERS COUNTY

COLORADO / KANSAS

Arriba
Flagler
Flagler SWA
Flagler Lake
Seibert
Vona
Stratton
Bethune
Burlington
Boyero
Aroya
Wild Horse
Kit Carson
Firstview
Cheyenne Wells
Arapahoe
Haswell
Galatea
Eads
Chivington
Brandon
Sheridan Lake
Towner
Sand Creek Massacre
Neesopah Res.
Neenoshe Res.
Neegronda Res.
Upper Queens Res.
Lower Queens Res.
Queens SWA
Adobe Creek Res.
Adobe Creek Res. SWA
May Valley
Wiley
Kornman
McClave
Hasty
Lake Hasty Rec. Area
Ft. Lyon
Las Animas
John Martin Res.
Caddoa
Prowers
Lamar
Carlton
Granada
Bristol
Hartman
Holly
Coolid
Purgatoire River SWA
John Martin SWA
Arkansas River
Smoky Hill River
Rush Creek
Sandy Creek
Big Sandy Creek

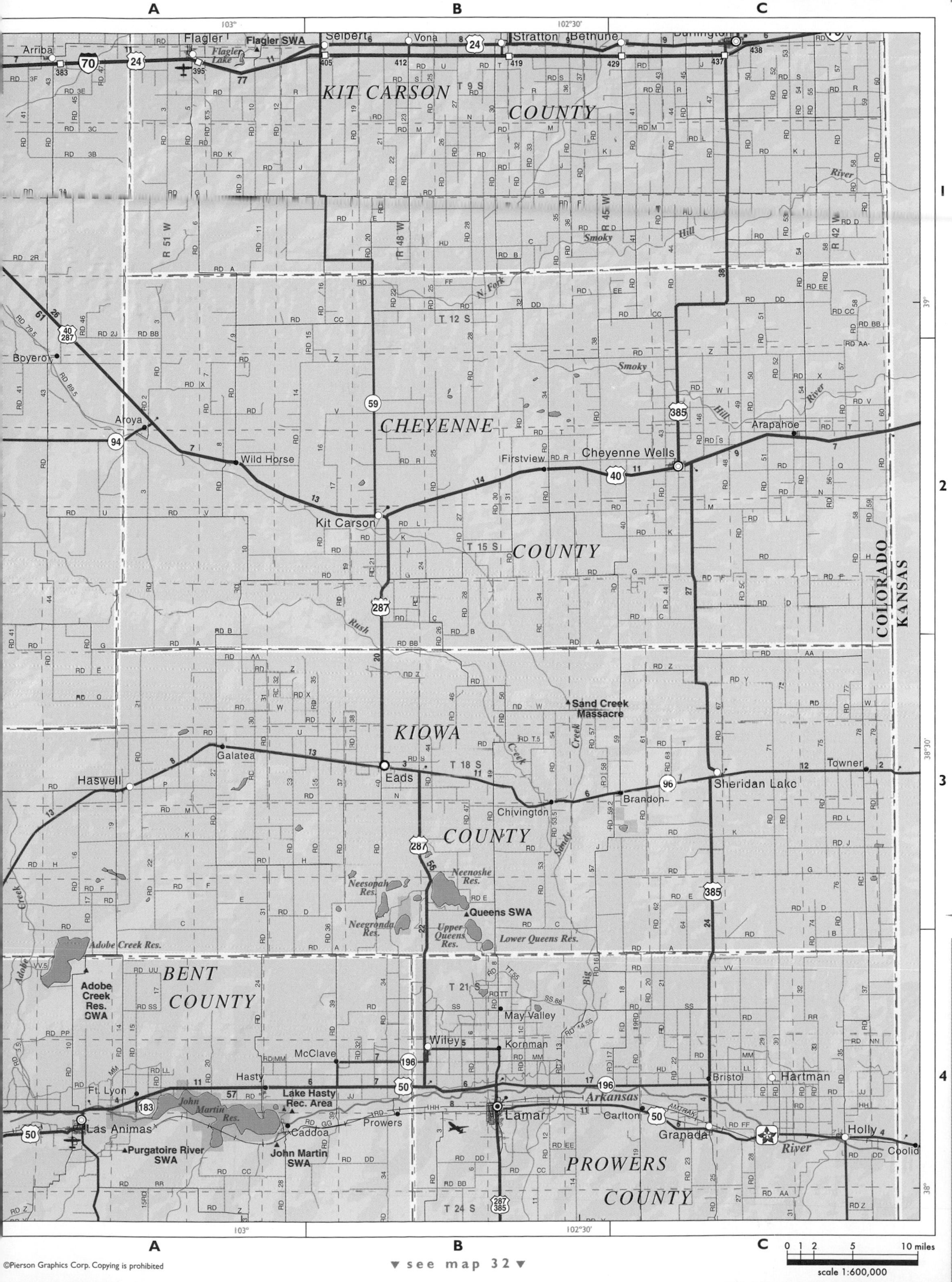

N. Fork

COLORADO RECREATIONAL

0 1 2 5 10 miles
scale 1:600,000

103°
102°30'
39°
38°30'
38°

T 9 S
T 12 S
T 15 S
T 18 S
T 21 S
T 24 S

R 51 W
R 48 W
R 45 W
R 42 W

Map Labels

Counties and Regions
- OURAY COUNTY
- MONTROSE COUNTY
- SAN MIGUEL COUNTY
- DOLORES COUNTY
- MONTEZUMA COUNTY
- UNCOMPAHGRE NATIONAL FOREST
- SAN JUAN NATIONAL FOREST
- MT. SNEFFELS WILDERNESS
- LIZARD HEAD WILDERNESS
- MESA VERDE NATIONAL PARK
- Hovenweep National Monument
- MANCOS STATE PARK
- Ute Mountain Indian Reservation
- Ute Mtn. Tribal Park
- Southern Ute Indian Reservation
- Navajo Indian Reservation

Towns and Places
- Vancorum
- Naturita
- Redvale
- Norwood
- Basin
- Dry Creek Basin SWA
- Miramonte SWA
- Lone Cone SWA
- Placerville
- Sawpit
- Vanadium
- Telluride
- Tellu...
- Ames
- Ophir
- Dunton
- Rico
- Slick Rock
- Egnar
- Northdale
- Dove Creek
- Cahone
- Pleasant View
- Yellow Jacket
- Lewis
- Dolores
- Lebanon
- Arriola
- Cortez
- Mancos
- Weber
- Hesperus
- La Plata
- Mayday
- Breen
- Kline
- Marvel
- Red Mesa
- Towaoc
- Ute Mountain
- Mancos River Trading Post
- 4 Corners
- La Plata
- Cedar Hill
- Riverside
- Durango
- Ft. Lewis Co
- Fort Lewis
- Hermosa
- Rockwood
- Tamarron Resort
- Purgatory
- Stoner
- Goodman
- Hesperus

Peaks and Passes
- Gypsum Gap Pass 6,100
- Mt. Sneffels 14,150
- Wilson Peak 14,017
- El Diente Peak 14,159
- Mt. Wilson 14,246
- Lizard Head Pass 10,222
- Grizzly Peak 13,280
- Coal Bank Pass 10,640
- OPHIR PASS

Water Features
- Gurley Reservoir
- Cone Reservoir
- Miramonte Reservoir
- Belmear Lake
- Groundhog Res.
- McPhee Reservoir
- Narraguinnep Res.
- Puett Reservoir
- Totten Reservoir
- Summit Res.
- Canyon Res.
- Mancos Lake
- Bauer Lake
- Mormon Res.
- Electra Lake
- Trout Lake
- Chapman Lake
- Dolores River
- Disappointment Creek
- Groundhog Creek
- San Miguel River
- West Dolores River
- Hermosa Creek
- Animas River
- La Plata River
- Mancos River
- McKenzie Creek
- Horsefly Creek
- Naturita Creek
- Galloway Rd

Highways
- 90, 97, 141, 145, 62, 24, 666, 184, 160, 550, 41, 46, 140

State/Border Labels
- UTAH
- ARIZ.
- COLORADO
- NEW MEXICO

0 1 2 5 10 miles
scale 1:600,000

109° 108°30' 108°
38° 37°30' 37°

OURAY
COUNTY

RIDGWAY
STATE PARK

Ridgway Res.
Silver Jack Res.

Ridgway

Owl Creek Pass
10,115

UNCOMPAHGRE

NATIONAL

FOREST

Sheep Mtn.
13,168

UNCOMPAHGRE

WILDERNESS

Uncompahgre Peak
14,309
Wetterhorn Peak
14,015

MT. SNEFFELS

Mt. Sneffels
14,150

WILDERNESS

Ouray

Camp Bird

Telluride
Historic Mining
District

Telluride

Blue
Lake

St. Paul
Ski Lodge

Ophir

OPHIR PASS

SAN JUAN

Gladstone

Red Mountain Pass
11,008

Storm Peak
13,487

Silverton
Historic Mining
District

COUNTY

Molas Pass
10,910

Coal Bank
Pass
10,640

Grizzly Peak
13,738

SAN JUAN

Canby Mtn.
13,478

HINSDALE

Redcloud Peak
14,034

Handies Peak
14,048

Sherman

Carson Peak
13,658

Pole Creek Mtn.
13,716

POWDERHORN

Powderhorn Lakes

GUNNISON

Devils Lake

Henson

Lake City

Golconda Resort
Slumgullion Pass
11,361

Lake
San Cristobal

Spring Creek
Pass - 10,906

COUNTY

Cebolla SWA

Cathedral

Los Pinos Pass
10,500

NATIONAL

La Garita

San Luis Peak
14,014

Steward Peak
13,983

FOREST

WILDERNESS

COCHETOPA

Cochetopa Dome
11,132

Dome
Lakes

North Pass
10,149

McDonough
Reservoir

Mesa Mtn.
12,958

RIO GRAND

Creede

Wagon Wheel Gap

MINERAL

Spar City

Lake
Humphries

Santa Maria
Reservoir

Brown
Lakes

COUNTY

MOUNTAINS

Metroz
Lake

South F

Alpi

Beaver Creek
Reservoir

SAN

Rio Grande Pyramid
13,821

JUAN

Ute
Lake

Rock Lake

WEMINUCHE

Granite
Lake

WILDERNESS

Cimmarrona Peak
12,575

CONTINENTAL

DIVIDE

South River Peak
13,149

Big
Meadows
Res

Wolf Creek Pass
10,857

Wolf
Creek

Alberta
Park Res.

North Mtn
12,754

Sunlight Peak
14,059

Mt. Eolus
14,084

Mt. Windom
14,087

Hazel Lake

Emerald
Lake

Williams Creek
Reservoir

NATIONAL

Silverton

Durango

Electra Lake

Rockwood

Hermosa

LA PLATA

Lemon Dam
Reservoir

Vallecito
Reservoir

City Reservoir

COUNTY

FOREST

Chimney Rock

Hatcher
Reservoir
Sullenburger
Res.

Pagosa Springs

Echo Canyon
Reservoir

Summit Peak
13,300

Blackhead Peak
12,495

SOUTH
SAN

Ft. Lewis
College

Durango

Gem Village

Bayfield

Oxford

Pastorius Res.

Southern Ute
Agency

Ignacio

Capote
Lake

Stollsteimer

Lonetree

ARCHULETA

Gramp Peak
12,145

Banded Peak
12,778

COUNTY

Spence Reservoir

Chromo

Chama Peak
12,019

Riverside

Cedar Hill

Allison

Arboles

NAVAJO
STATE PARK

Pagosa
Junction

COLORADO

NEW MEXICO

Navajo Reservoir

Jicarilla Apache

Indian Reservation

CARSON

NATL. FOREST

Lumberton

©Pierson Graphics Corp. Copying is prohibited.

scale 1:600,000

0 1 2 5 10 miles

◄ see map 29 ►

A   B   C

106°30'   106°   105°30'

COLORADO RECREATIONAL

West Pass Creek
Cochetopa Dome ×11,132
North Pass 10,149
Cochetopa Pass 10,032
COCHETOPA HILLS
Hayden Peak 12,130
Villa Grove
Valley View Hot Springs
Mineral Hot Springs
SANGRE
Rainbow Lake
Brush Creek Lakes
Electric Peaks 13,621
SAN ISABEL
The Pines
Westcliffe
114

1

Devils Knob 8,938 ×
Saguache
SAGUACHE
Tracy Mtn. 11,017
285
Moffat
Crestone
RIO GRANDE
Rito Alto Peak 13,794
NATIONAL
Mt. Adams ×13,931
Kit Carson Peak 14,165
Humboldt Peak ×14,064
Crestone Peak 14,294
Crestone Needle 14,197
WET
FOREST
Mesa Mtn. 12,958
COUNTY
Russell Lakes SWA
Russell Lakes
Mishak Lakes
BACA
Cottonwood Creek
Deadman
GRANT
Great Sand Dunes
15

RIO GRANDE
La Garita
La Garita Creek
Carnero Creek
17
San Luis Creek
National Monument
Wagon Wheel Gap
149
Center
112
Hooper
SAN LUIS STATE PARK
150

2

Alpine
Hanna
Rio
Del Norte
RIO GRANDE
285
Mosca
San Luis Res.
Ellingwood Point 14,042
Little Bear Peak 14,037
160
South Fork
NATIONAL
Sevenmile Plaza
Grande
COUNTY
Torres
Homelake
Sherman Lake
SAN LUIS VALLEY
ALAMOSA
Metroz Lake
Beaver Creek Reservoir
FOREST
Monte Vista
Parma
Rio Grande SWA
COUNTY
Wolf Creek
North Mtn. 12,754
Fuchs Reservoir
Bennett Peak 13,203
Monte Vista NWR
Adams State College
Alamosa
160
Blanca
CONTINENTAL
Summitville
Jasper
FOREST
Alamosa NWR
Ft. Garland
370
371
368
SANGRE de CRISTO

3

Summit Peak 13,300
Platoro Res.
Platoro
Kerr Lake
Big Lake
Red Mtn. 12,018
Terrace Res.
Estrella
GRANT
Blackhead Peak ×12,495
Rio Blanco River
Conejos Peak 13,172
Blue Lake
SOUTH
SAN JUAN
La Jara Reservoir
La Jara Reservoir SWA
CONEJOS
Capulin
La Jara
136
Sanford
San Acacio
142
15
285
Culebra
WILDERNESS
Gramp Peak 12,145 ×
Victoria Lake
DIVIDE
La Jara SWA
Romeo
Manassa
Los Cerritos
Mesita
159

4

ARCHULETA
Banded Peak ×12,778
Trujillo Meadows Res.
Piñorealosa Mtn. 10,984
Fox Creek
COUNTY
Guadalupe
Conejos
Lobatos
17
Chama Peak ×12,019
Cumbres Pass 10,022
Cumbres
CUMBRES
Conejos Ranch
Antonito
Cove Lake Reservoir
Jaroso
Garcia
COUNTY
San Antonio
COLORADO
NEW MEXICO
CARSON
NATIONAL
Los Pinos
Ute Mtn. ×10,093
Costill

0 1 2   5   10 miles
scale 1:600,000

©Pierson Graphics Corp. Copying is prohibited

A B C

105° 104°30'

Grape Creek
De Weese Res.
T 21 S
RD 265
RD 271
Wetmore
Adobe Peak 10,188
Hardscrabble
Siloam
PUEBLO STATE PARK 45
19
50
98
Vineland
Avondale
209
96
50
RD 260
RD 34
15
McKenzie Junction
96
SILOAM RD 207
RED CREEK
SPRINGS
GALBREATH
RD 208
Salt Creek
94
25
South
8
302
36TH LN
40TH LN
44TH LN
55TH LN
Apple LN
River

Silver Cliff
Querida
Rosita
WET MTN.
VALLEY COUNTY
CUSTER COUNTY
RD 271
RD 858
RD 306
San Isabel
Fairview
Beulah
78
Rock
21
WATER BARREL
BERGEMAN RD
RD 227
Stem Beach
91
Lime
88
87
St. Charles Res.
PUEBLO COUNTY
Huerfano Lake
Dotson Reservoir
OLSON
HUCKLEBER

165
Valley View
Pueblo Mtn. Park
St. Charles Peak 11,784
San Isabel
Beckwith Reservoir
74
77
49
83
Burnt Mill
CEDARWOOD RD
Cedarwood
VIGIL & ST. VRAIN GRANT
703
RD 333
RD 319

Lake Isabel
NATIONAL
12
Rye
165
71
Colorado City
PICKNEY RD
MUSTANG RD
RD 701
705
Cedar Crest
73

Greenhorn
Greenhorn Mtn. 12,349
FOREST
67
RD 112
25
RD 111
103
122
123
RD 125
RD 130
RD 123
24
RD 311

Gardner
69
Farisita
5
RD 555
RD 560
540
RD 616
LASCAR
64
RD
Orlando Res.
River
120
121
Cucharas Reservoir
10

Mosca Pass 9,750
Malachite
Sharpsdale
Huerfano
Red Wing
Badito
Delcarbon
60
59
55
RD 640
RD 103
RD 610
Maria Res.
River
RD 210
LAS ANIMAS COUNTY
Apishapa SWA

Carbonate Mtn. 12,308
T 27 S
RD 559
HUERFANO
521
52
50
Walsenburg
Cuchara Junction
214
211
RD 212
R 53 W

Mt. Lindsey 14,042
Little Bear Peak 14,037
North La Veta Pass 9,413
Pass Creek Pass 9,400
Mt. Maestas 11,569
LATHROP STATE PARK
Horseshoe Lake
Martin Lake
Walsenburg Res.
49
85 87
Saliba Lake
77

La Veta Pass 9,382
La Veta
160
Cucharas
COUNTY
Monson
42
41
160
019
350

Fort Garland
Fort Garland
73
SAN ISABEL NATIONAL FOREST
Three Bridges
12
RD 440
ROUSE
Santa Clara Creek
34
31
30
Seven Lakes Res.

COSTILLA
159
16
Mountain Home Res.
Napolean Peak 11,866
Cuchara Mountain Resort
East Spanish Peak 12,683
West Spanish Peak 13,626
Aguilar
27
RD 65 W
Model Reservoir
Mode
Earl

San Luis
Trinchera Peak 13,517
CUCHARA FOREST
Cordova Pass 11,005
Cucharas Pass 9,941
Gulnare
Ludlow
Ludlow Monument
23
25
Hoehne
AMTRAK

Chama
San Pablo
De Anza Peak 13,333
Monument Lake
North Lake
Spanish Peaks SWA
Boncarbo
18
15
239
El Moro
Beshoar
160

San Francisco
Sanchez Reservoir
Culebra Peak 14,047
Monument Park
Vigil
PARK PLATEAU
RD 32.5
RD 30.1
Medina Plaza
Cokedale
Madrid
Jansen
Trinidad
Historic Area
Barela

Culebra Range
CULEBRA RANGE
Stonewall
Weston
12
3
Sogundo
Valdez
Trinidad Lake
TRINIDAD STATE PARK
Starkville
Fisher Peak 9,627

196
Amalia
Tercio
BEAUBIEN & MIRANDA MAXWELL GRANT
Bosque del Oso SWA
RATON MESA
Morley
Raton Pass 7,843

COLORADO
NEW MEXICO
25
Raton

105°30'
105°
104°30'
37°

A B C

0 1 2 5 10 miles

scale 1:600,000

COLORADO RECREATIONAL

▼ see map 31 ▼

A   B   C

◄ see map 30 ►

COLORADO RECREATIONAL

PUEBLO COUNTY

North Avondale
Boone
Vineland
Avondale
Olson
Huerfano Lake
Nepesta
Dotson Res.
Cedar Crest

VIGIL & ST. VRAIN GRANT

Olney Springs
King Center
Crowley
Ordway
Sugar City
Lake Henry
Lake Meredith
Breckenridge
Timber Lake
Horse Creek Res.

Fowler
Manzanola
Vroman
Hays
Cheraw
Cheraw Res.

OTERO

Rocky Ford
Swink
North La Junta
La Junta
Hawley
Bent's Old Fort NHS
Arkansas River

COUNTY

Setchfield SWA

COMANCHE

Timpas
Higbee

NATIONAL

GRASSLAND

David Canyon

Apishapa SWA

Delhi

Houghton

Thatcher

Pinon Canyon

Military Reservation

Pinon Park

PURGATOIRE CANYON

Seven Lakes Res.
Tyrone

Model
Model Res.

Earl

Hoehne

LAS ANIMAS

El Moro
Beshoar
Purgatoire River

Trinidad
Historic Area

COUNTY

Villegreen

Tobe

Kim

Walts Corner

Starkville
Fisher Peak
9,627

RATON MESA

Barela

Trinchera
8.8

Branson

Morley

Raton Pass
7,834

COLORADO

NEW MEXICO

0 1 2   5   10 miles

scale 1:600,000

A   B   C

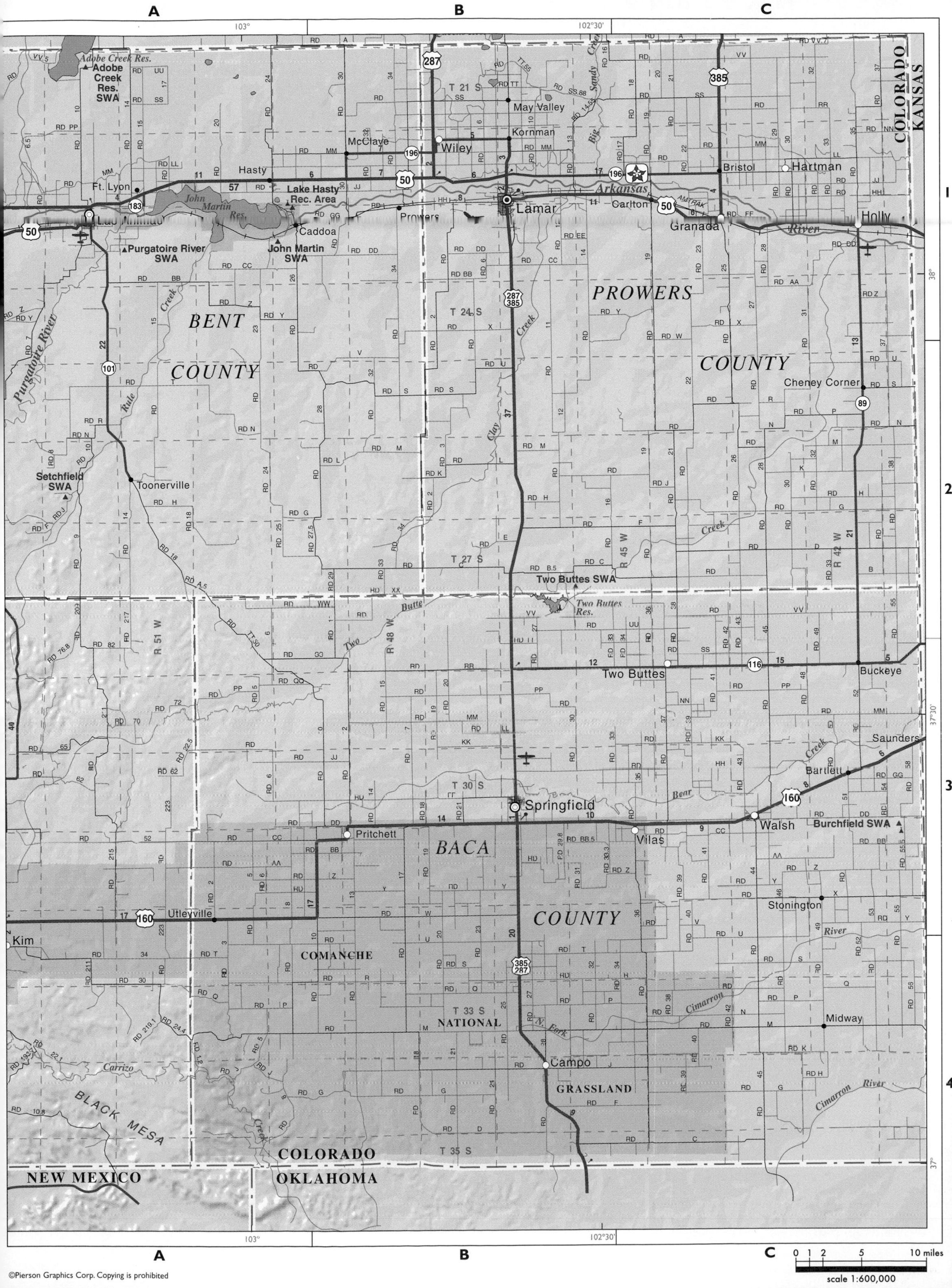

COLORADO
KANSAS

Adobe Creek Res.
▲ Adobe Creek Res. SWA

RD PP
Ft. Lyon
183
50
Las Animas
50
101
Purgatoire River SWA
John Martin Res.

McClave
Hasty
Lake Hasty Rec. Area
Caddoa
John Martin SWA
Prowers

287
196
Wiley
50
196
Kornman
May Valley

Lamar
Carlton
50
AMTRAK
Bristol
Hartman
Granada
Holly
Arkansas River

287
385

BENT COUNTY

PROWERS COUNTY

T 24 S
Clay Creek

Cheney Corner
89

Setchfield SWA
Toonerville

R 45 W

R 42 W
R 33 W

Two Buttes SWA
Two Buttes Res.

T 27 S

Two Buttes
116
Buckeye

R 51 W
R 48 W
Two Butte Creek

Saunders
Bartlett
160
Burchfield SWA
Walsh
Stonington

Springfield
Vilas
Bear Creek

Pritchett

BACA COUNTY

160
Utleyville
Kim

COMANCHE

385
287
Midway
Cimarron River

T 33 S

NATIONAL

Campo
GRASSLAND
N. Fork

BLACK MESA

T 35 S

COLORADO
OKLAHOMA

NEW MEXICO

103°
102°30'
102°30'

A
B
C

0 1 2 5 10 miles
scale 1:600,000

COLORADO RECREATIONAL

NATIONAL PARKS & MONUMENTS

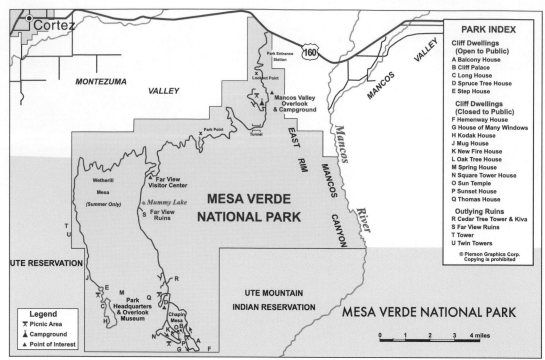

PARK INDEX

Cliff Dwellings
(Open to Public)
A Balcony House
B Cliff Palace
C Long House
D Spruce Tree House
E Step House

Cliff Dwellings
(Closed to Public)
F Hemenway House
G House of Many Windows
H Kodak House
J Mug House
K New Fire House
L Oak Tree House
M Spring House
N Square Tower House
O Sun Temple
P Sunset House
Q Thomas House

Outlying Ruins
R Cedar Tree Tower & Kiva
S Far View Ruins
T Tower
U Twin Towers

© Pierson Graphics Corp.
Copying is prohibited

Legend
✗ Picnic Area
▲ Campground
▲ Point of Interest

Mesa Verde National Park
(27 B-3) South of US Hwy 160, 10 miles E of Cortez. Pre-Columbian Pueblo Indians built these well preserved cliff dwellings, which were abandoned at about the same time as the Hovenweep ruins. The park is well developed with facilities for camping and hiking. (970) 529-4465.

Rocky Mountain National Park
(6 A-4) Just W of Estes Park on US. Hwy 34. The park contains over 400 square miles of mountain peaks, lakes and valleys, straddling the Continental Divide. America's highest continuous paved road, Trail Ridge Road attains an elevation of 12,183 feet. Hiking trails, camping and picnic facilities are numerous, but fill to overflow proportions in the summer months. (970) 586-1206. 5 miles NE OF Granby on US Hwy 34. This large recreation area wraps around Lake Granby and Shadow Mountain Lake at the SW corner of Rocky Mountain National Park. Every sort of water sport and camping are provided. (970) 498-1100.

Arapaho National Recreation Area (10 A-2) Five miles NE OF Granby on US Hwy 34. This large recreation area wraps around Lake Granby and Shadow Mountain Lake at the SW corner of Rocky Mountain National Park. Water sports, fishing and camping. (970) 498-1100.

Bent's Old Fort National Historical Site (25 C-4) On State Hwy 194, about 8 miles NE of La Junta. An outpost of civilization on the Santa Fe Trail and center of fur trading activity, the fort has been restored to its 1845 appearance. Picnic areas, but no camping or hiking. (719) 383-5010.

Black Canyon of the Gunnison National Monument (22 A-3) On State Hwy 347, about 14 miles NE of Montrose. This steep gorge cut by the Gunnison River averages over 2,000 feet deep, yet is only about half a mile wide. The canyon is in seemingly perpetual shadow. Camping is available, but check in with park rangers before attempting any hiking into the canyon. There are no marked trails. (970) 641-2337.

Colorado National Monument (21 A-1) On State Hwy 340, 10 miles W of Grand Junction. Sheer cliffs, canyons, fossils and prehistoric ruins, mark this colorful monument sitting on a mesa high above the Colorado River. Hiking, camping and picnic areas are available. (970) 858-3617.

Curecanti National Recreation Area (22 B-3) On US Hwy 50 between Gunnison & Montrose. Three lakes comprise the recreation area. Many recreational opportunities exist including hiking, boating, fishing, camping and cross-country skiing. (970) 641-2337.

Dinosaur National Monument (1 A-2) North of US Hwy 40 in the extreme NW corner of the state. Attractions include dinosaur fossils, spectacular scenery, hiking, and white water rafting and camping on the Green and Yampa Rivers. (970) 374-3000.

Florissant Fossil Beds National Monument (24 A-2) South of US Hwy 24, 32 miles W of Colorado Springs. Find fossilized insects, leaves and petrified Sequoia stumps from the Oligocene period (30 million years ago) on the site of an ancient volcano. There are no camping facilities, but hiking trails and picnic areas are available. (719) 748-3253.

Great Sand Dunes National Monument (29 C-2) On State Hwy 150, 34 miles NW of Alamosa. North America's tallest sand dunes rise 700 feet above the floor of the San Luis Valley, at the foot of the Sangre de Cristo Mountains. Camping and hiking are available. (719) 378-2312.

Hovenweep National Monument (27 A-3) Southwest of US Hwy 666 in the SW corner of state. The monument consists of a collection of pueblos, towers and cliff dwellings created by pre-Columbian Pueblo Indians and abandoned 700 years ago. Camping, hiking and picnic areas are available. (970) 749-0510.

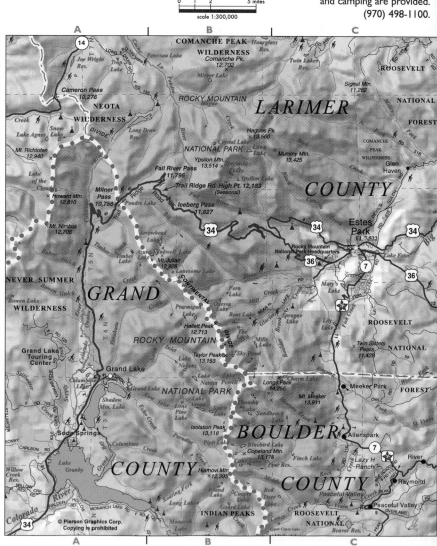

COLORADO SKI AREAS

DENVER INTERNATIONAL AIRPORT

Denver, Colorado
www.flydenver.com

**Transportation Service From
Denver Internation Airport
to the Following Resort Areas:**

Aspen/Snowmass . Colorado Airport Shuttle • (970) 920-9124
. . . . Colorado Mountain Express • (800) 525-6363
Estes Park . . . . Emerald Taxi • (970) 586-1992
Glenwood Springs
. . . . Colorado Mountain Express • (800) 525-6363
Grand Lake . . . . Home James • (800) 451-4844
Monarch . . . . Timberline Express • (800) 288-1375
Summit County (Breckenridge, Keystone,
    Copper Mountain, Dillon)
. . . . Resort Express • (800) 334-7433
Steamboat Springs . . . . Alpine Taxi • (800) 343-7433
. . . . Steamboat Express • (800) 545-6050
Vail/Beaver Creek
. . . . Colorado Mountain Express • (800) 525-6363
. . . . Vans to Vail • (800) 525-6363
Winter Park . . . . Home James • (800) 451-4844

- **AGTS Trains - AGTS Level**
  Trains to and from concourses
- **Auto Passenger Drop Off - Level 6**
- **Auto Passenger Pick Up- Level 4**
- **Baggage Claim - Level 5**
- **Commercial Drop Off - Level 5**
  Vans, Limos, Buses, Cabs
- **Commercial Pick Up - Level 5**
  Vans, Limos, Buses, Cabs
- **Public Parking _ Levels 1-5**
- **Ticketing Level - Level 6**
  Departures

Important Numbers

- DIA Information 303-342-2000
- DIA Paging 303-342-2300
- DIA Parking Info 303-DIA-PARK (303-342-7275)
- DIA Ground Transportation Shuttle Service 303-342-4059
- RTD Information . . . . 303-299-6000 or 800-366-7433
- RTD TDD 303-299-6098
- RTD Web Site . . . . www.RTD-denver.com

Concourse C
American
ATA
Delta
Midwest Express
Northwest
Sun Country
TWA
US Airways
Vanguard
Charters & Commuters

Concourse B
Air Canada
United
United Express

Concourse A
America West
British Airways
Continental
Frontier
Korean Air
Mexicana

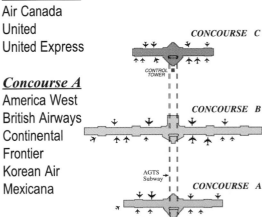

CAR RENTAL LOCATIONS

TO DENVER   PEÑA   BLVD

RETURN TO AIRPORT →

E. 78th AVE   E. 78th AVE (Service Road)

E. 75th AVE

E. 71st AVE

0   1/4   1/2
Miles

GUN CLUB RD
JACKSON GAP RD
OAK HILL ST
PATSBURG ST
POWHATON ST
ROBERTDALE ST
TITUS ST
UNDERGROVE ST
SHADY GROVE ST
HARRY B. COMBS PKWY
UNDERGROVE CIR
VANDRIVER ST
E. 75th CIR
E. 80th AVE

AIRBORNE
FEDERAL EXPRESS
UNITED CARGO
UNITED KITCHEN
VEHICLE STORAGE
AIRPORT MAINTENANCE
COMMERCIAL STAGING AREA
TENDER FUELING SITE
CONTINENTAL KITCHEN
Vehicle Service Road

© Pierson Graphics Corp.
Copying is strictly Prohibited

COLORADO SKI AREAS

COLORADO

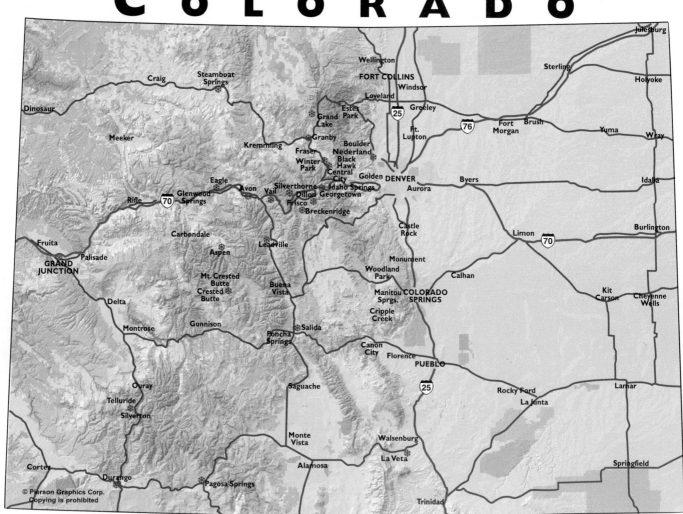

ARAPAHOE BASIN
P.O. Box 8787
Arapahoe Basin, Colorado 80435

STATISTICS
Base Elevation: 10,800'
Peak Elevation: 13,050'
Vertical Rise: 2,250'
Number of Lifts: 5
Number of Trails: 61
Skiable Acres: 490
Longest Run: 1.5 Miles
Lift Capacity: 6,066 Skiers/Hour
Half Pipe: No
Snowboard Park: No
Average Snowfall: 367"
Child Care: Yes

PHONE NUMBERS
Main: (888) ARAPAHOE / (970) 468-0718
Reservations & Snow Report: (888) ARAPAHOE
Ski School: (970) 496-7007
www.arapahoebasin.com

Arapahoe Basin opened in 1946, living up to its nickname, the Legend, by remaining the highest lift-served terrain (13,050 feet) in North America. KBCO radio's annual Cardboard Derby is held in January, a downhill race for crafts made of cardboard, paper, tape, glue and string. Snowshoeing, ice skating, cross-country and telemark skiing, snowmobiling and sleigh rides are other popular outdoor activities.

Aspen Highlands

Beginner **20%** Intermediate **33%** Advanced **17%** Expert **30%**

ASPEN HIGHLANDS
Aspen Skiing Company
P.O. Box 1248
Aspen, Colorado 81612

STATISTICS
Base Elevation: 8,040'
Peak Elevation: 11,675'
Vertical Rise: 3,635'
Number of Lifts: 6
Number of Trails: 118
Skiable Acres: 680
Longest Run: 3.5 Miles
Lift Capacity: 5,700 Skiers/Hour
Half Pipe: No
Snowboard Park: Yes
Average Snowfall: 300"
Child Care: Yes

PHONE NUMBERS
Main: (800) 525-6200 / (970) 925-1220
Reservations: (888) 452-2409
Snow Report: (888) ASPEN-SNO
Ski School: (800) 525-6200 / (970) 925-1220
www.skiaspen.com

*B*eautiful views and skiing in the trees are two of Aspen Highland's hallmarks. Annual events include the Wintersköl winter carnival in mid-January, the Ski-Whee, a cardboard derby using homemade cardboard sleds, and KSPN radio's anniversary party, Blitzenbanger. Tired of skiing and boarding? Try dogsled rides, sleigh rides, snowcat tours, snowshoe nature tours, snowmobiling, cross-country skiing, ice climbing, ice fishing, tubing, and ice skating.

ASPEN HIGHLANDS

ELEVATION TOP:	11,675 ft/3559 m
VERTICAL RISE:	3,635 ft/1108 m
SKIABLE TERRAIN:	680 acres/261 hectares
LONGEST RUN:	3.5 miles/5.63 km
LIFTS:	2 high-speed quad chairs, 3 double chairs, 1 triple
LIFT CAPACITY:	5,700 skiers per hour
AVERAGE ANNUAL SNOWFALL:	300 inches/762 cm
SNOWMAKING CAPABILITIES:	110 acres/44.5 hectares (20% of area)
EASIEST TERRAIN:	20%
MORE DIFFICULT TERRAIN:	33%
MOST DIFFICULT TERRAIN:	17%
EXPERT TERRAIN:	30%
SEASON DATES:	December 11, 1998 — April 4, 1999

ASPEN HIGHLANDS
TRAIL MAP AND SKIER GUIDE

- Easiest Trails
- More Difficult
- Most Difficult
- Expert Only
- Lifts
- High-Speed Quad
- Least Difficult Way Down
- High Traffic Area Ski Courteously
- Danger
- Ski Patrol
- Emergency Phones
- Closed Area Do Not Enter
- NASTAR
- Warming Hut
- Group Picnic Area
- Picnic Tables
- Ski School
- Ski Check
- Tickets
- On-Mountain Concierge
- Aspen Highlands Sports
- Restaurant
- Restrooms
- Buses
- Day Parking
- Handicapped Access
- Ticket Information Office
- Mountain Photo

SYMBOLS AND COLOR CODES INDICATE THE RELATIVE SKIING DIFFICULTY FOR SLOPES AND TRAILS ON ASPEN HIGHLANDS ONLY. FOR YOUR OWN PROTECTION, DO NOT START DOWN A TRAIL OR SLOPE UNTIL YOU KNOW ITS DEGREE OF DIFFICULTY AND NEVER SKI A CLOSED TRAIL.

FOR MORE INFORMATION ON THE ASPEN HIGHLANDS VILLAGE OF TOMORROW, INQUIRE ABOUT OUR BASE AREA MAP.

ASPEN MOUNTAIN

ASPEN MOUNTAIN
Aspen Skiing Company
P.O. Box 1248
Aspen, Colorado 81612

STATISTICS
Base Elevation: 7,945'
Peak Elevation: 11,212'
Vertical Rise: 3,267'
Number of Lifts: 8
Number of Trails: 76
Skiable Acres: 675
Longest Run: 3 Miles
Lift Capacity: 10,755 Skiers/Hour
Half Pipe: No
Snowboard Park: No
Average Snowfall: 300"
Child Care: Yes

PHONE NUMBERS
Main: (800) 525-6200 / (970) 925-1220
Reservations: (888) 452-2409
Snow Report: (888) ASPEN-SNO
Ski School: (800) 525-6200 / (970) 925-1220
www.skiaspen.com

Sorry, no snowboarding.

Photos courtesy of Aspen Skiing Company / Burnham Arndt, Petter McBride, Biege Jones

*O*nce famous as a silver-mining town, Aspen still has a working mine on the mountain. The mountain is not for beginners; there are no green runs. Aspen lends itself to events such as the 24 Hours of Aspen Ski Race. Teams ski around the clock, resting only on the 14 minute lift ride to the top of the course. For other outdoor activities try dogsledding, snowcat tours, snowshoe nature tours, hot air ballooning, ice climbing, ice fishing, sleigh rides, ice skating, cross-country skiing, tubing, and snowmobiling.

ASPEN MOUNTAIN

ELEVATION TOP:	11,212 ft/3418 m
VERTICAL RISE:	3,267 ft/996 m
SKIABLE TERRAIN:	675 acres/273 hectares
LONGEST RUN:	3 miles/4.83 km
LIFTS:	Silver Queen Gondola, 1 high-speed quad chair, 1 high-speed double chair, 2 quad chairs, 3 double chairs
LIFT CAPACITY:	10,755 skiers per hour
AVERAGE ANNUAL SNOWFALL:	300 inches/762 cm
SNOWMAKING CAPABILITIES:	210 acres/88 hectares (33% of area)
EASIEST TERRAIN:	None
MORE DIFFICULT TERRAIN:	35%
MOST DIFFICULT TERRAIN:	35%
EXPERT TERRAIN:	30%
SEASON DATES:	November 21, 1998 — April 18, 1999

ASPEN MOUNTAIN
TRAIL MAP AND SKIER GUIDE

More Difficult	⚠ Danger	🎫 Tickets		
Most Difficult	Ski Patrol	Ski School		
Expert Only	Restrooms	Restaurant		
Lifts	NASTAR	Picnic Tables		
High-Speed Quad	Self Timer Course	Ski Rental		
High Speed Double	Lockers	Buses		
Gondola	Compromise Mine	On-Mountain Concierge		
Special Events Lift Limited Operation	Ski Check	Performance Center		
High Traffic Area Ski Courteously	Mountain Photo	Powder Tours Registration		
Closed Area Do Not Enter	Retail Shop	Ticket Information Offices		
	Handicapped Access	XC Skiing		

SYMBOLS AND COLOR CODES INDICATE THE RELATIVE SKIING DIFFICULTY FOR SLOPES AND TRAILS ON ASPEN MOUNTAIN ONLY. FOR YOUR OWN PROTECTION, DO NOT START DOWN A TRAIL OR SLOPE UNTIL YOU KNOW ITS DEGREE OF DIFFICULTY AND NEVER SKI A CLOSED TRAIL.

Beaver Creek

Beginner **34%** Intermediate **39%** Advanced **17%** Expert **10%**

BEAVER CREEK
P.O. Box 7
Vail, Colorado 81658

STATISTICS
Base Elevation: 7,400'-8,100'
Peak Elevation: 11,440'
Vertical Rise: 4,040'
Number of Lifts: 14
Number of Trails: 146
Skiable Acres: 1,625
Longest Run: 3.5 Miles
Lift Capacity: 24,739 Skiers/Hour
Half Pipe: Yes
Snowboard Park: Yes
Average Snowfall: 331"
Child Care: Yes

PHONE NUMBERS
Main: (970) 845-6610
Reservations & Snow Report: (800) 427-8216
Ski School: (970) 845-5300
www.snow.com

*B*eaver Creek, Vail's younger sister, opened in the winter of 1980. The ski resort had originally been planned by developers for the 1976 Winter Olympics, but Colorado voters overwhelmingly defeated the scheme. The annual Snowshoe Shuffle is the largest snowshoe race in North America held the first Saturday in April. The ski resort boasts the only outdoor escalator in the US. Other outdoor activities include dogsledding, hot air ballooning, snowshoeing, cross-country skiing, ice fishing, ice skating, snowmobiling, tubing, and sleigh rides to Beano's Cabin for gourmet dining in the woods.

&. Beaver Creek's Adaptive Disabled Skier's Program is taught by PSIA/Adaptive Certified or Disabled Sports Instructors. Adaptive ski equipment rentals are available at the ski school.

© Dan Cosey / Vail Resorts / Beaver Creek

Berthoud Pass

Beginner 20% Intermediate 30% Advanced 25% Expert 25%

BERTHOUD PASS SKI AREA
P.O. Box 3314
Winter Park, Colorado 80482

STATISTICS
Base Elevation: 11,307'
Peak Elevation: 12,407'
Vertical Rise: 1,100'
Number of Lifts: 2
Number of Trails: 67
Skiable Acres: 1300
Longest Run: .75 Miles
Half Pipe: Yes
Snowboard Park: Yes
Average Snowfall: 500"
Child Care: No

PHONE NUMBERS
Main: (303) 569-0100
Snow Report: (800) SKI-BERT
Ski School: (800) SKI-BERT
www.berthoudpass.com

© Byron Hetzler / Berthoud Pass Ski Area

Berthoud Pass Ski Area was one of the first ski areas in Colorado, and home to the first double chairlift in North America. Besides skiing and boarding, try snowshoeing, telemark skiing, cross-country skiing and complimentary mountain tours conducted by ski patrol members.

Breckenridge

Beginner 14% Intermediate 26% Advanced 22% Expert 38%

BRECKENRIDGE SKI RESORT
P.O. Box 1058
Breckenridge, Colorado 80424

STATISTICS
Base Elevation: 9,600'
Peak Elevation: 12,998'
Vertical Rise: 3,398'
Number of Lifts: 23
Number of Trails: 139
Skiable Acres: 2,043
Longest Run: 3.5 Miles
Lift Capacity: 30,625 Skiers/Hour
Half Pipe: Yes
Snowboard Park: Yes
Average Snowfall: 300"
Child Care: Yes

PHONE NUMBERS
Main: (800) 789-SNOW / (970) 453-5000
Reservations: (800) 221-1091
Snow Report: (800) 404-3535
Ski School: (888) LRN-2SKI
www.snow.com

© Bob Winsett / Vail Resorts / Breckenridge

BRECKENRIDGE SKI RESORT

Breckenridge is one of the most popular snowsports destinations in North America and home to Mach 1, one of the most challenging mogul runs on the freestyle World Cup schedule. Snowboarders can thrash in two terrain gardens complete with jumps and half-pipes. Or, if that is too strenuous, try snowmobiling, snowshoeing, ice skating, ice fishing, cross-country skiing, dogsledding, and dinner sleigh rides.

♿ The Breckenridge Outdoor Education Center (800-383-2632 or 970-453-6422) offers skiing lessons to adults and children with disabilities and serious illnesses. Instructors are PSIA certified and/or outdoor educators who are experienced working with all types of disabilities.

PEAK 9 Summit Elevation: 13,198 ft. / 4,024 m

643 ft. / 4,157 m

PEAK 8 Summit Elevation: 12,998 ft. / 3,963 m

PEAK 7 Summit Elevation: 12,671 ft. / 3,865 m

Ski Area Boundary

IMPERIAL BOWL

LAKE CHUTES

WHALE'S TAIL

PEAK 7 BOWL

Foot Access Peak 7

Ski Area Boundary

6 Chair
11,788 ft / 3,394 m

T-Bar 12,141 ft / 3,702 m

Foot Access Peak 8

PEAK 9 CHUTES

Foot Access Peak 9

HORSESHOE BOWL

NORTH BOWL

ART'S BOWLE

PEAK 9
11,460 ft / 3,494 m

Boneyard

CONTEST BOWL

Tele

Sadie

The End

TO PEAK 8

Peak 9
Restaurant

Vista Haus
11,059 ft / 3,372 m

CUCUMBER BOWL

PEAK 7 GLADES

Tom's Baby Sluce Box

TO PEAK 8

GoldKing

TO PEAK 8

TO PEAK 9

Freeway

Peak 7 Road

Midway Load

Ski Area Boundary

Kinder Carpet

Bergenhof Restaurant

Castle Carpet

Beaver Run Resort

The Great Divide Lodge

King's Crown Rd.

Breckenridge Nordic Center

Maggie Restaurant

Ski Hill Road

The Village at Breckenridge Resort

Village Carpet

Dredge Boat Lot

Park Avenue

Main Street

Miners Parking Lot

Tailings Parking Lot

Park Avenue

To Hwy 9 to Denver

Buttermilk Mountain

Beginner **35%** Intermediate **39%** Advanced **26%** Expert **0%**

BUTTERMILK MOUNTAIN

Aspen Skiing Company
P.O. Box 1248
Aspen, Colorado 81612

STATISTICS
Base Elevation: 7,870'
Peak Elevation: 9,900'
Vertical Rise: 2,030'
Number of Lifts: 7
Number of Trails: 43
Skiable Acres: 420
Longest Run: 3 Miles
Lift Capacity: 7,500 Skiers/Hour
Half Pipe: Yes
Snowboard Park: Yes
Average Snowfall: 200"
Child Care: Yes

PHONE NUMBERS
Main: (970) 925-1220
Reservations: (888) 452-2409
Snow Report: (888) ASPEN-SNO
Ski School: (800) 525-6200 / (970) 925-1220
www.skiaspen.com

Photos courtesy of Aspen Skiing Company / Burnham Arndt; Petter McBride; Biege Jones

Known as a good beginner's resort, Buttermilk also has enough challenging runs to satisfy all levels of expertise. Boarderfest in mid-December is a weekend long event for snowboarders only. No skiers allowed. In the meantime, try ice skating, snowshoe nature tours, dogsled, sleigh rides, cross-country skiing, hot air ballooning, ice climbing, ice fishing, snowmobiling, tubing, and snowcat tours.

BUTTERMILK MOUNTAIN

ELEVATION TOP:	9,900 ft/3018 m
VERTICAL RISE:	2,030 ft/618 m
SKIABLE TERRAIN:	420 acres/170 hectares
LONGEST RUN:	3 miles/4.83 km
LIFTS:	1 high-speed quad chair; 5 double chairs; 1 handletow
LIFT CAPACITY:	7,500 skiers per hour
AVERAGE ANNUAL SNOWFALL:	200 inches/508 cm
SNOWMAKING CAPABILITIES:	108 acres/44 hectares (27% of area)
EASIEST TERRAIN:	35%
MORE DIFFICULT TERRAIN:	39%
MOST DIFFICULT TERRAIN:	26%
EXPERT TERRAIN:	None
SEASON DATES:	December 11, 1998— April 4, 1999

BUTTERMILK MOUNTAIN
TRAIL MAP AND SKIER GUIDE

- Easiest Trails
- More Difficult
- Most Difficult
- Lifts
- High-Speed Quad
- Easiest Route
- Closed Area Do Not Enter
- Caution Blind Skier
- Snowboard Park
- Slow Skiing
- Ski Patrol
- Ski School
- Emergency Phones
- Warming Hut
- Buttermilk Sports
- Sack Lunch Area
- Handicapped Access
- Ticket Information Office
- Mountain Photo
- Tickets
- On-Mountain Concierge
- Ski Check
- Restaurant
- Picnic Tables
- Child Care Facilities
- Fort Frog
- Buses
- Day Parking
- Self Timer Course
- Retail Shop

SYMBOLS AND COLOR CODES INDICATE THE RELATIVE SKIING DIFFICULTY FOR SLOPES AND TRAILS ON BUTTERMILK MOUNTAIN ONLY. FOR YOUR OWN PROTECTION, DO NOT START DOWN A TRAIL OR SLOPE UNTIL YOU KNOW ITS DEGREE OF DIFFICULTY AND NEVER SKI A CLOSED TRAIL.

Beginner **21%** Intermediate **25%** Advanced **36%** Expert **18%**

COPPER MOUNTAIN RESORT
P.O. Box 3001
Copper Mountain, Colorado 80443

STATISTICS
Base Elevation: 9,712'
Peak Elevation: 12,313'
Vertical Rise: 2,601'
Number of Lifts: 20
Number of Trails: 118
Skiable Acres: 2,433
Longest Run: 2.8 Miles
Lift Capacity: 30,630 Skiers/Hour
Half Pipe: Yes
Snowboard Park: Yes
Average Snowfall: 280"
Child Care: Yes

PHONE NUMBERS
Main: (970) 968-2882
Reservations: (800) 458-8386
Snow Report: (800) 789-7609
Ski School: (970) 968-2882 ext. 6331
www.ski-copper.com

Photo by Ben Blankenburg / Copper Mountain Resort

Copper Mountain has Colorado's first six-passenger chairlift capable of transporting 3,000 skiers per hour. The ever-popular Eenie Weenie Bikini Ski Contest happens annually the second weekend in April. Other activities include cross-country and telemark skiing, tubing, ice skating, and snowmobiling. Nighttime activities under the lights include tubing and ice skating. Try Dining in the Woods, a sleigh ride to a miner's cabin for a western-style dinner and cowboy entertainment.

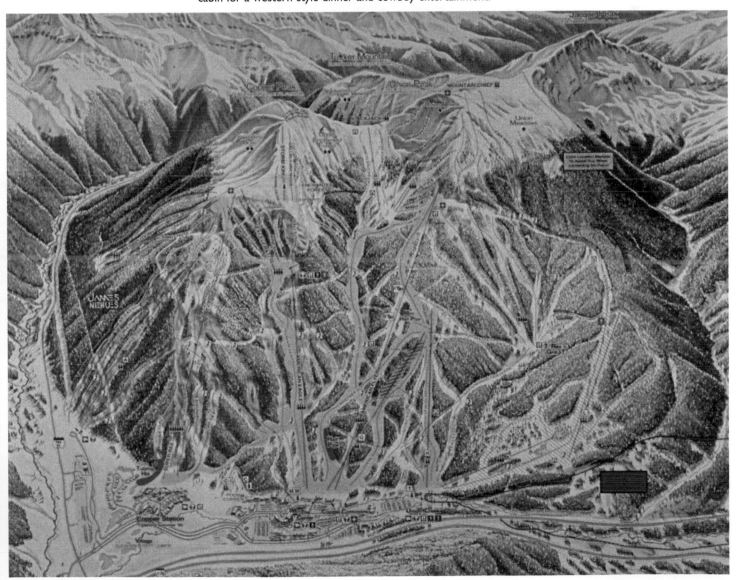

COLORADO SKI AREAS

CRESTED BUTTE MOUNTAIN RESORT
P.O. Box A, 500 Gothic Road
Mt. Crested Butte, Colorado 81225

STATISTICS
Peak Elevation: 12,162'
Vertical Rise: 3,062'
Number of Lifts: 13
Number of Trails: 85
Skiable Acres: 1160
Longest Run: 2.6 Miles
Lift Capacity: 16,560 Skiers/Hour
Half Pipe: Yes
Snowboard Park: Yes
Average Snowfall: 300"
Child Care: Yes

IMPORTANT PHONE NUMBERS
Main: (970) 349-2333
Reservations: (800) 544-8448
Snow Report: (888) TO-POWDER / (970)349-2323
Ski School: (800) 444-9236
www.crestedbutteresort.com

Photos courtesy of Crested Butte Mtn. Resort / Tom Stillo Photographer

Crested Butte is host annually to the US Extreme Skiing and Snowboarding Championships, the Saab US Extreme Free Skiing Championships, and the Sector Sport Watches US No Limits Extreme Snowboarding Championships. Other outdoor activities include snowmobiling, cross-country and telemark skiing, ice skating, winter mountaineering, ice fishing, bobsledding, tubing, dogsledding, snowshoeing, ice climbing, and sleigh rides.

The Adaptive Sports Center of Crested Butte (970-349-5075) offers instruction to people with both physical and cognitive-related disabilities. Adaptive equipment is available.

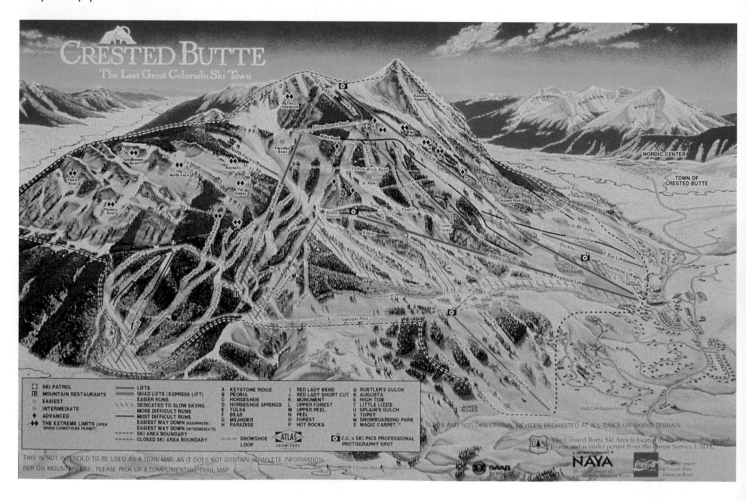

$\mathcal{C}$uchara

CUCHARA MOUNTAIN RESORT
946 Panadero Avenue
Cuchara, Colorado 81055

STATISTICS
Base Elevation: 9,248'
Peak Elevation: 10,810'
Vertical Rise: 1,562'
Number of Lifts: 4
Number of Trails: 24
Skiable Acres: 230
Longest Run: 2.75 Miles
Lift Capacity: 5,000 Skiers/Hour
Half Pipe: Yes
Snowboard Park: Yes
Average Snowfall: 230"
Child Care: Yes

PHONE NUMBERS
Main, Snow Report
    and Reservations: (888) 282-4272
Ski School: (719) 742-3163 ext.233
www.cuchara.com

Beginner 40% **Intermediate** 40% **Advanced** 20% **Expert** 0%

Photo courtesy of Cuchara Mountain Resort

$\mathcal{C}$uchara has the distinction of being the Colorado ski resort closest to Texas. The resort offers all types of skiing including downhill, cross-country, and telemark. Other activities include snowshoeing, dogsled rides, sleigh rides, ice skating, snowmobiling, tubing and snowblading.

♿ Cuchara Mountain Resort has a new center for Adaptive Ski Instruction.

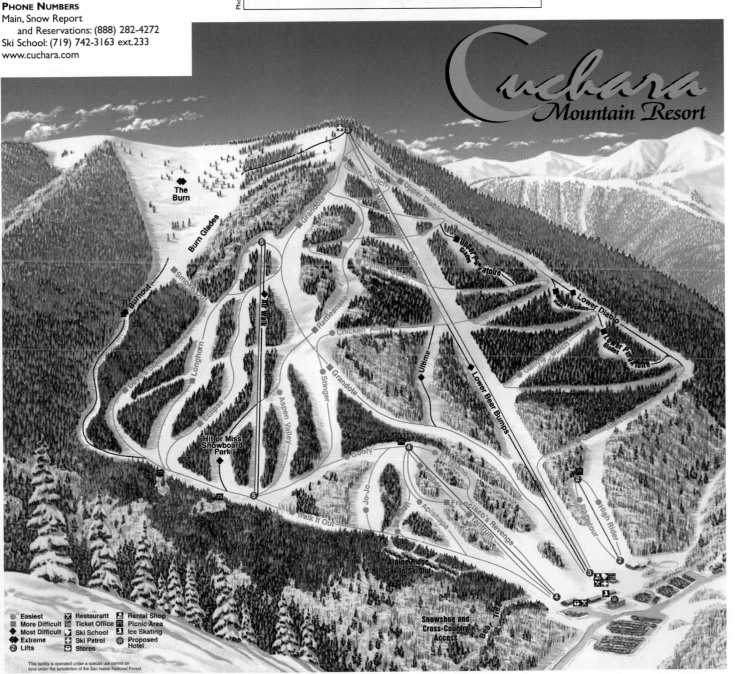

LEGEND
● Easiest
■ More Difficult
◆ Most Difficult
◆◆ Extreme
❷ Lifts

🍴 Restaurant
🎫 Ticket Office
🎿 Ski School
✚ Ski Patrol
🏪 Stores

🏪 Rental Shop
🍽 Picnic Area
⛸ Ice Skating
🏨 Proposed Hotel

This facility is operated under a special use permit on land under the jurisdiction of the San Isabel National Forest.

Beginner 20% | Intermediate 50% | Advanced 15% | Expert 15%

Eldora Mountain Resort

P.O. Box 1697
Nederland, Colorado 80466

STATISTICS
Base Elevation: 9,200'
Peak Elevation: 10,600'
Vertical Rise: 1,400'
Number of Lifts: 10
Number of Trails: 52
Skiable Acres: 495
Longest Run: 2 Miles
Lift Capacity: 11,500 Skiers/Hour
Half Pipe: Yes
Snowboard Park: Yes
Average Snowfall: 311"
Child Care: Yes

PHONE NUMBERS
Main: (888) 2-ELDORA
Snow Report: (303) 440-8700
Ski School: (303) 440-8700
www.eldora.com

Photos courtesy of Eldora Mountain Resort

Eldora was the first ski area in Colorado to build a half-pipe. The Skiesta in April is Eldora's annual celebration of spring. The Spring Triathlon adds to the fun with a competition combining skiing, snowshoeing and skating. The Eldora Nordic Center rents equipment for snowshoeing and cross-country skiing. The ski area is the closest to Denver offering skiing and snowboarding

♿ The Eldora Special Recreation Program (303-442-0606) has weekend programs for physically and mentally challenged people in January, February and March.

Mountain Statistics
Longest Run: 2 miles
10 Lifts:
    2 quad chairlifts
    1 triple chairlift
    4 double chairlifts
    3 surface lifts
Top Elevation: 10,600 ft.
Base Elevation: 9,200 ft.
Vertical Rise: 1,400 ft.

Mountain Operations
Weekdays   9:00 a.m. to 4 p.m.
Weekends/Holidays 8:30 a.m. to 4 p.m.

Ski Season
Mid-November to Mid-April
Snowmaking is utilized throughout most of the area to assist Mother Nature.

CONTINENTAL DIVIDE

SUMMIT ELEVATION - 10,600'

CORONA BOWL

CHALLENGE MOUNTAIN   INDIAN PEAKS   THE LOOKOUT

TRAIL MAP LEGEND
Easiest
More Difficult
Difficult
Most Difficult
Terrain Parks & Half Pipe
Lift Line
Area Boundary
Snowshoe Trail
Road
First Aid
Slow Skiing Area

BASE ELEVATION - 9,200'

A portion of Eldora Mountain Resort is located in the Roosevelt National Forest and is under permit from the Forest Service, USDA.

Howelsen Hill

Beginner 25% | Intermediate 25% | Advanced 40% | Expert 10%

HOWELSEN HILL SKI AREA
P.O. Box A 775088
Steamboat Springs, Colorado 80477

STATISTICS
Base Elevation: 6,696'
Peak Elevation: 7,136'
Vertical Rise: 440'
Number of Lifts: 3
Number of Trails: 15
Skiable Acres: 150
Longest Run: 1 Miles
Lift Capacity: 2,057 Skiers/Hour
Half Pipe: Yes
Average Snowfall: 250"
Child Care: No

PHONE NUMBERS
Main & Snow: (970) 879-8499
Reservations: (800) 525-2628
www.ci.steamboat.co.us

The Howelsen Ski Area, the oldest continuously operating ski area in Colorado, first opened in 1915 to promote Nordic skiing and jumping. The Nordic Combined Cup has been held there since 1994 and there are hopes that the event will become an annual one leading to the 2002 Winter Olympics. There is also an annual Winter Carnival. Howelsen offers snowshoe and cross-country ski trails, ski jumping, freestyle and Nordic jump training at the Olympic Jump Training Center, and a covered ice skating rink. Night skiing is also available.

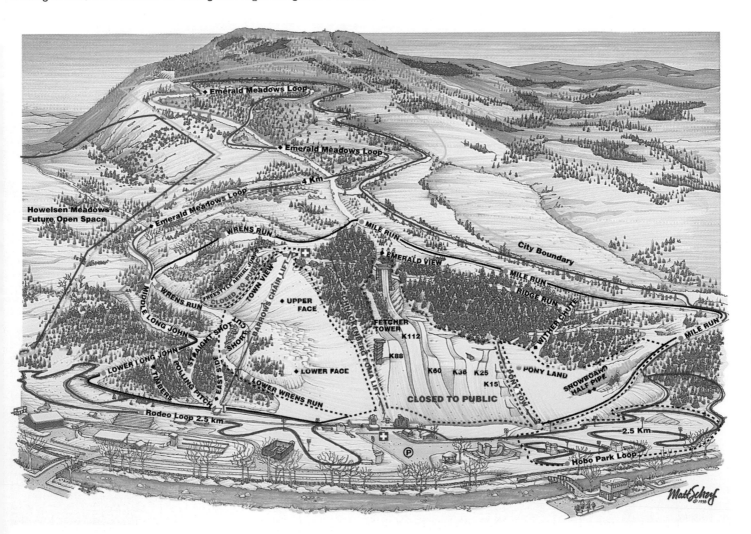

KEYSTONE

KEYSTONE
P.O. Box 38
Keystone, Colorado 80435

STATISTICS
Base Elevation: 9,300'
Peak Elevation: 12,220'
Vertical Rise: 2,900'
Number of Lifts: 20
Number of Trails: 116
Skiable Acres: 1,861
Longest Run: 3 Miles
Lift Capacity: 27,873 Skiers/Hour
Half Pipe: Yes
Snowboard Park: Yes
Average Snowfall: 230"
Child Care: Yes

PHONE NUMBERS
Main: (800) 468-5004 / (970) 496-2316
Reservations: (800) 427-8216
Snow Report: (970) 496-1111
Ski School: (800) 255-3715
www.keystone.snow.com

© Dave Nagel / Vail Resorts / Keystone

Keystone Mountain/North Peak/The Outback ski areas are located on National Forest System land and are under permit from the Forest Service, USDA.

This is not the official 1998/99 Keystone Ski Resort trail map. Pick up an official trail map when you arrive at the resort.

*K*eystone's night skiing is the largest operation of its type in North America. You can ski 17 lighted trails over 235 acres. The resort also has the largest Zamboni-maintained outdoor ice rink on the continent. Other outdoor activities include a lighted tubing hill, cross-country skiing, snowshoeing, ice fishing, ice skating, snowmobiling, dogsledding, monthly moonlight tours for cross-country skiers and snowshoers, sleigh rides and dinner in a cabin in the woods.

The Keystone Ski School (800-255-3715), in conjunction with the Breckenridge Outdoor Education Center, offers snowboarding classes and clinics in Area 51, a 20 acre terrain park.

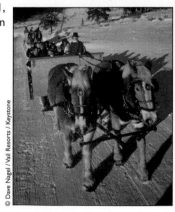

© Dave Nagel / Vail Resorts / Keystone

*L*oveland

LOVELAND SKI AREA
P.O. Box 899
Georgetown, Colorado 80444

STATISTICS
Base Elevation: 10,600'
Peak Elevation: 13,010'
Vertical Rise: 1,171
Number of Lifts: 11
Number of Trails: 70
Skiable Acres: 1365
Longest Run: 2 Miles
Lift Capacity: 14,293 Skiers/Hour
Half Pipe: No
Snowboard Park: Yes
Average Snowfall: 400"
Child Care: Yes

PHONE NUMBERS
Main: (800) 736-3SKI / (303) 569-3203
Reservations: (800) 255-LOVE
Snow Report: (303) 571-5554 or (800) 736-3SKI
Ski School: (303) 571-5580 ext.170
www.skiloveland.com

© Ben Blankenburg / Loveland Ski Area

The Ridge at Loveland straddles the Continental Divide at 13,010 feet and is considered the highest skiable terrain and has the highest quad chair lift in North America. On-hill rental cabins are available for groups of 20 or more. The Day-Tripper Program outfits unprepared skiers or snowboarders with everything needed for a day of skiing or boarding with everything from clothing to equipment to sunscreen. And, of course, a lift ticket. On Valentine's Day you can participate in The Marry Me and Ski Free event. Other activities at Loveland include cross-country and telemark skiing, snowshoeing, and snowmobiling.

ℳonarch

Beginner **21%** Intermediate **37%** Advanced **42%** Expert **0%**

MONARCH SKI & SNOWBOARD AREA
#1 Powder Place
Monarch, Colorado 81227

STATISTICS
Base Elevation: 10,790'
Peak Elevation: 11,961'
Vertical Rise: 1,171'
Number of Lifts: 4
Number of Trails: 54
Skiable Acres: 670
Longest Run: 2 Miles
Lift Capacity: 4,500 Skiers/Hour
Half Pipe: No
Snowboard Park: Yes
Average Snowfall: 350"
Child Care: Yes

PHONE NUMBERS
Main: (888) 996-SNOW / (719) 539-3573
Reservations: (800) 332-3668
Snow Report: (800) 228-7943
Ski School: (800) 996-7669
www.skimonarch.com

ℳonarch opened in 1939, and became the first Colorado ski area to include snowboarding in its name in 1996, Monarch Ski and Snowboard Area. Annual events include the New Year's Eve Evening of Lights parade with on-slope fireworks and the Media Challenge race for skiing members of the Colorado news media. Monarch offers some of the steepest snowcat skiing and snowboarding terrain with 900 acres above timberline. Other activities include cross-country skiing, ice fishing, snowmobiling, and ice climbing.

Photo courtesy of Monarch Ski & Snowboard Area

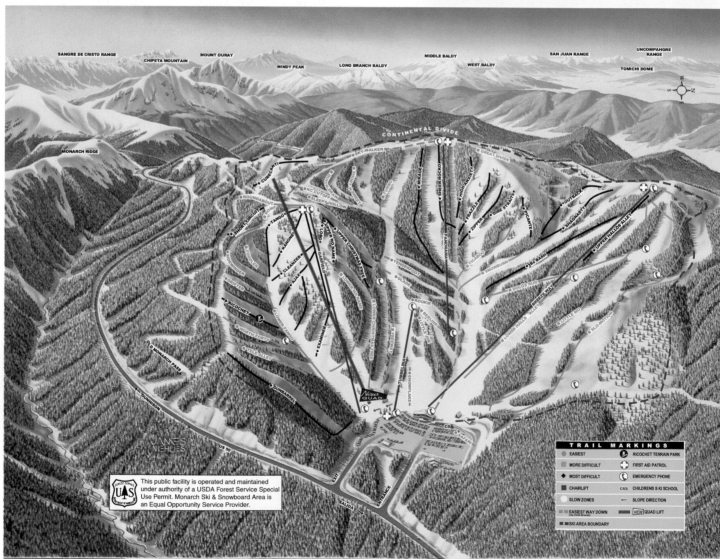

TRAIL MARKINGS

EASIEST	Ⓡ RICOCHET TERRAIN PARK
MORE DIFFICULT	✚ FIRST AID PATROL
MOST DIFFICULT	☎ EMERGENCY PHONE
CHAIRLIFT	CSS CHILDRENS S KI SCHOOL
SLOW ZONES	SLOPE DIRECTION
EASIEST WAY DOWN	NEW QUAD LIFT
SKI AREA BOUNDARY	

Powderhorn

POWDERHORN RESORT
P.O. Box 370
Mesa, Colorado 81643

STATISTICS
Base Elevation: 8,200'
Peak Elevation: 9,850'
Vertical Rise: 1,650
Number of Lifts: 4
Number of Trails: 27
Skiable Acres: 510
Longest Run: 2.2 Miles
Lift Capacity: 4,370 Skiers/Hour
Half Pipe: Yes
Snowboard Park: Yes
Average Snowfall: 250"
Child Care: No

PHONE NUMBERS
Main: (970) 268-5700
Reservations: (800) 241-6997 / (970) 268-5040
Snow Report: (970) 268-5700
Ski School: (970) 268-5355
www.powderhorn.com

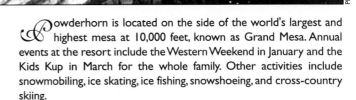

Photos courtesy of Powderhorn Resort

Powderhorn is located on the side of the world's largest and highest mesa at 10,000 feet, known as Grand Mesa. Annual events at the resort include the Western Weekend in January and the Kids Kup in March for the whole family. Other activities include snowmobiling, ice skating, ice fishing, snowshoeing, and cross-country skiing.

♿ The Colorado Discover Ability program at Powderhorn (970-268-5700) offers adaptive ski programs for most special needs.

⛷ POWDERHORN RESORT

Mountain Statistics
Base Elevation: 8,200 ft.   Summit Elevation: 9,850 ft.   Vertical Drop: 1,650 ft.
Skiable Acres: 510 total acres—20% Beginner, 50% Intermediate, 15% Advanced, 15% Expert
Average Snowfall: 250 inches
Lifts: 4 lifts total—1 Quad, 2 Doubles and 1 Surface Lift
Winter Season: Early December – Early April

SKIER'S RESPONSIBILITY CODE
Powderhorn Resort is committed to promoting skier safety. In addition to traditional alpine skiers, you may be joined by snowboarders, telemark or cross-country skiers, skiers with disabilities or skiers with adaptive equipment. Always show courtesy to others and be aware that there are elements of risk in skiing that common sense and personal awareness can help reduce. All skiers must adhere to the Skier's Responsibility Code.
1. Ski under control and in such a manner that you can stop or avoid other skiers or objects.
2. When skiing downhill or overtaking another skier, you must avoid the skier below you.
3. You must not stop where you obstruct a trail or are not visible from above.
4. When entering a trail or starting downhill, yield to other skiers.
5. All skiers shall wear retention straps or other devices to help prevent runaway skis.
6. You should keep off closed trails and out-of-bound areas and observe all posted signs.

COLORADO SKI AREAS

Purgatory

Beginner **23%** Intermediate **51%** Advanced **21%** Expert **5%**

PURGATORY RESORT
#1 Skier Place
Durango, Colorado 81301

STATISTICS
Base Elevation: 8,793'
Peak Elevation: 10,822'
Vertical Rise: 2,029'
Number of Lifts: 11
Number of Trails: 75
Skiable Acres: 1200
Longest Run: 2 Miles
Lift Capacity: 13,600 Skiers/Hour
Half Pipe: Yes
Snowboard Park: Yes
Average Snowfall: 263"
Child Care: Yes

PHONE NUMBERS
Main & Snow Report: (970) 247-9000
Ski School: (970) 247-9000
www.ski-purg.com

Photo courtesy of Purgatory Resort

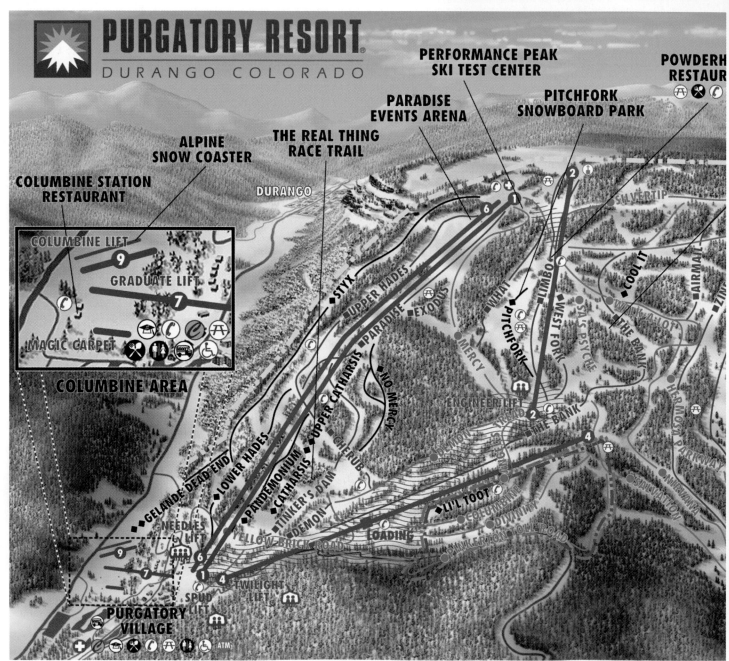

PURGATORY RESORT
DURANGO COLORADO

PERFORMANCE PEAK
SKI TEST CENTER

POWDERH
RESTAUR

PARADISE
EVENTS ARENA

PITCHFORK
SNOWBOARD PARK

ALPINE
SNOW COASTER

THE REAL THING
RACE TRAIL

COLUMBINE STATION
RESTAURANT

DURANGO

SILVERTIP

COLUMBINE LIFT
9

GRADUATE LIFT
7

MAGIC CARPET

COLUMBINE AREA

COOL IT

AIRMAIL
ZIN

STYX

UPPER HADES

WHAT
PITCHFORK

LIMBO

SA'S PSYCHE
WEST FORK

EXODUS

PARADISE

NO MERCY

MERCY

THE BANK

ENGINEER LIFT
2

GELANDE DEAD END

LOWER HADES

PANDEMONIUM

UPPER CATHARSIS

CATHARSIS

CHERUB

TINKER'S DAM

THE BANK

4

HERMOSA PARKWAY

NEEDLES
LIFT

YELLOW BRICK ROAD

DEMON

LI'L TOOT

LOADING

COLUMBIN
DIVINITY

SALVATION

9

7

6
1
4

TWILIGHT
LIFT

PINKERTON TOLLEROAD

SPUD

PURGATORY
VILLAGE

ATM

Famous for snowcat powder skiing in the backcountry of the San Juan Mountains, Purgatory is also home to one of the best Colorado winter carnivals, Snowdown. Sunday mornings should be reserved for free guided mountain nature tours. Outdoor snow activities include a lighted tubing hill, guided snowmobiling, ice fishing, ice skating, ice climbing, cross-country skiing, snowshoeing, tubing, dinner sleigh rides, and gold-medal trout fishing.

♿ The Adaptive Sports Association (970-259-0374), a Durango-based non-profit organization, offers ski instruction to physically and developmentally disabled adults and children. Instructors are volunteers trained to work with all types of disabilities.

LEGEND

▬▬ LIFT	✚ SKI PATROL	
▬ ▬ HIGH SPEED LIFT	ⓢ SKI SCHOOL	
●— EASIEST	ⓒ EMERGENCY PHONE	
■— MORE DIFFICULT	ⓒ CONCIERGE	
◆— MOST DIFFICULT	ⓧ RESTAURANT	
◆◆ EXPERT ONLY	ⓟ PICNIC AREA	
░░ SKI AREA BOUNDARY	ⓦ REST ROOMS	
▬ SLOW SKIING ZONE	ATM ATM MACHINE	
▬ ▬ FAMILY SKI ZONE	ⓢ SKI SHUTTLE	
▬ — SKI ONLY ZONE	⛪ MOUNTAIN CHAPEL	

NON-DENOMINATIONAL WORSHIP SERVICE EVERY SUNDAY AT 2:00 P.M.

Mountain users should be advised that a green circle, blue square or black diamond trail at Purgatory Resort is not necessarily the same as a similarly rated trail at another area. The system is a relative system, therefore, the symbols on the Purgatory Resort trail map are valid only at our area. Mountain users should work their way up, beginning with the easiest trails until they are familiar with the trails at the area.

LIFT TYPE

1. SPUD DOUBLE
2. ENGINEER DOUBLE
3. HERMOSA PARK EXPRESS QUAD
4. TWILIGHT DOUBLE
5. GRIZZLY DOUBLE
6. NEEDLES TRIPLE
7. GRADUATE TRIPLE
8. LEGENDS TRIPLE
9. COLUMBINE TRIPLE
10. MAGIC CARPET

Purgatory Resort is located in the San Juan National Forest and is under permit from the Forest Service - USDA. Operated by Durango Ski Corporation. Purgatory Resort is an equal opportunity service provider.

Silver Creek Golf & Ski Ranch

Beginner **30%** ● Intermediate **50%** ■ Advanced **20%** ◆ Expert **0%** ◆◆

SILVER CREEK GOLF & SKI RANCH

P.O. Box 1110
Silver Creek, Colorado 80446

STATISTICS

Base Elevation: 8,202'
Peak Elevation: 9,202'
Vertical Rise: 1,000'
Number of Lifts: 5
Number of Trails: 33
Skiable Acres: 251
Longest Run: 1.5 Miles
Lift Capacity: 5,400 Skiers/Hour
Half Pipe: No
Snowboard Park: Yes
Average Snowfall: 180"
Child Care: Yes

PHONE NUMBERS

Main: (800) 754-7458 / (970) 887-3384
Reservations and Snow Report: (888) 283-7458
Ski School: (888) 283-7458
www.silvercreek-resort.com

Silver Creek was the first Colorado ski area to unveil the strange-looking snow-bike. The annual Firefighter's Feud pits teams from various fire departments dressed in full gear racing in slalom and obstacle courses carrying 40 feet of fire hose. Some of the many outdoor activities include snowmobiling, sleigh rides, hot air ballooning, snowshoeing, ice skating, ice fishing, and cross-country skiing. Day or night skiing, snow biking, and tubing are available on lighted slopes.

♿ The Silver Creek Adaptive Sports Center (888-283-7458) has programs for all physically challenged skiers.

Ski Cooper

SKI COOPER
P.O. Box 896
Leadville, Colorado 80461

STATISTICS
Base Elevation: 10,500'
Peak Elevation: 11,700'
Vertical Rise: 1,200'
Number of Lifts: 4
Number of Trails: 26
Skiable Acres: 365
Longest Run: 1.4 Miles
Lift Capacity: 3,300 Skiers/Hour
Half Pipes: No
Snowboard Parks: Yes
Average Snowfall: 250"
Child Care: Yes

PHONE NUMBERS
Main: (719) 486-3684
Reservation: (800) 748-2057
Snow Report: (719) 486-2277
Ski School: (719) 486-3684
www.skicooper.com

Photo courtesy of Ski Cooper

The first lift was installed in 1942 by the Tenth Mountain Division, and was the longest in the US at the time. The annual Crystal Carnival highlights include snow sculptures, a parade of lights and ski-joring. Another popular event is the Tenth Mountain Division Ski-In and Reunion races, which are open to all. Other things to do in the snow include snowshoeing, winter bike races, fly fishing, ice skating, cross-country skiing, snowmobiling, and snowcat skiing on Chicago Ridge with a 1,500 foot vertical drop.

The Ski Cooper Ski School (719-486-3684) offers lessons for blind and physically disabled skiers.

SNOWMASS

Beginner **10%** Intermediate **52%** Advanced **18%** Expert **20%**

Photos courtesy of Aspen Skiing Company / Burnham Arndt, Petter McBride, Biege Jones

SNOWMASS
Aspen Skiing Company
P.O. Box 1248
Aspen, Colorado 81612

STATISTICS
Base Elevation: 8,104'
Peak Elevation: 12,510'
Vertical Rise: 4,406'
Number of Lifts: 17
Number of Trails: 83
Skiable Acres: 2,580
Longest Run: 4.16 Miles
Lift Capacity: 24,321 Skiers/Hour
Half Pipe: Yes
Snowboard Park: Yes
Average Snowfall: 300"
Child Care: Yes

PHONE NUMBERS
Main: (800) 526-6200 / (970) 925-1220
Reservations: (888) 452-2409
Snow Report: (888) ASPEN-SNO
www.skiaspen.com

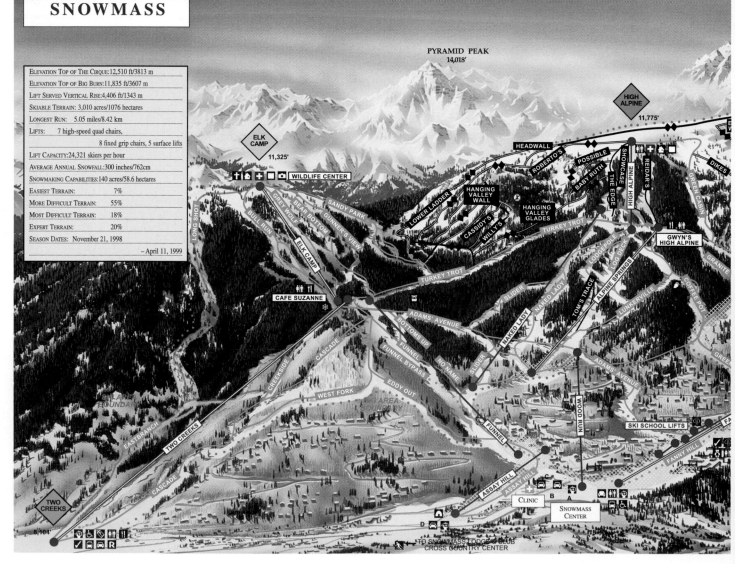

SNOWMASS

Elevation Top of The Cirque:	12,510 ft/3813 m
Elevation Top of Big Burn:	11,835 ft/3607 m
Lift Served Vertical Rise:	4,406 ft/1343 m
Skiable Terrain:	3,010 acres/1076 hectares
Longest Run:	5.05 miles/8.42 km
Lifts:	7 high-speed quad chairs, 8 fixed grip chairs, 5 surface lifts
Lift Capacity:	24,321 skiers per hour
Average Annual Snowfall:	300 inches/762cm
Snowmaking Capabilities:	140 acres/58.6 hectares
Easiest Terrain:	7%
More Difficult Terrain:	55%
Most Difficult Terrain:	18%
Expert Terrain:	20%
Season Dates:	November 21, 1998 – April 11, 1999

$\mathcal{S}$nowmass has a new surface chair that operates solely on wind power. The Snowmass Mardi Gras is a fun-filled week of treasure hunts, contests, and music. The Snowmass Banana Season offers another week of fun featuring the Great Banana Hunt and the Chicken Legs contest. When not hitting the slopes, try dogsled rides, snowshoe nature tours, sleigh rides, ice skating, cross-country skiing, snowmobiling, and snowcat rides.

♿ Challenge Aspen and Blind Outdoor Leisure Development (970-923-0578) offers instruction to skiers with any physical and/or mental disabilities from beginning downhill skiing to a full racing program. Adaptive equipment and ski buddies are available.

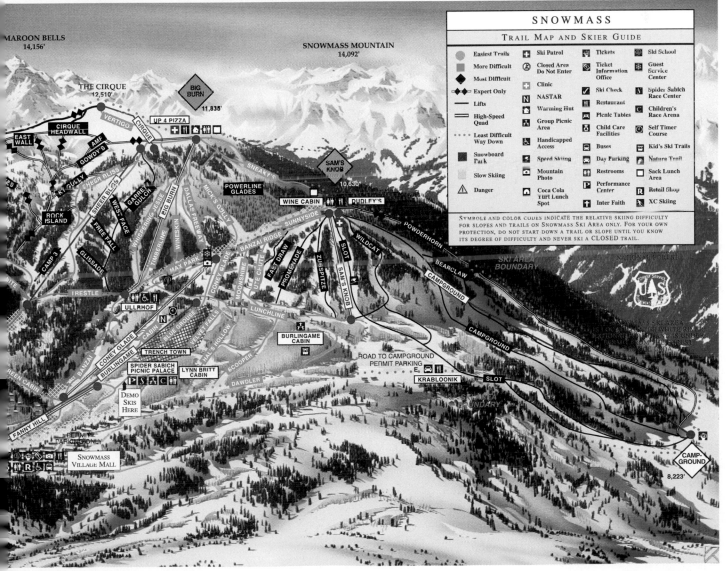

Steamboat

Photo courtesy of Steamboat Ski Area

Beginner **13%** Intermediate **56%** Advanced **31%** Expert **0%**

STEAMBOAT
2305 Mt. Werner Circle
Steamboat Springs, Colorado 80487

STATISTICS
Base Elevation: 6,900'
Peak Elevation: 10,568'
Vertical Rise: 3,668'
Number of Lifts: 22
Number of Trails: 140
Skiable Acres: 2,939
Longest Run: 3 Miles
Lift Capacity: 34,658 Skiers/Hour
Half Pipe: Yes
Snowboard Park: Yes
Average Snowfall: 300"
Child Care: Yes

PHONE NUMBERS
Main: (970) 879-6111
Reservations: (800) 922-2722 / (970) 879-0740
Snow Report: (970) 879-7300
Ski School: (800) 525-6200 / (970) 925-1220
www.steamboat-ski.com

The biggest and weirdest event of the winter season is the Annual Coors Cowboy Downhill featuring professional rodeo cowboys competing in such non-rodeo events as ski-joring and slalom racing. The event is held in January to coincide with the National Western Stock Show in Denver. Other activities include cross-country skiing, dogsledding, tubing, hot air ballooning, hot springs, sleigh rides, snowmobiling, snowshoeing, snowcat powder tours, ice fishing, ice skating, and ice climbing. Resort personnel guide snowshoe tours for all ability levels.

♿ The Perfect Turn Ski School (970-879-6111 ext. 531) at Steamboat offers ski instruction to the physically and developmentally challenged. Adaptive sports equipment is available.

Sunlight Mountain

Beginner **20%** Intermediate **55%** Advanced **20%** Expert **5%**

SUNLIGHT MOUNTAIN RESORT

10901 County Road 117
Glenwood Springs, Colorado

STATISTICS
Base Elevation: 7,885'
Peak Elevation: 9,895'
Vertical Rise: 2,010'
Number of Lifts: 4
Number of Trails: 63
Skiable Acres: 467
Longest Run: 2.5 Miles
Lift Capacity: 4,600 Skiers/Hour
Half Pipe: No
Snowboard Park: Yes
Average Snowfall: 300"
Child Care: Yes

PHONE NUMBERS
Main: (800) 445-7931 / (970) 945-7491
Reservations: (888) 488-4737
Snow Report: (970) 945-7491 ext. 239
Ski School: (970) 945-7491
www.sunlightmtn.com

Sunlight has the longest snowmobile trail system in Colorado, linking with Powderhorn over 100 miles away. The Ski Spree Winter Carnival features both ski and snowboard competitions and fun events such as a parade and fireworks. Other things to do include ice skating, snowmobiling, cross-country skiing, hot air ballooning, hot springs, snowcat tours, snowshoeing, ice skating, sleigh rides, and year-round gold-medal trout fishing.

Telluride

TELLURIDE SKI RESORT

P.O. Box 11155
Telluride, Colorado 81601

STATISTICS

Base Elevation: 8,725'
Peak Elevation: 12,247'
Vertical Rise: 3,522'
Number of Trails: 64
Number of Lifts: 13
Skiable Acres: 1,050
Longest Run: 2.85 Miles
Lift Capacity: 12,076 Skiers/Hour
Half Pipe: Yes
Snowboard Park: Yes
Average Snowfall: 300"
Child Care: Yes

PHONE NUMBERS

Main: (800) 801-4832 / (970) 728-6900
Reservations: (888) 355-8743
Snow Report: (970) 728-7425
Ski School: (800) 801-4832
www.telski.com

Beginner **21%** Intermediate **47%** Advanced **15%** Expert **17%**

Photo by Doug Berry / Telluride Ski & Golf Company

Photo by T.R. Youngstrom / Telluride Ski & Golf Company

Telluride celebrates the advent of spring with Surf the Rockies, two weeks of snowboarding and other snow-related fun and games. Other activities include heli-skiing, cross-country skiing, hut tours, snowshoeing, ice skating, tubing, hot air ballooning, ice climbing, mountaineering, sleigh rides, snowmobile tours, dogsledding, snow-biking, tubing, fly fishing, and free snowshoe nature tours led by members of the US Forest Service.

♿ The Telluride Adaptive Ski Program (970-728-7537), non-profit organization dedicated to making quality skiing and mountain accessibility available to people with disabilities. The program offers ski lessons, ski buddies, guide services and equipment rental for disabled people of all ages and levels of ability. A volunteer program is available for people who want to assist disabled skiers.

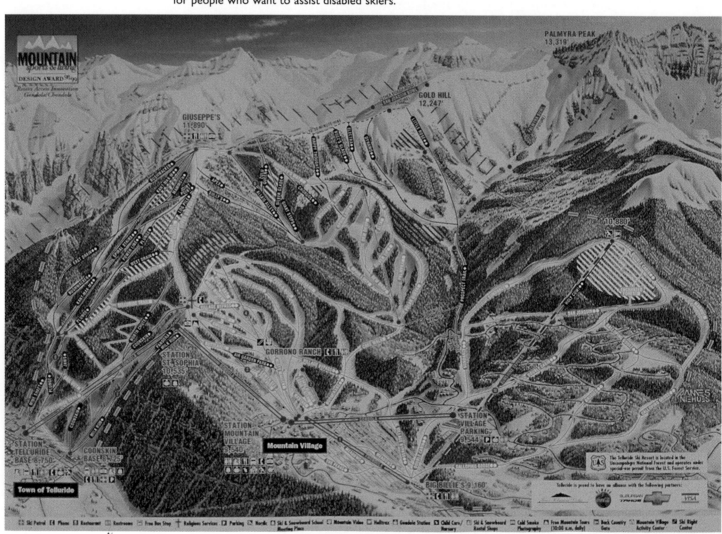

Vail

Beginner **0%** Intermediate **13%** Advanced **87%** Expert **0%**

© Jack Affleck/Vail Resorts/Vail

VAIL
P.O. Box 7
Vail, Colorado 81658

STATISTICS
Base Elevation: 8,120'
Peak Elevation: 11,450'
Vertical Rise: 4,000'
Number of Lifts: 31
Number of Trails: 174
Skiable Acres: 4,644
Longest Run: 4.5 Miles
Lift Capacity: 52,500 Skiers/Hour
Half Pipe: Yes
Snowboard Park: Yes
Average Snowfall: 335"
Child Care: Yes

PHONE NUMBERS
Main: (800) 525-2287 / (970) 476-5601
Reservations & Snow Report: (800) 427-8216
Ski School: (970) 476-3239 / (800) 475-4543
www.snow.com

© Jack Affleck / Vail Resorts / Vail

Back Bowls

Vail's Legendary Back Bowls offer
acres of wide-open, natural skiing.
Certain trails are only occasionally
groomed and you may encounter
unmarked obstacles. Visibility and
snow conditions can change
quickly. The majority of trails in the
Back Bowls are recommended
for ADVANCED SKIERS ONLY.
 When skiing the Back Bowls:
1) Check the lift status signs at the
top of the mountain before entering
the Back Bowls; 2) Enter through
open gates only, never cross
any closure rope for any reason;
and 3) Ski with a companion.

CATEGORY III
Future Skiing Terrain

Category III will be our largest expansion ever,
opening 2,200 acres in two new areas,
Pete's Bowl and Super Bowl. This ideal,
north-facing terrain offers all levels of skiers
excellent early and late skiing conditions and
features a mix of open bowl and gladed tree runs.

*Trademark, Celestial Seasonings, Inc., Boulder, Colorado.

Vail

Beginner 21% **Intermediate** 31% **Advanced** 48% **Expert** 0%

© Dann Coffey / Vail Resorts / Vail

For those who like to play in the snow after dark, Vail offers , tubing, ice skating, and snowmobile tours. Other activities include dogsledding, hot air ballooning, snowshoeing, bobsledding, cross-country skiing, ice fishing, sleigh rides, snowbiking, snowcat tours, and laser tag, bobsledding, cross-country skiing, ice fishing, ice skating, sleigh rides, snowbiking, snowcat powder tours, snowmobiling, and tubing. Vail has over 4,600 acres of skiable terrain, the most in the United States.

♿ Vail Ski and Snowboard School (970-476-3239 or 800-475-4543) offers private ski lessons taught by PSIA/Adaptive Certified or Disabled Sport Instructors. The school has adaptive sport equipment available.

© Jack Affleck / Vail Resorts / Vail

TWO ELK LODGE™ ELEVATION 11,220' - 3,420m **CAMP 1** **PHQ** (PATROL HEADQ 11,250'-3,430

NORTHEAST BOWL

Legend:
- Express Lifts
- Downloading Lift
- Most Difficult ◆ ◆◆
- More Difficult ■
- Easiest ●
- Chairlift
- Surface Lift
- Area Boundary/Closure (do not cross)
- Road or Catwalk (may include flat terrain)
- Nordic Or Snowshoe Trail
- Practice Park
- Brewery
- Picnic Area
- Adaptive Skiing Office
- Recreational Ski Racing
- Rossignol International Test Center
- Sunday Services
- Automated Teller Machine
- Bus Stop (every 10 minutes)

ALL GUEST SERVICES include the following:
- Accessibility For Individuals With Disabilities
- Retail/Rental
- Dining
- Table Service Dining
- Snowboard Zone
- Slow Zone
- Ski School
- Overnight Storage

Pick up a Children's Adventures Map at any Ski School location for more information on the following:
- Children's Skiing Centers
- Children's Adventures

GOLDEN PEAK™ ELEVATION 8,217'-2,505m

VAIL VILLAGE ELEVATION 8,200'-2,500m FREE BUS

TO DENVER 100 MILES TO BRECKENRIDGE//KEYSTONE - 35 MILES I-70

Vail Mountain facilities, operated by Vail Associates, Inc., are located within the White River National Forest and are under permit from the Forest Service, U.S.D.A.

Many winter activities take place in the White River National Forest. Learn about all of the recreation available on United States Forest Service land by visiting the Holy Cross Ranger District in Minturn or by calling 827-5715.

© Jack Affleck / Vail Resorts / Vail

GAME CREEK BOWL™ Enter through open gates only.
The only way out is up Chair 7. Chairlift normally closes at 3:30 pm.

WILDWOOD™
ELEVATION
10,981'-3,347m

LOST BOY

WOODS GLADE

WILD CARD

THE WOODS

DEALER'S CHOICE

BACCARAT

SHOWBOAT

DEUCES WILD

FARO

OUZO

GAME CREEK EXPRESS™ LIFT

OUZO GLADE

GAME CREEK
CLUB
(Members)

GAME TRAIL

7

WINDOWS ROAD

BUCKSKIN GLADE

RAMSHORN

THE SKIPPER

HUNKY DORY

KANGAROO CORNICE

WILDWOOD EXPRESS™ LIFT

THE MEADOWS

LOOK MA

S. LOOK MA

CHALLENGE

MID-VAIL EXPRESS

LOVEREASY

PICKEROON

BERRIES

LODGEPOLE

EAGLE'S NEST RIDGE

9

15

18

**Adventure
Ridge™**

19

26

EAGLE'S NEST™
ELEVATION 10,350'-3,155m

POWERLINE GLADE

MOUNTAINTOP EXPRESS™ LIFT

ZOT

WHISTLE PIG

ESPRESSO

MID-VAIL™
ELEVATION 10,150'-3,094m

16

SPRUCE FACE

BEARTREE

COLD FEET

ATM

AVANTI EXPRESS™ LIFT

AVANTI

COOKSHACK

PICKEROON

BERRIES

LODGEPOLE

COLUMBINE

HEDGES

OWL'S ROOST

MINNIE'S LIFT

BORN FREE

CUB'S
WAY

BWANA

SIMBA

GITALONG ROAD

GITALONG ROAD

TOURIST TRAP

COMPROMISE

BEEN THERE

DONE THAT

BOBSLED

BLACK
FOREST RACE
ARENA

27

27

2

AVANTI

THE CHUTES

1

CUB'S WAY

LION'S WAY

DO THE DEW

MINNIE'S MILE

BORN FREE

8

PRIDE PARK

SAFARI

PRIDE EXPRESS™ LIFT

26

**CLOSED
AREA**
JAMES
NIEHUES

VISTA BAHN EXPRESS™ LIFT

GIANT STEPS

GIANT STEPS LIFT

INTERNATIONAL

GITALONG ROAD

9

BORN FREE

POST ROAD

THE
GLADE

BWANA

LOOK

BORN FREE EXPRESS™ LIFT

EAGLE BAHN EXPRESS™ GONDOLA

POST ROAD

CHEETAH GULCH

CHEETAH

SIMBA

SAFARI

DOWNLOAD
CHAIR 20

20

CASCADE VILLAGE LIFT

GITALONG ROAD

BEAR TREE

CHICKEN LEGS

VAIL VILLAGE CATWALK

VILLAGES CATWALK

LIONSHEAD CATWALK

BWANA

SAFARI

SIMBA

CASCADE WAY

**CASCADE
VILLAGE**
20

8
19

LIONSHEAD
ELEVATION 8,120'-2,475m

ATM

FREE BUS

H
HOSPITAL

I-70

TO BEAVER CREEK® RESORT 10 MILES
TO VAIL/EAGLE COUNTY AIRPORT 35 MILES

Winter Park / Mary Jane

Beginner **9%** Intermediate **22%** Advanced **13%** ◆ Expert **56%** ◆◆

WINTER PARK RESORT

P.O. Box 36
Winter Park, Colorado 80482

STATISTICS

Base Elevation: 9,000'
Peak Elevation: 12,060'
Vertical Rise: 3,060'
Number of Lifts: 20
Number of Trails: 134
Skiable Acres: 2,886
Longest Run: 5.1 Miles
Lift Capacity: 34,910 Skiers/Hour
Half Pipe: Yes
Snowboard Park: Yes
Average Snowfall: 370"
Child Care: Yes

PHONE NUMBERS

Main: (970) 726-5514 / (303) 892-0961
Reservations: (800) 729-5813
Snow Report: (303) 572-SNOW
Ski School: (970) 726-1551
www.skiwinterpark.com

Photo courtesy of Winter Park Resort

Winter Park receives an average of 370 inches (31 feet) of snow annually and has the distinction of being the only ski area in Colorado with direct train service from Denver. Annual events include the Christmas Eve Torchlight Parade, the Wells Fargo Cup pro-ski Race, and the Ocean Spray Spring Splash on closing day. Other activities include snowshoe tours, snowcat tours, guided moonlight snowmobile tours, tubing, ice skating, hot air balloons, ice fishing, snowshoeing, cross-country skiing, sleigh rides and dog sled rides.

♿ The National Sports Center for the Disabled (970-726-1540, www.nscd.org) at Winter Park offers sports programs for adults and children with over 45 physical and mental disabilities. Programs for downhill skiing, cross-country skiing, snowboarding, snowshoeing, and overnight Nordic ski trips. There is even a ski racing training camp.

Wolf Creek

WOLF CREEK SKI AREA

P.O. Box 2800
Pagosa Springs, Colorado 81147

STATISTICS

Base Elevation: 10,300'
Peak Elevation: 11,904'
Vertical Rise: 1,604'
Number of Lifts: 5
Number of Trails: 50
Skiable Acres: 1,581
Longest Run: 2 Miles
Lift Capacity: 5,800 Skiers/Hour
Half Pipe: No
Snowboard Park: No
Average Snowfall: 465"
Child Care: No

PHONE NUMBERS

Main: (970) 264-5639
Snow Report: (800) SKI-WOLF
Ski School: (970) 264-5639
www.wolfcreekski.com

Wolf Creek has been owned by the same family for over 20 years. The resort holds Fun Races throughout the year for all ages and abilities. All types of skiing are available including cross-country skiing, telemark, and snowcat tours to the backcountry for skiers and snowboarders.

WOLF CREEK
THE MOST SNOW IN COLORADO®

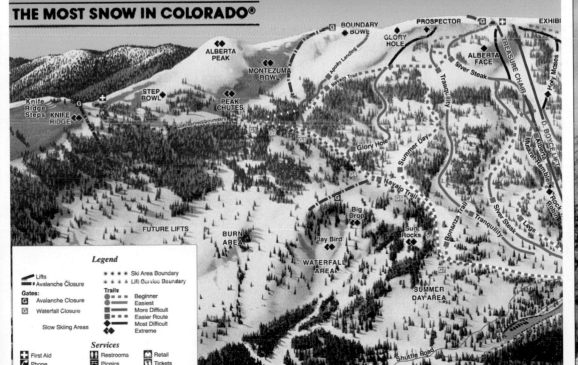

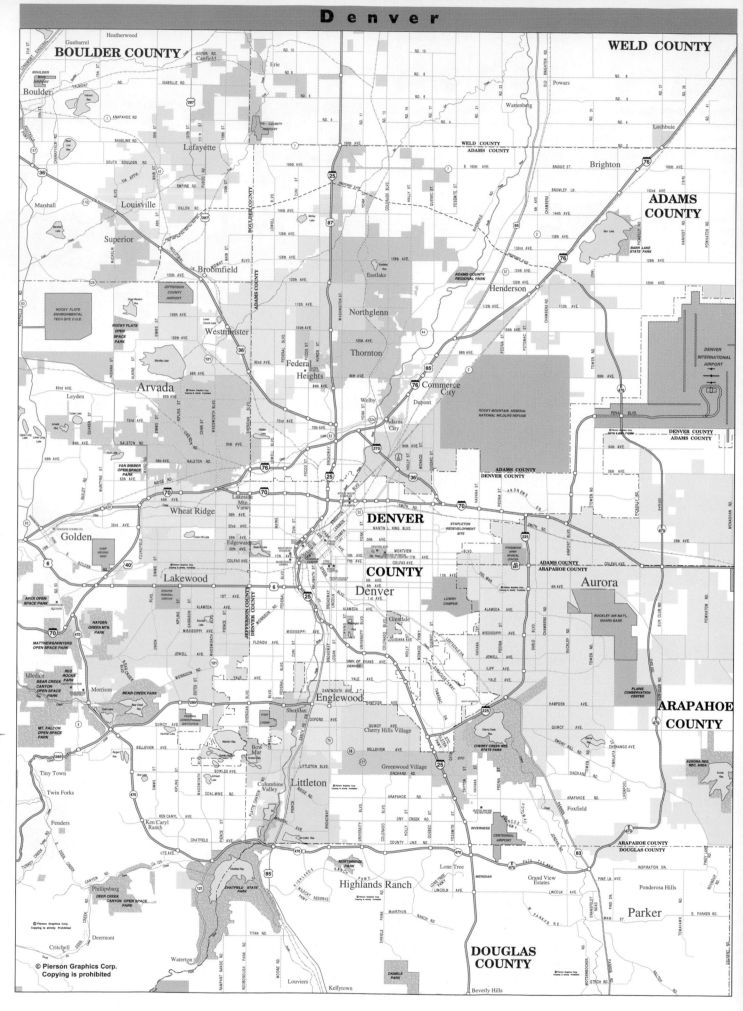

*D*enver

Points of Interest: Denver Art Museum, Four Mile Historic Park, City Park, Denver Botanic Gardens, Six Flags Elitch Gardens, Governor's Mansion, Denver Zoo, IMAX Theater, The Denver Museum of Natural History, Molly Brown House, State Capitol, US Mint, Ocean Journey

Annual Events:

National Western Stock Show & Rodeo	January	(303) 297-1166
Cinco de Mayo Celebration	Early May	(303) 534-8342
Norwest Culture-Fest	Mid-May	(303) 871-4626
Capitol Hill People's Fair	Memorial Day Weekend	(303) 830-1651
Cherry Creek Arts Festival	July 4th Weekend	(303) 355-2787
Sprint International at Castle Pines	August	(800) 755-1986
A Taste of Colorado	Labor Day Weekend	(303) 478-7878
John Elway Golf Classic	Late May	(303) 790-7300
Aurora Gateway to the Rockies Parade	Mid-September	(303) 361-6169
Great American Beer Festival	October	(303) 399-1859
Denver International Film Festival	October	(303) 321-FILM
Parade of Lights	Early December	(303) 478-7878

Seasonal Sporting Events: Denver Broncos NFL Football, Denver Nuggets NBA Basketball, Colorado Rapids MLS Soccer, Colorado Rockies NL Baseball, Colorado Avalanche NHL Hockey

Denver Metro Convention and Visitors Bureau — 1555 California St. — (303) 892-1112

HOSPITALS

Avista Adventist Hospital	100 Health Park Dr.	(303) 673-1000
Littleton Adventist Hospital	7700 S. Broadway	(303) 730-8900
Porter Adventist	2525 S. Downing St.	(303) 778-1955
St. Anthony Central Hospital	4231 W. 16th Ave.	(303) 629-3511
St. Anthony North Hospital	2551 W. 84th Ave.	(303) 426-2151
Children's Hospital	1056 E. 19th Ave.	(303) 861-8888
Craig Hospital	3425 S. Clarkson St.	(303) 789-8000
Denver Health Medical Center	777 Bannock St.	(303) 436-6000
Lutheran Med. Ctr.	8300 W. 38th Ave.	(303) 425-4500
St. Joseph Hospital	1835 Franklin St.	(303) 837-7111
Medical Center of Aurora, The	1501 S. Potomac St.	(303) 695-2600
Medical Center of Aurora-North	700 Potomac St.	(303) 363-7200
National Jewish Med & Resrch. Ctr.	1400 Jackson St.	(303) 388-4461
North Suburban Med. Ctr.	9191 Grant St.	(303) 451-7800
Presbyterian/St. Luke's Med. Ctr.	601 E. 19th Ave.	(303) 839-1000
Rose Medical Center	4567 E. 9th Ave.	(303) 320-2121
Swedish Medical Center	501 E. Hampden Ave.	(303 788-5000
University Hosp.	4200 E. 9th Ave.	(303) 372-0000
VA Medical Center	1055 Clermont St.	(303) 399-8020

PUBLIC TRANSIT

RTD	1600 Blake St.	(303) 299-6000
Amtrak	Union Station	(303) 534-2812

BUS STATION

Greyhound Bus Lines	1055 19th Ave.	(303) 292-6111

AIRPORT

Denver International Airport		(303) 270-1670

COLLEGES

Arapahoe Comm. College	2500 W. College Dr.	(303) 797-5900
Comm. College of Aurora	16000 E. Center Tech. Pkwy.	(303) 360-4700
Comm. College of Denver	1111 W. Colfax Ave.	(303) 556-2600
Front Range Comm. College	3645 W. 112th Ave.	(303) 404-5550
Metro State College	1006 11th St.	(303) 556-3058
Red Rocks Comm. College	13300 W. 6th Ave.	(303) 914-6269

Regis University	3333 Regis Blvd.	(303) 556-2523
Teikyo-Loretto Heights University	3001 S. Federal Blvd.	(303) 936-8441
Univ. of Colo.- Denver	1200 Larimer St.	(303) 556-2704
University of Denver	2199 S. University Blvd.	(303) 871-2000

MUSEUMS

Black American West Museum & Heritage Center	3091 California St.	(303) 292-2566
Buffalo Bill Memorial Museum & Grave	987 Lookout Mtn. Rd.	(303) 526-0747
Byers Evans House	1310 Bannock St.	(303) 620-4795
Children's Museum	2121 Children's Mus. Dr.	(303) 433-7444
Colorado History Museum	1300 Broadway	(303) 866-3682
Colorado Railroad Museum	17155 W 44th Ave.	(303) 279-4591
Denver Art Museum	14th & Bannock St.	(303) 640-2789
Denver Firefighters Museum	1326 Tremont Pl.	(303) 892-1436
Denver Museum of Miniatures and Dolls	1880 Gaylord St.	(303) 322-3704
Four Mile Historic Park	715 S. Forest St.	(303) 399-1859
Mizel Museum of Judaica	560 S Monaco Pkwy.	(303) 333-4156
Molly Brown House Museum	1340 Pennsylvania St.	(303) 832-4092
Denver Museum of Natural History	2001 Colorado Blvd.	(303) 322-7009
Museo de las Americas	861 Santa Fe Dr.	(303) 571-4401
Museum of Computer Technology	1640 Grant St.	(303) 832-8080
Pearce-McAllister Cottage	1880 Gaylord St.	(303) 322-1053
Plains Conservation Center	21901 E Hampden Ave.	(303) 693-3621
Stiles African American Heritage Center	2607 Glenarm Pl.	(303) 294-0597
Vance Kirkland Foun. & Museum	1311 Pearl St.	(303) 832-8576
Wings Over The Rockies Aviation & Space Museum	7711 E Academy Pkwy.	(303) 360-5360

NEWSPAPERS

Denver Post	1560 Broadway	(303) 820-1010
Denver Rocky Mountain News	400 W. Colfax Ave.	(303) 892-5000

Points of Interest

Denver Botanic Gardens	1005 York St.	(303) 331-4000
Denver Public Library	10 W. 14th Ave. Pkwy.	(303) 640-6200
Denver Zoo	2300 Steele St.	(303) 331-4100
Gates Planetarium	Mus. of Natural History	(303) 370-6351
Larimer Square	1400 Block of Larimer St.	(303) 534-2367
Ocean Journey	700 Water St.	(303) 561-4450
Six Flags Elitch Gardens	I-25 & Speer Blvd.	(303) 595-4386
State Capitol	Colfax at Sherman St.	(303) 866-2604
U. S. Mint	W. Colfax at Cherokee St.	(303) 844-3582
Post Office (Main Branch)	951 20th St.	(800) 275-8777
Denver Public Library	10 W. 14th Ave. Pkwy.	(303) 640-8800
Police Department	1331 Cherokee St.	(303) 640-2011
Fire Department	745 W. Colfax Ave.	(303) 640-3435

*D*enver was founded in 1859 when town promoters jumped a claim staked out by the St. Charles Town Company on the present site of downtown. Named for the governor of Kansas Territory, Denver City and its rival sister city Auraria became the supply point for the entire Pikes Peak mining region. The two towns merged to become Denver in 1861, the same year Colorado Territory was established. By 1867 Denver beat out Golden to become the permanent capital of the territory. The arrival of the railroads in 1871 and achieving statehood in 1876 accelerated Denver's growth, as did gold and silver discoveries in Aspen, Leadville and Cripple Creek. By 1890 Denver was established as the undisputed metropolis of the Rocky Mountain Region. Today the Denver metro area is the largest urban center between California and the Midwest.

COLORADO SKI TOWNS

Colorado Springs

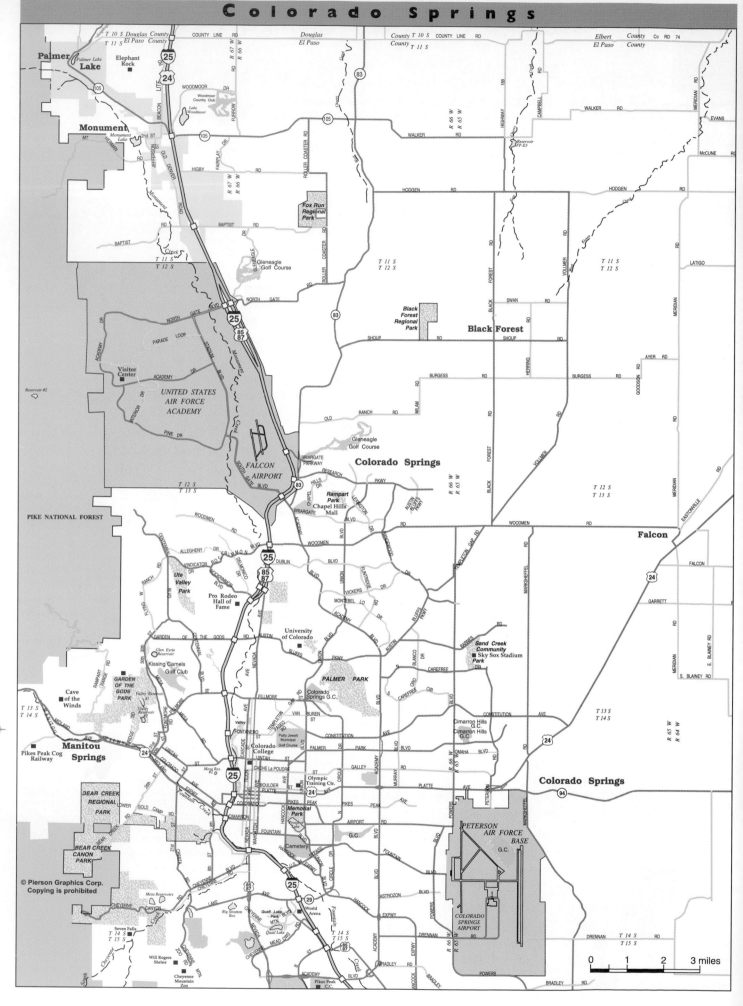

COLORADO SKI TOWNS

Colorado Springs

Points of Interest: U. S. Air Force Academy, Cheyenne Mountain Zoo, Garden of the Gods, Cave of the Winds, Pioneers Museum, Seven Falls, Pikes Peak Hwy. Toll Road, Pikes Peak Cog Railway, U. S. Olympic Complex, Pro Rodeo Hall of Fame, World Figure Skating Hall of Fame, The Broadmoor Hotel, Manitou Springs Historic District, NORAD, Pikes Peak International Raceway

Annual Events!

The Great Fruitcake Toss	January	(800) 642-2567
Carnivale & Gumbo Cookoff	February	(719) 685-5089
El Cinco de Mayo	Early May	(719) 635-7506
Territory Days Celebration	Mid-May	(719) 471-0545
Celebration of the Arts & Lilac Festival	Mid-May	(719) 685-4882
Hell on a Hillside Bicycle Race	June	(719) 591-4671
Pikes Peak Hill Climb	July 4th	(719) 685-4400
Colorado Springs Opera Festival	July, August	(719) 473-0073
Pikes Peak or Bust Rodeo	Early August	(719) 635-3548
Pikes Peak Marathon Run	Mid-August	(719) 473-2625
Mountain Music Festival	Late August	(719) 591-4671
CO Springs Annual Balloon Classic	Early September	(719) 471-4833
Buffalo Barbecue	Late September	(719) 685-5089
Oktoberfest	Early September	(719) 635-7506
Victorian Christmas at Miramont Castle	November, December	(719) 685-1011

Visitor Info. Chamber of Comm.	2 N. Cascade	**(719) 635-1551**

Hospitals

St. Francis Hospital	825 E. Pikes Peak Ave.	(719) 636-8800
Memorial Hospital	1400 E. Boulder	(719) 365-5000
Penrose Comm. Hospital	3205 N. Academy Blvd.	(719) 591-3000
Penrose Hospital	2215 N Cascade Ave.	(719) 776-5000

Public Transit

Springs Transit (CTM)	127 E. Kiowa	(719) 475-9733
Greyhound Bus Lines	327 S. Weber	(719) 635-1505

Airport

Colo. Springs Mun. Airport	7770 Drennan Rd.	(719) 550-1972

Colleges

Colorado College	14 E. Cache La Poudre	(719) 389-6000
Regis Univ.-Colo. Springs	7450 Campus Dr.	(719) 264-7070
Univ. of Colo.-Colo. Springs	PO Box 7150	(719) 262-3000
US Air Force Academy	2346 Academy Dr.	(719) 333-1818
Pikes Peak Comm. College	5675 S. Academy Blvd.	(719) 576-7711
Post Office - Main Branch	201 E. Pikes Peak Ave.	(719) 570-5343

Libraries

Fine Arts Center Library	30 W. Dale	(719) 634-5581
Penrose Public Library	20 N. Cascade Ave.	(719) 531-6333
Cheyenne Mtn. Branch	1791-D S. 8th St.	(719) 633-6278
East Library	5550 N. Union Blvd	(719) 531-6333

Public Golf Courses

Appletree Golf Course	10150 Rollng Ridge Rd.	(719) 382-3518
Cherokee Ridge Golf Course	1850 Tuskegee Pl.	(719) 597-2637
Elmwood Golf Course	1910 Airport Rd.	(719) 422-0220
Gleneagle Golf Club	345 Mission Hill Wy.	(719) 488-0900
Pine Creek Golf Club	9850 Divot Tr.	(719) 594-9999
Patty Jewett Golf Course	900 E. Espanola	(719) 578-6825
Sand Creek Golf Course	6865 Galley Rd.	(719) 597-9396
Valley Hi Golf Course	610 S. Chelton Rd.	(719) 578-6926

Museums

Am. Numismatic Assoc.	818 N. Cascade Ave.	(719) 632-2646
Children's Museum of Colorado Springs	750 Citadel Dr. E.	(719) 574-0077
Fine Arts Center	30 W. Dale	(719) 634-5581
Hall of Presidents Wax Museum	1050 S. 21st	(719) 635-3553
John May Museum Center	710 Rock Creek Canyon Rd.	(719) 576-0450
Manitou Cliff Dwellings Museum	Hwy. 24 (Manitou Spgs.)	(719) 685-5242
McAllister House Museum	423 N. Cascade Av.	(719) 635-7925
Nikola Tesla Museum of Science & Ind	2220 E. Bijou St.	(719) 475-0918
Pioneers Museum	215 S. Tejon	(719) 578-6650
Pro Rodeo Hall of Fame/ Mus. of Amer. Cowboy	101 Pro Rodeo Dr.	(719) 593-8847
Rock Ledge Ranch Hist. Site	30th St. & Gateway Rd.	(719) 578-6777
Rocky Mtn. Motorcycle Museum & Hall of Fame	308 E. Arvada St.	(719) 633-6329
US Olympic Complex	One Olympic Plaza	(719) 578-4644
Van Briggle Art Pottery	600 S. 21st St.	(719) 633-7729
Western Mus. of Mining	125 Gleneagle Dr.	(719) 488-0880
World Figure Skating Hall of Fame & Museum	20 1st St.	(719) 635-5200
Police Department	224 E. Kiowa	(719) 578-6762
Fire Department	31 S. Weber	(719) 578-7050

Newspapers

Colorado Springs Gazette	30 S. Prospect	(719) 632-5511

Colorado Springs was founded in 1858. The new settlement was named El Paso because of its proximity to the Ute Pass Trail. For a few years, in the 1860s, the town became the territorial capital, renamed Colorado City. With the arrival of the railroad, the area began to grow. In 1871 William J. Palmer, railroad baron and former Civil War general, purchased 10,000 acres of land east of Colorado City, which was a wild and wooly industrial town complete with saloons and other dens of iniquity. Palmer wanted to build a temperate, family-oriented community filled with churches, schools and parks. The new town, called Fountain Colony, was a planned community with no industry allowed and laws against the manufacture and sale of alcoholic beverages. The town was remained dry until the repeal of Prohibition in 1933. Sinners had to make the trek to Colorado City or Manitou Springs.

With the arrival of the railroad, the area was publicized as a scenic wonderland and health resort. Many tuberculosis patients came west to recuperate in the healthful mountain air. The natural wonders of the region and easy accessibility by rail attracted tourists, particularly Easterners and Europeans in such numbers that the town earned the nickname "Little London." Fountain Colony was renamed Colorado Springs to lure tourists, used to the fashionable spas of the East. The town became the first resort community west of Chicago, even though the actual hot springs were in Manitou Springs, five miles away.

Economically, Colorado Springs differed from other towns in the state. Most of them based their existence on mining or agriculture, usually ranching. Colorado Springs economic base was tourism. So many rich Easterners built summer homes that, between 1900 and 1910, Colorado Springs was the wealthiest city per capita in the U. S.

In modern times, tourism is still the main industry in the Springs, but government is also a major contributor. The city is now the seat of El Paso County and home to the Air Force Academy, the North American Air Defense Command (NORAD) buried deep inside Cheyenne Mountain, Fort Carson and Peterson Air Force Base.

COLORADO SKI TOWNS

Aspen

Points of Interest: The Aspen Mountains, Maroon Bells, Hallam Lake Wildlife Sanctuary, Wheeler Opera House, Aspen Art Museum, Independence Pass, Ashcroft Ghost Town, Wheeler-Stallard House Museum, founded in 1879

Annual Events:

Chocolate Classic	Mid-February	(970) 920-5357
Snowmass Mardis Gras Celebration	Late February	(970) 923-2000
America's Uphill	Mid March	(970) 925-1220
Aspen Shortsfest	Early April	(970) 925-6882
Canine Uphill Snowshoe Race	Early April	(970) 925-1069
Food & Wine Magazine Classic	Mid-June	(800) 262-7736
Aspen Music Festival & School	June-August	(970) 925-3254
International Design Conference	June	(970) 925-2257
Janus Jazz Aspen at Snowmass	June	(800) SNOWMASS
Snowmass Hot Air Balloon Festival	Late June	(800) 332-3245
Aspen Theater in the Park	Summer	(970) 920-5770
Dance Aspen	July, August	(303) 925-1940
Americruise Music & Fireworks Extravaganza	Mid-July	(303) 925-1940
Rocky Mtn. Brewers Fest	Late July	(303) 925-1940
Snowmass Village Children & Family Festival	Early August	(800) SNOWMASS
Aspen Harvestfest	September	(970) 925-3721
Snowmass Labor Day Music Festival	September	(800) 332-3245
MotherLode Volleyball Classic	Early September	(970) 925-6882
Aspen Ruggerfest	Mid-September	(970) 920-1042
Aspen Film Festival	Late September	(970) 925-6882
Silver Barons Ball	Early December	(800) 525-6200

Photos courtesy of Aspen Skiing Company/Biege Jones, Burnham Arndt, Peter McBride

Visitor Information			
	Visitor Center	425 Rio Grande Pl.	(970) 925-1940
Reservations			(800) 262-7736
Hospital	Aspen Valley Hospital	401 Castle Creek Rd.	(970) 925-1120
Public Transit	RFTA	51 Service Ctr. Dr.	(970) 925-8484
Aspen Parking Information			(970) 920-5267
Airport	Aspen-Pitkin County Airport	Sardy Field	(970) 920-5380
College	Colorado Mtn. College	221 High School Rd.	(970) 925-7740
Post Office		235 Puppy Smith St.	(970) 925-7523
Libraries	Pitkin County Library	120 N. Mill St.	(970) 925-7124
Museums	Aspen Art Museum	590 N. Mill St.	(970) 925-8050
	Wheeler-Stallard House/Aspen Historical Soc.		
		620 W. Bleeker St	(970) 925-3721
Ski Areas	Aspen Highlands	1600 Maroon Creek Rd.	(970) 925-5300
	Aspen Mountain		(970) 925-1220
	Buttermilk		(970) 925-1220
	Snowmass		(970) 923-2010
Recreation	Red Brick Arts & Recreation Ctr.	100 E. Hallam St.	(970) 920-5140
Windstar Land Conservancy		2317 Snowmass Creek Rd. (Snowmass)	(970) 927-4777
Public Golf Course	Aspen Munic. Golf Course	408 E. Cooper St.	(970) 925-2145
Police Department		506 E. Main St.	(970) 920-5400
Fire Department		420 E. Hopkins Ave.	(970) 925-5532
Newspapers	Aspen Daily News	315 E. Hyman Ave.	(970) 925-2220
	Aspen Times	310 E. Main St.	(970) 925-3414

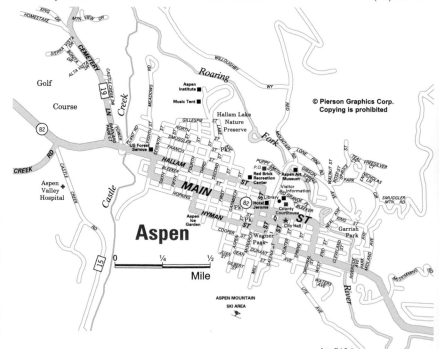

© Pierson Graphics Corp.
Copying is prohibited

Aspen

Aspen began as a small mining camp called Ute City, eventually growing to become a world-class ski resort and summer playground. Jerome B. Wheeler increased the city's wealth by opening a bank and reopening an abandoned silver smelter in 1880. By 1885 Aspen had electric lights and, two years later, service by two railroads. One million dollars worth of silver ore was shipped in the first month alone. In 1892, one-sixth of all the silver mined in the US came from the Aspen area. One year later the price of silver plummeted in the financial panic of 1893. So did the population, dropping from a peak of 15,000 to less than 500. The little mountain town began to bloom again when the first ski resort was built in 1936. In 1948 Chicago industrialist Walter Paepcke converted the small ski resort into the year-round health, sports and cultural center that is Aspen today.

Avon

Population: 2,437　✳　Elevation: 7,430　✳　Area Code: 970　✳　See Map 13　✳　Eagle, Co., CO 81620

Points of Interest: Beaver Creek Resort, Vail Center for the Arts at Beaver Creek

Annual Events:

Avon Winter Carnival	January	(970) 949-4280
Sweet Heart 5K Run/Walk	Mid-February	(970) 949-4280
Easter Egg Hunt	Early April	(970) 949-4280
Avon Festival of Nations	Mid-June	(970) 949-4280
LaCrosse Tournament	Late June, Early July	(970) 748-4032
Salute to the USA	4th of July	(970) 949-4280
High Country Triathlon/Duathlon	Late July	(970) 949-4280
Bob Summer Fest	Mid-August	(970) 949-4280
Beaver Creek Culinary Fest	September	(800) 525-3875
Avon Fall Festival Race	Early September	(970) 949-4280

Avon was founded in 1884, but not incorporated until 1978. The town, ten miles west of Vail and just north of Beaver Creek, was named after the Avon River by a homesick Englishman.

© Pierson Graphics Corp.
Copying is prohibited

Avon

0　　¼　　½
Mile

Arrowhead

Beaver Creek

Beaver Creek Golf Course

Beaver Creek Resort

Visitor Information	**Chamber of Commerce**	**260 Beaver Crk. Pl.**	**(970) 949-4385**
Hospital	Vail Valley Med. Ctr.	181 W. Meadow Dr.	(970) 476-2451
Public Transit	Avon/Beaver Creek Transit	500 Swift Gulch Rd.	(970) 949-6121
	Eagle County Regional Transit	48 E. Beaver Creek Blvd.	(970) 748-0702
Airport	Eagle County Airport	0215 Eldon Wilson Rd., Eagle	(970) 524-9490
Post Office		111 W. Beaver Creek Blvd.	(970) 949-4057
Library	Avon Public Library	200 Benchmark Rd.	(970) 949-6797
Ski Area	Beaver Creek /Vail Resorts		(800) 525-2257
Public Golf Course	Eagle Vail Golf Club	431 Eagle Drive	(970) 949-5267
Recreation Center		325 Benchmark Rd.	(970) 949-9191
Fire Department		351 Benchmark Rd.	(970) 949-6425
Police		400 Benchmark Rd.	(970) 949-5312
Newspaper	Avon/Beaver Creek Times		(970) 949-4402

Breckenridge

Points of Interest: Breckenridge Ski Resort, Riverwalk Center, Edwin Carter Museum.

Annual Events:

International Snow Sculpting Championships	Early January	(970) 453-6018
Ullr Fest Winter Carnival	January	(970) 453-6018
April Fool's Day Parade & Celebration	Early April	(970) 453-6018
A Taste of Breckenridge	Mid-May	(970) 453-5960
Steve Watson Golf Classic	Mid-June	(970) 453-9679
Breckenridge Music Festival	Summer	(970) 453-9142
4th of July Celebration & Fine Arts Fair	July	(970) 453-6018
Genuine Jazz in July	Mid-July	(970) 453-6018
No Man's Land	Early August	(970) 453-6018
Gathering at the Great Divide	Late August, Early September	(970) 547-9326
Labor Day Weekend Blues Festival		(970) 453-6018
Breckenridge Film Festival	Mid-September	(970) 453-6200
Oktoberfest Celebration	Late September	(970) 453-6200
Continental Divide Hot Air Balloon Fest	Late November, Early December	(970) 453-6018

Central Reservations			**(800) 221-1091**
Visitors Information	Breckenridge Resort Chamber	311 S. Ridge	**(970) 453-2918**
Hospital	Summit Medical Center	Hwy. 9 at School Rd., Frisco	(970) 668-3300
Public Transit	Summit Stage		(970) 668-0999
Colleges	Colorado Mountain College	103 S Harris	(970) 453-6757
Post Office		300 S. Ridge	(970) 453-2310
Libraries		504 Airport Rd.	(970) 453-6098
Museums	Summit Historical Society	309 N. Main St.	(970) 453-9022
	Edwin Carter Museum	111 N Ridge	(970) 453-9022
	Country Boy Mine		
Public Golf Course	Breckenridge Golf Club	200 Clubhouse Dr.	(970) 453-9104
Recreation Center		0800 Airport Rd.	(970) 453-1734
	Breckenridge Ice Arena	0189 Boreas Pass Rd.	(970) 547-9974
Police Department		150 Ski Hill Rd.	(970) 453-2941
Fire Department:		316 N. Main St.	(970) 453-2474
Newspapers	Summit Daily News	40 W. Main St., Frisco	(970) 668-3998
Summit County Breckenridge Journal			(970) 453-9192

Breckenridge

B reckenridge was named after Vice President John Cabell Breckinridge in an attempt to get a post office located in the town. When Breckinridge was commissioned a general in the Confederate Army at the start of the Civil War, the citizens of the town, loyal to the Union, changed the spelling of the town name in protest. The history of Breckenridge is not much different from other Colorado mountain towns. It fell on hard times when the gold mines began to play out. Better times came in 1961 with the development of the Breckenridge ski area. It is the biggest ski area in Summit County with 16 ski lifts, and 112 designated trails on 2000 skiable acres. Summer vacations in Breckenridge offer activities as different as shopping and mountain biking. The Breckenridge Historic District contains over 40 well-preserved Victorian buildings.

© Bob Winsett / Vail Resorts / Breckenridge

Crested Butte

Population: 1,079 ❋ Elevation: 8,885 ❋ Area Code: 970 ❋ See Map 22 ❋ Gunnison Co., CO 81224

Points of Interest: Crested Butte Ski Resort, mountain biking, Chairlift rides, Crested Butte Mtn. Heritage Museum & Mountain Bike Hall of Fame, Crested Butte National Historic District, Rocky Mountain Biological Laboratory in Gothic

Annual Events:

US Extreme Skiing Championships	February	(970) 349-2201
Alley Loop Cross Country Ski Race	February	(970) 349-6438
Dannon Winterfest	February	(970) 349-2201
Al Johnson Mem. Uphill-Downhill Tele-Ski Race	Late March	(800) 323-2453
US Extreme Snowboarding Championships	March, April	(970) 349-2201
Flauschink Festival	Mid-April	(970) 349-2201
Crested Butte Fat Tire Festival	Late June	(802) 226-7411
Crested Butte Wildflower Fest	Mid-July	(970) 349-2571
Aerial Weekend	Late July	(800) 545-4505
Dansummer	July	(800) 323-2453
Crested Butte Reel Festival	August	(970) 349-7487
Crested Butte Festival of the Arts	Early August	(970) 349-6438
Mt. Crested Butte Micro Brewery Festival	Late August	(800) 545-4505
Paragon People's Fair	Early September	(800) 323-2453
Pearl Pass Mountain Bike Tour	Mid-September	(800) 545-4505
Town Tree Lighting	Mid-December	(800) 323-2453

Crested Butte, and its much younger sibling, Mt. Crested Butte, three miles away, reside in a high mountain valley. The valley was once the summer hunting grounds of the Utes until the arrival of gold and silver miners in the 1880s. Crested Butte incorporated when the Denver And Rio Grande Railroad arrived from Gunnison. Coal was discovered in the late 1880s, allowing the town to survive after the gold and silver played out. When the ski area opened in the early 1960s, the village of Mt. Crested Butte grew around the foot of the ski runs. The skiing, both cross-country and downhill, is said to be some of the best in the state. Crested Butte is the place where Colorado mountain biking was born. Fat Tire Week in July is the place to be for mountain bike competition at its best.

Photo courtesy of Crested Butte Mtn. Resort/Grafton Smith Photography

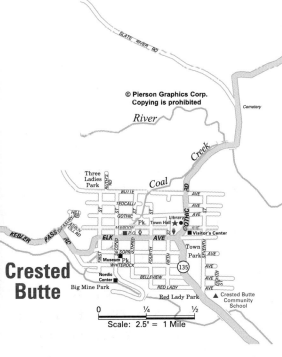

© Pierson Graphics Corp.
Copying is prohibited

Scale: 2.5" = 1 Mile

Visitor Information	Chamber of Commerce	601 Elk Ave.	(800) 545-4505
	Central Reservations	601 Elk Ave.	(800) 215-2226
Hospitals	Gunnison Valley Hospital	214 E. Denver Ave., Gunnison	(970) 641-1456
Bus Station TNM & O (Greyhound)	Gunnison		(970) 642-0060
Public Transportation	Mountain Express	801 Butte Ave.	(970) 349-5616
Airport	Gunnison County Airport	S. Boulevard Ave., Gunnison	(970) 641-2304
Post Office		217 Elk Ave., Mt. Crested Butte	(970) 349-5568
Library	Old Rock Community Library	507 Maroon Ave.	(970) 349-6535
Museums	Crested Butte Mountain Heritage Museum	200 Sopris Ave.	(970) 349-1880
	Mountain Bike Hall Of Fame & Museum	200 Sopris Ave.	(970) 349-6817
	Crested Butte Center for the Arts	606 6th St.	(970) 349-7487
Ski Areas	Crested Butte Mountain Resort	12 Snowmass Rd., Mt. Crested Butte	(800) 544-8448
Police Department		508 Maroon Ave	(970) 349-5231
	Mt. Crested Butte Police	911 Gothic Rd.	(970) 349-6516
Fire Department		306 Maroon Ave.	(970) 349-5333
Newspapers	Crested Butte Chronicle & Pilot	500 Belleview Ave	(970) 349-6114

Dillon

Points of Interest: Dillon Schoolhouse Museum, Dillon Reservoir, Dillon Amphitheater

Annual Events:

Colorado Soap Box Derby	Early June	(970) 668-2050
Taste of the Summit	Late June	(970) 468-3400
Independence Day Celebration	Early July	(970) 668-5800
Dillon Open Regatta	Early August	(970) 262-5824
Chamber of Commerce	**11 S. Summit Blvd**	**(970) 668 5800**
Summit Medical Center	Hwy. 9 at School Rd., Frisco	(970) 668-3300
Summit Stage Bus		(970) 668-0999
Post Office	224 Dillon Mall Ave.	(970) 468-2501
The Dillon School House Museum	403 La Bonte	(970) 468-2207
Ski Areas	Keystone	(800) 468-5004
	Arapahoe Basin	(800) ARAPAHOE
Police Department	275 Lake Dillon Dr.	(970) 468-6078
Fire Department	401 Blue River Pkwy.	(970) 468-2823

Dillon was founded around the same time as Silverthorne. The present town is not the original one; it has had three different townsites over the years. The first town was built east of the Snake River. When the railroad arrived a few years later, Dillon was moved to be closer to the depot. In the 1950s, Denver, 73 miles to the east, was rapidly outgrowing its water supply so plans were made to dam the Blue River to create a reservoir. The town of Dillon was right where the new lake would form when the dam was in place. Because Dillon Reservoir was to be a source of drinking water, all traces of the town had to be removed. Every structure was demolished and hauled away. The new Dillon grew on its present site in 1961 and is now a popular winter and summer resort.

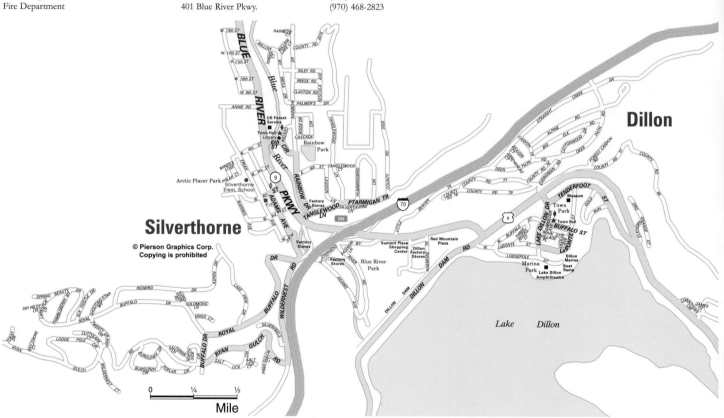

© Pierson Graphics Corp.
Copying is prohibited

Silverthorne

Silverthorne was founded in 1881 by Judge Marshal Silverthorne on 160 acres of land he purchased from the US Government. He developed a new, more efficient way to extract gold from the Blue River, eventually obtaining a patent for the process called the Silverthorne Placer. Silverthorne is now the home of the Silverthorne Factory Shops, a factory outlet mall featuring 70 stores.

Points of Interest: Prime Outlets - Silverthorne shopping mall

Annual Events:

Mountain Community Fair	Early July	(970) 262-2261

Chamber of Commerce		**11 S. Summit Blvd.**	**(970) 668-5800**
Hospital	Summit Medical Center	Hwy. 9 at School Rd., Frisco	(970) 668-3300
Public Transit	Summit Stage Bus		(970) 668-0999
Bus Station	Greyhound Trailways Bus	471 Rainbow Dr.	(970) 468-1938
Colleges	Colorado Mtn. College	151 W. 4th St.	(970) 468-5989
Post Office		390 N. Brian Ave.	(970) 468-8112
Library	Silverthorne Town Hall Library	601 Center Cir.	(970) 468-5887
Recreation Center		430 Rainbow Dr.	(970) 262-7370
Public Golf Course	Eagle's Nest Golf Course	1695 Chipmunk	(970) 468-0681
Ski Areas (see above)			
Police Department		601 Center Cir.	(970) 262-7320
Fire Department		401 Blue River Pkwy.	(970) 468-2823

Durango

When the Durango and Rio Grande Railroad bypassed Animas City two miles to the south, preferring to build its own townsite, everyone immediately packed up and moved to the new town of Durango. By the end of the year Durango boasted 2,500 souls, 20 saloons and 134 businesses. It became the haunt of ranchers, rustlers, miners, claim jumpers and railroad workers. Vigilantes struggled to keep order in the lawless town. Because of the railroad, Durango became the regional center for supplying the mines and smelting the ore they produced. With the silver bust of 1893, the town subsisted as a shipping center for ranchers and farmers in the Animas Valley. Its proximity to Mesa Verde National Park, established in 1903, and access to the many recreational activities available in the area ensured that Durango would become the major tourist destination it is today.

Points of Interest: Durango/Silverton Narrow Gauge Railroad, Mesa Verde National Park, Purgatory Ski Resort, Vallecito Reservoir, Trimble Hot Springs

Photo courtesy of Purgatory Resort

Annual Events:

Durango Meltdown Bluegrass Festival	April	(800) 525-8855
Iron Horse Bicycle Classic	Late May	(970) 259-4621
Animas Music Festival	Early June	(970) 259-2606
4th of July Festival	July	(800) 525-8855
Music in the Mountains	Late July, Early August	(970) 385-6820
Durango Fiesta Days	Late July, Early August	(970) 385-6820
Main Avenue Juried Arts Festival	August	(970) 259-2606
La Plata County Fair	August	(800) 525-8855
Colorfest Celebration	September, October	(970) 247-0312
Four Corners Iron Horse Motorcycle Rally	Early September	(970) 563-4171
Western Movie Festival	September	(800) 525-8855
Durango Cowboy Gathering	October	(970) 259-2165
Caroling Procession & Lighting of Durango	November	(800) 525-8855

Visitor Information	Chamber of Commerce	111 S. Camino del Rio	(970) 247-0312
Central Reservations		945 Main Ave.	(800) 525-0892
Hospitals	Mercy Med. Center	375 E. Park Ave.	(970) 247-4311
Airport	Durango-La Plata County Airport	100 Airport Rd.	(970) 247-8143
Bus Station	Greyhound TNM&O	275 E. 8th Ave.	(970) 259-2755
Public Transit	Durango Opportunity Bus	2301 Main Ave.	(970) 247-3577
	Durango LIFT	105 Sawyer	(970) 259-5438
Train Depot	Durango & Silverton Narrow Gauge Railroad	479 Main Ave.	(970) 247-2733
Colleges	Fort Lewis College	1000 Rim Dr.	(970) 247-7184
Post Office		222 W. 8th Ave.	(970) 247-3434
Libraries	Durango Public Library	1188 E. 2nd Ave.	(970) 385-2970
	Southwest Library System	1060 Main Ave.	(970) 247-4782
Museums	Animas Museum	31st St. & W. 2nd Ave.	(970) 259-2402
	Children's Museum of Durango	802 E. 2nd Ave.	(970) 259-9237
	Durango & Silverton Narrow Gauge RR Mus.	479 Main Ave.	(970) 247-9302
Public Golf Courses	Hillcrest Golf Course	2300 Rim Dr.	(970) 247-1499
	Dalton Ranch Golf Club	589 County Rd. 252	(970) 247-8774
Recreation Centers	Durango Rec. Ctr.	486 Florida Rd.	(970) 247-9999
Ski Area	Purgatory	175 Beatrice Dr.	(970) 247-9000
	Chapman Hill	500 Florida Rd.	(970) 385-2967
Police Department	990 E. 2nd Ave.		(970) 385-2900
Fire Department			(970) 385-2850
Newspapers	Durango Herald	1275 Main Ave.	(970) 247-3504

Photo courtesy of Purgatory Resort

$\mathcal{E}$agle/ Eagle Valley

Points of Interest: Eagle County Historical Society Museum.

Annual Events:

Ditch Day Ski Event	March	(970) 328-5220
Eagle Flight Days	Late June	(970) 328-5220
Eagle County Fair & Rodeo	Late July, Early August	(970) 328-5220
Screaming Eagle Golf Tournament	Mid-September	(970) 328-5220
Christmas on Broadway	Early December	(970) 328-5220
Citizen of the Year Extravaganza	Mid-December	(970) 328-5220

Visitor Information	Tourist Information Center	100 Fairgrounds Rd.	(970) 328-6464
Hospital	Vail Valley Medical Center	181 Meadow Dr., Vail	(970) 476-2451
Public Transportation	Eagle County Reg. Transp. Authority		(970) 748-0702
	Greyhound	432 Grand	(970) 328-2305
Airport	Eagle County Reg. Airport	1193 Cooley Mesa Rd., Gypsum	(970) 524-9490
College	Colorado Mtn. College	139 Broadway	(970) 328-6304
Post Office		264 Chambers Ave.	(970) 328-6828
Library	Eagle Public Library	600 Broadway	(970) 328-8800
Museum			
Eagle County Historical Soc. Museum		Chambers Park	(970) 328-6464
Police Department		108 W. 2nd St.	(970) 328-6351
	Eagle County Sheriff	855 E. Chambers Ave.	(970) 328-8500
	Eagle Ranger District Office	125 W. 5th St.	(970) 328-6388
Fire Department		425 E. 3rd St.	(970) 328-6343
Newspaper	Vail Daily		(970) 949-0555

Eagle, the seat of Eagle County, and the surrounding valley were the summer hunting and fishing grounds of the Utes before the arrival of Europeans. The first known visitation occurred in 1840 when Kit Carson led the Fremont party through the valley. Formerly part of Summit County, Eagle County became a separate entity in 1883 with the town of Red Cliff, named for the surrounding red quartzite cliffs, as the county seat. In 1921 the county seat was moved to the town of Eagle. Several sites in the town are listed in the National Register of Historic Places.

$\mathcal{E}$stes $\mathcal{P}$ark

Points of Interest: Trail Ridge Road, Old Fall River Road, Stanley Hotel, Enos Mills Cabin, Moraine Park Museum, Estes Park Area Historical Museum, Key Room, MacGregor Ranch Museum, Rocky Mountain National Park.

Annual Events:

Artwalk & Jazz Festival	2nd Week in May	(800) 44-ESTES
Wool Market	Early June	(800) 44-ESTES
Scandinavian Mid-Summer Fest	Late June	(800) 44-ESTES
Rooftop Rodeo & Parade	Early-Mid-July	(800) 44-ESTES
Best of the West Estes Brewfest	Mid-August	(970) 586-5124
September Festival Month	September	(800) 44-ESTES
Longs Peak Scottish Highland Festival	Mid-September	(800) 44-ESTES
Autumn Gold Festival of Brats & Band	Late September	(800) 44-ESTES
Catch the Glow Christmas Parade	Late November	(800) 44-ESTES

Visitor Information

Chamber of Commerce	500 Big Thompson Ave.	(800) 44-ESTES	(970) 586-4237
Hospitals	Estes Park Med. Ctr.	555 Prospect Ave.	(970) 586-2317
Public Transit	Estes Park Trolley	870 West Ln.	(970) 586-8866
Post Office		215 W. Riverside Dr.	(970) 586-8177
Libraries	Estes Park Library	335 E. Elkhorn Ave.	(970) 586-8116
Museums	Enos Mills Cabin Museum	6760 Co. Hwy. 7	(970) 586-4706
	Estes Park Historical Museum	200 4th St.	(970) 586-6256
	MacGregor Ranch Museum	180 MacGregor Ave.	(970) 586-3749
Public Golf Courses	Estes Park Golf Club	1080 S. St. Vrain Ave.	(970) 586-8146
Lake Estes Exec. Golf Club		690 Big Thompson Ave.	(970) 586-8176
Cross Country Skiing/ Winter Rec.		YMCA of the Rockies	(970) 586-3341
Police Department		170 MacGregor Ave.	(970) 586-4000
Fire Department		170 MacGregor Ave.	(970) 586-4000
Newspapers	Estes Park Trail Gazette	251 Moraine Ave.	(970) 586-3356

Estes Park was first settled by cattle rancher Joel Estes in 1859. The harsh winter of 1866 changed his mind. He sold out and moved his family and herd to warmer pastures. The next year Griffith J. Evans acquired some of the land and built cabins to accommodate travelers coming to the area to explore and climb. One of his guests, the English Earl of Dunraven, was so impressed by what he saw that he tried to buy Estes Park to use as an exclusive hunting preserve. He was unable to purchase land under the Homestead Act as a foreign national. Not to be denied, he pulled off a classic land grab scheme by using drifters', fictitious and, even, dead people's names to buy 160 acre parcels. He then consolidated all the individual claims into the Estes Park Company, known locally as the English Company. In 1907 he sold out to the Stanley brothers of Stanley Steamer fame who built the Stanley Hotel. Estes Park has long been a resort area and is the eastern gateway to Rocky Mountain National Park.

Frisco

Points of Interest: Frisco Historic Park, Frisco Nordic Center

Annual Events:

Frisco Gold Rush	Mid-February	(800) 424-1554
Ten Mile One Mile Kayak Races	Early June	(800) 424-1554
Run the Rockies	Late June	(800) 424-1554
Frisco's Fantastic 4th of July	July	(800) 424-1554
Music on Main Street	Mid-July	(970) 668-5276
Yettes on the Rockies	Early August	(970) 191 1661
Founders Day	Late August	(800) 424-1554
Colorado Barbecue Challenge	Late August	(800) 424-1554
Old Fashioned Christmas	Early December	(800) 424-1554

Chamber of Commerce	11 S. Summit Blvd.	(970) 668-5800
Visitor Information		
Summit Medical Center	Hwy. 9 at School Rd.	(970) 668-3300
Public Transit	Summit Stage Bus	(970) 668-0999
College		
Colorado Mountain College	602 Galena	(970) 668-0855
Post Office	35 W. Main	(970) 668-5505
Library	37 County Rd. 1005	(970) 668-5555
Frisco Historic House & Museum	120 Main	(970) 668-3428
Ski Area	Copper Mtn. Resort	(800) 458-8386
Police Department	1 Main St.	(970) 668-3579
Fire Department	401 Blue River Pkwy., Silverthorne	(970) 468-2823
Newspapers		
Summit Daily News	40 W. Main St.	(970) 668-3998
Summit Sentinel	40 W. Main St.	(970) 668-0750

Frisco grew up as a center of logging and mining in the early 1880s. Legend says that it was named after the California city of San Francisco in the hopes that it would become as prosperous. During the mining boom in the area, and being the geographic center of Summit County, Frisco became a hub for stagecoach and rail travel. The town is now a popular resort and home of the Frisco Nordic Center located on a peninsula on Dillon Reservoir. The Center has 35 kilometers of set track.

Georgetown

Points of Interest: Georgetown Loop Railroad, Hamill House Museum, Georgetown Energy Museum, Hotel de Paris

Annual Events:

Poverty Follies	April	(303) 569-2888
4th of July Parade	July	(800) 472 8230
Georgetown to Idaho Springs Half Marathon	Early August	(800) 472-8230
Hoe Down at the Hamill House	August	(303) 569-2840
Fund Raising Auction	Mid-August	(800) 472-8230
Autumn Jazz & Leaves Fest	September	(303) 569-2300
Christmas Tree Lighting	Late November	(800) 472-8230
Christmas Market	Early December	(800) 472-8230
Christmas at the Hamill House	Early December	(800) 472-8230
Marry Me & Ski for Free	Mid-February	(800) 736-3SKI

Visitor Information	Central Reservations	1009 Griffith	(303) 569-2665
Hospital	Summit Med Ctr.	Hwy. 9 at School Rd., Frisco	(970) 668-3300
Railroad	Georgetown Loop	1106 Rose	(303) 569-2403
Post Office		700 6th	(303) 569-2771
Library	John Tomay Mem. Library	605 6th St.	(303) 569-2620
Museums	Georgetown Energy Museum	600 Main St.	(303) 569-3557
	Hamill House	305 Argentine	(303) 569-2840
	Hotel de Paris	409 6thSt.	(303) 569-2311
Ski Area	Loveland		(800) 736-3SKI
Police			(303) 569-3232
Fire			(303) 569-3232
Newspaper	Clear Creek Courant	1634 Miner, Idaho Springs	(303) 567-4991

When the Griffith brothers, George and David, discovered gold in a little beaver flat on Clear Creek in 1859, they thought they had finally succeeded as miners. The Griffith Lode was worth $500. Rather than move on yet again, the brothers decided to stay put. They went back to Kentucky, retrieved the rest of the family and set up shop in the canyon, founding George's Town, or Georgetown, as it came to be called. Georgetown became the third largest town in Colorado by 1876 with several hotels, five churches, four fire companies, two newspapers, a telegraph office, a waterworks and a bank. Until silver was discovered in Leadville, Georgetown was known as the Silver Queen, the most important silver camp in the Rockies. The crash of the silver market in 1893 plunged Georgetown into a seventy-year dark age, not relieved until it was designated a historical landmark district. The many Victorian buildings preserved in the town and the nearby Georgetown Loop Historic Mining District and Railroad Park have revitalized Georgetown into a popular tourist destination.

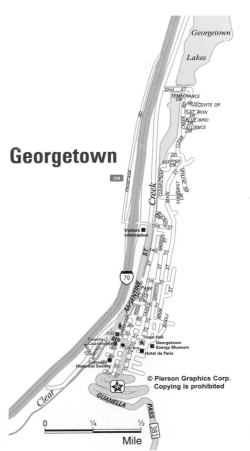

Glenwood Springs

Points of Interest: Hot Springs Pool, Vapor Caves, Hotel Colorado, Ski Sunlight, Frontier Historical Museum, Doc Holliday Tombstone, Glenwood Canyon

The healing properties of the hot water springs and vapor caves at Glenwood were used by the Ute tribe for centuries. In 1860 Captain Richard Sopris became, perhaps, the first outsider to take advantage of the benefits. When he became ill while exploring the Eagle River Valley, the Utes took him to the springs to recuperate. In 1885 Walter Deveraux bought the hot springs and began developing the town and tourism. Both were aided by the arrival of the Durango and Rio Grande Railroad in 1887. The elegant Hotel Colorado, built in 1893, became the playground of the era's rich and famous, introducing polo as a popular pastime for those who could afford it. Glenwood teams won many national polo championships. Today, Glenwood Springs is a popular tourist destination with many opportunities for outdoor recreation year round.

Photo courtesy of the Hot Springs Pool

Annual Events:

Ski Spree	February	(970) 945-6589
March Music Madness	March	(970) 945-6589
Rallye Glenwood Springs	Mid-June	(970) 945-6589
Glenwood Springs Dance Festival	June, July	(970) 945-6589
Glenwood Springs Summer of Jazz	June, July	(970) 945-6589
Strawberry Days	Late June	(970) 945-6589
4th of July Fireworks Display	July	(970) 945-6589
Doc Holidays	Mid-August	(970) 945-6589
Fall Arts Festival	Late September	(970) 945-6589
Tri Glenwood Triathlon	September	(970) 945-6589

Visitor Information

	Chamber Resort Assn.	1102 Grand Ave.	(970) 945-6589
Hospital	Valley View Hospital	1906 Blake Ave.	(970) 945-6535
Bus Station	Greyhound Bus Lines	118 W. 6th St.	(970) 945-8501
Public Transit	Roaring Fork Transit Assoc. (RFTA)		(970) 925-8484
	Ride Glenwood Springs		(970) 945-2575
Train	Amtrak	413 7th St.	(970) 945-9563
Airport	Glenwood Springs Munic. Airport	1172 Airport Center Rd.	(970) 945-2385
Colleges	Colorado Mountain College	215 9th St.	(970) 945-8691
	Regis University	1402 Blake Ave.	(970) 945-0624
Post Office		113 9th St.	(970) 945-5611
Libraries	Glenwood Springs Library	413 9th St.	(970) 945-5958
	Colorado Mtn. College Library	3000 County Rd. 114	(970) 945-7481
Museum	Frontier Historical Museum	1001 Colorado Ave.	(970) 945-4448
Public Golf Courses	Glenwood Springs G. C.	193 Sunny Acres Rd. (RD 193)	(970) 945-7086
	Westbank G. C.	1007 Westbank Rd.	(970) 945-7032
Ski Area	Sunlight Mountain Resort	10901 117 Rd.	(970) 945-7491
Police Department		823 Blake Ave.	(970) 945-8566
Fire Department		806 Cooper Ave.	(970) 945-6161
Newspapers	Glenwood Independent	1001 Grand Ave.	(970) 945-6300
	The Glenwood Post	2014 Grand Ave.	(970) 945-8515

COLORADO SKI TOWNS

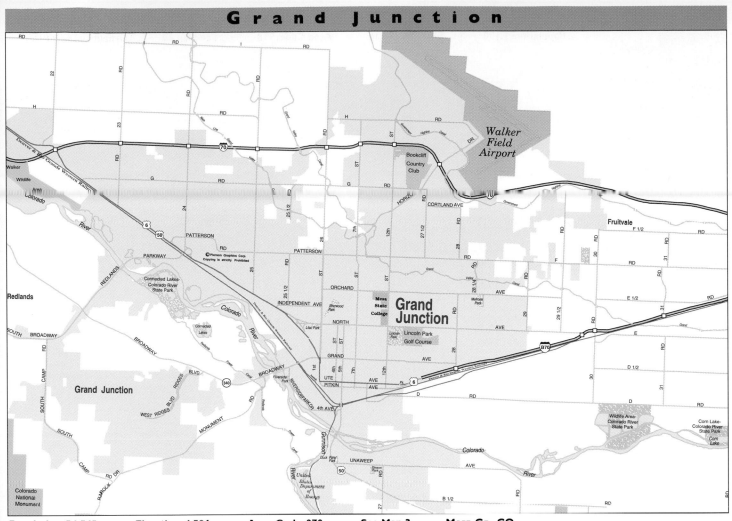

Population: 34,540   **Elevation: 4,586**   **Area Code: 970**   **See Map 3**   **Mesa Co., CO**

Points of Interest: Colorado National Monument, Museum of Western Colorado, Cross Orchards Living History Farm, Dinosaur Valley, Two Rivers Plaza Convention Center, Mesa State College, Western Colorado Center for the Arts, Rabbit Valley Dinosaur Quarry founded in 1881, Winery tours.

Annual Events:

St. Patrick's Day Parade	Mid-March	(800) 962-2547
Southwest Fest	Mid-April	(970) 245-2926
Western Colorado Heritage Days	Late April	(970) 242-0971
Cinco de Mayo	Early May	(970) 242-3214
Grand River Indian Artists Gathering	Mid May	(970) 242-0971
Jr. College World Series Baseball Tourn.	May	(970) 242-3214
Country Jam USA	June	(800) 962-2547
Colorado Stampede Rodeo	June	(970) 242-3214
Norwest Art & Jazz Fest	Mid-June	(970) 245-2926
4th of July Parade & Fireworks	July	(970) 242-3214
Dinosaur Days	Mid-July	(970) 245-2926
Mesa County Fair	July	(970) 242-3214
Kokopelli Marathon/Half Marathon/50K	September	(970) 242-3214
Tour of the Vineyards Bicycle Tour	September	(970) 242-3214
Colorado Mtn. Winefest	Mid-September	(800) 962-2547
Celtic Festival & Highland Games	Late September	(970) 243-5119
Marching Band Festival	October	(970) 242-3214
Oktoberfest	October	(970) 242-3214
Riverfront 5K Run/Walk	October	(970) 242-3214
Apple Jubilee	Early October	(970) 242-0971
Rim Rock Run	November	(970) 242-3214
Winter Festival/Parade of Lights	Early December	(970) 245-2926
Boars Head Christmas Feast	December	(970) 242-3214

Visitor Information

Chamber of Commerce	360 Grand Ave.	(970) 242-3214
Hospitals		
Veterans Adm. Med. Ctr.	2121 North Ave.	(970) 242-0731
Community Hospital	2021 N. 12th St.	(970) 242-0920
St. Mary's Hospital	2635 N. 7th St.	(970) 244-2273
Greyhound Bus Lines	230 S. 5th St.	(970) 242-6012
Amtrak	399 S. 1st St.	(970) 241-2733
Walker Field Airport	2828 Walker Field Dr.	(970) 244-9100
Mesa State College	12th & North Ave.	(970) 248-1786
Post Office	241 N. 4th St.	(970) 244-3400
Mesa County Library	530 Grand Ave.	(970) 243-4783
Museums		
Cross Orchards Farm	3073 F Rd.	(970) 434-9814
DooZoo Children's Museum	635 Main St.	(970) 241-5225
Dinosaur Valley Museum	362 Main St.	(970) 243-3466
Mus. of Western Colorado	248 S. 4th St.	(970) 242-0971
Western Colorado Ctr. for the Arts	1803 N. 7th St.	(970) 243-7337
Public Golf Courses		
Chipeta Golf Course	222 29 Rd.	(970) 245-7177
Lincoln Park Golf Course	12th & North Ave.	(970) 242-6394
Tiara Rado Golf Course	2063 S. Broadway	(970) 245-8085
Ski Area	Powderhorn	(970) 268-5700
Police Department	625 Ute Ave.	(970) 244-3555
Fire Department	330 S. 6th St.	(970) 244-1400
Newspaper		
Daily Sentinel	734 S. 7th St.	(970) 242-5050

With a population of over 30,000, Grand Junction is the largest town between Salt Lake City and Denver. First settled in 1881, irrigation projects gave the valley around Grand Junction the basis for its farming industry. Once the railroad arrived the next year, the area grew rapidly, becoming famous for its fine fruits including cherries, apricots and grapes. During the early and mid1900s, oil and uranium were discovered around Grand Junction. The town suffered many boom and bust cycles because of dependence on mineral production. Tourism is now becoming a major industry due to the many outdoor activities available affording along with agriculture, a more stable economic base for the region.

Granby

Points of Interest: Silver Creek Resort, Lake Granby

Annual Events:

Firefighters' Feud	March	(800) 247-2635
Granby Ice Fishing Derby	March	(800) 247-2635
Easter Service & Egg Hunt	Early April	(800) 247-2635
Kids Buckaroo & Adult Open Rodeo	June	(800) 247-2635
4th of July Parade & Barbecue	Early July	(800) 247-2635
Michael Martin Murphy's Westfest	July	(800) 247-2635
Arts & Crafts Fest	August	(800) 247-2635
Labor Day Festival	Early September	(800) 247-2635
Fall Fashion Show	October	(800) 247-2635
Cowboy Christmas Ski Race	Mid-December	(800) 247-2635
Hometown Christmas	Mid-December	(800) 247-2635
New Year's Eve Parade & Fireworks	Late December	(800) 247-2635

Visitor Information			
	Granby Chamber of Commerce	81 W. Jasper Ave.	(970) 887-2311
Hospital	Kremmling Mem. Hospital	214 S. 4th, Kremmling	(970) 724-3442
Bus Station	Greyhound	516 E. Agate Ave.	(970) 887-2411
Airport	Granby Airport	1023 County Rd 610	(970) 887-9926
Post Office		54 Zero	(970) 887-3612
Library	Granby Library	13 E. Jasper Ave.	(970) 887-2149
Snow Mountain Ranch YMCA of the Rockies			(970) 887-2152
Ski Area	Silver Creek		(800) 754-7458
Police Department			(970) 725-3343
Newspapers	The Daily Tribune	424 E. Agate Ave.	(970) 887-3334

Granby was founded in 1905 when the Moffat Railroad entered the Fraser Valley. Incorporated in 1906, the town was named for Granby Hillyer, the US District Attorney for Colorado in appreciation for services to the state. Within a year the town grew to 30 buildings, including four saloons, two livery stables, two hotels, two restaurants, a church and a schoolhouse. The valley attracted ranchers, making cattle one of the mainstays of the local economy. As tourism became more profitable than herding cattle, many ranches have since been converted into guest ranches, offering a real western experience for city folk. The 4th of July fireworks show in Granby is the biggest one in the state, drawing 75,000 people each year.

Grand Lake

Points of Interest: Rocky Mtn. National Park, Kauffman House, a refurbished turn-of-the-century log hotel, Shadow Mountain Lake, and Grand Lake recreation

Annual Events:

Grand Lake Ice Fishing Derby	March	(800) 531-1019
Grand Lake High Altitude Sled Dog Championships	March	(800) 531-1019
Grand Spring Fishing Derby	Early May	(800) 531-1019
Grand Lake Pro-Am Scramble	Mid-June	(970) 627-8008
4th of July Fireworks Extravaganza	July	(970) 627-3402
Legends of Grand Lake/Western Week/ Buffalo Barbecue	Mid-July	(800) 531-1019
Grand Lake Regatta & Lipton Cup Races		(970) 627-3377
Daven Haven Downs Turtle Races & Reptilian Ball	Mid-August	(800) 531-1019
Grand Lake Pro Am Scramble	Late August	(800) 531-1019
Lariat International Golf Tournament	Early September	(800) 531-1019
Old Fashioned Christmas	Mid-Late December	(970) 627-3402

Visitor Information			
	Chamber of Commerce	928 Grand Ave.	(970) 627-3372
Hospital	Kremmling Mem. Hospital	214 S. 4th, Kremmling	(970) 726-5488
Public Transportation	Amtrak	205 Fraser Ave, Fraser	(970) 726-8816
Bus Station	Greyhound	516 E. Agate, Granby	(970) 887-2411
Airport	Grand County Airport, Granby		(970) 725-3347
Post Office		520 Center Dr.	(970) 627-3340
Library	Juniper Library at Grand Lake	315 Pitkin St.	(970) 627-8353
Museum	Kauffman House	Pitkin St.	(970) 627-3402
Public Golf Course	Grand Lake Golf Course	1415 County Rd 45	(970) 627-8008
Ski Area	Silver Creek	US Hwy. 40, East of Granby	(800) 754-7458
Fire Department		316 Garfield	(970) 627-8428
Newspaper	Grand Lake Prospector	424 E. Agate Ave., Granby	(970) 887-3334

Gold was discovered in the mountains around Grand Lake, the largest glacial lake, and the largest natural lake, in Colorado. The little town began as a supply depot for the prospectors heading up into the high country to try their luck. The beautiful lake, with its forested shores, developed into a resort in the late 1800s. By the early 1900s, wealthy families from Denver and back East were building summer homes around the lake. The lake was an ideal place to sail, so the Grand Lake Yacht Club was founded in 1905, the highest yacht club in the world. Regattas are held frequently throughout the short summer sailing season. Besides the obvious summer attractions, Grand Lake offers such winter sports as snowmobiling, cross-country skiing and snowshoeing.

Gunnison

Points of Interest: Western State College, Pioneer Museum, the Black Canyon of the Gunnison, Crested Butte Ski Area, Curecanti National Recreation Area, Alpine Tunnel, Aberdeen Quarry, founded in 1879

Annual Events:

Winter Carnival	January	(800) 274-7580
Hottest Cold Spot in the Nation Celebration	February	(800) 274-7580
Blue Mesa Fishing Tournament	Early May	(800) 274-7580
Mammoth Bass Gamefish & Reserve Fishing Tourn.	May	(888) 323-2453
Rage in the Sage Race	Early June	(800) 274-7580
White Water Festival	Mid-June	(970) 641-1501
Wildflower Festival	July	(800) 323-2453
Cattlemen's Days Celebration & Rodeo	July	(800) 323-2453
4th of July Celebration	July	(800) 274-7580
Art in the Park	Late July	(800) 274-7580
Land of the Rainbow Quilt Festival	August	(800) 323-2453
Festival of Country Arts	Late August	(800) 274-7580
Sugarplum Festival	November	(800) 274-7580
Parade of Lights	Early December	(800) 274-7580

Visitor Information	Chamber of Commerce	500 E. Tomichi	(800) 274-7580
Hospital	Gunnison Valley Hospital	214 E. Denver Ave.	(970) 641-2695
Bus Station	Greyhound TNM&O	821 W. Tomichi Ave.	(970) 641-0060
Airport	Gunnison County Airport	S. Boulevard Ave.	(970) 641-2304
College	Western State College	600 N. Adams St.	(970) 943-0120
Post Office		200 N. Wisconsin St.	(970) 641-1884
Libraries	Ann Zugelder Library	307 N. Wisconsin St.	(970) 641-3485
	Savage Library	Western State College	(970) 944-2103
Museums	Pioneer Museum	S. Adams & E. Hwy. 50	(970) 641-4530
Public Golf Courses	Dos Rios Country Club	501 Dos Rios on the Gunnison	(970) 641-1482
Recreation Center	Gunnison Warming House		(970) 641-8061
Ski Areas	Crested Butte	12 Snowmass Rd., Mt. Crested Butte	(970) 349-2333
	Cranor Hill Ski Area		(970) 641-4655
	Monarch		(888) 996-7669
Police Department			(970) 641-8000
Fire Department			(970) 641-1241
Newspapers	Gunnison Country Times	218 N. Wisconsin St.	(970) 641-1414

Gunnison

The Gunnison River Valley was first explored in 1776 by the Escalante-Dominguez party who were looking for a route between the missions at Santa Fe, New Mexico and Monterey, California. During the early 1800s, mountain men trapped and hunted in the valley and surrounding mountains, trading their furs at Bent's Fort and Taos. Captain John Gunnison was sent by the US government to survey the area for a suitable route for a transcontinental railroad in 1853. Gunnison, for whom the town, river and valley were named, and several members of his team were killed a few months later in Utah in a skirmish with a local native tribe. The valley was settled by farmers and gold miners in the 1870s. The railroad pushed through in 1880 putting Gunnison on the map as the regional trade center and county seat. The town, home of Western State University, now depends on tourism, education and ranching for its livelihood.

Photo courtesy of Monarch Ski & Snowboard Area

Photo courtesy of Monarch Ski & Snowboard Area

La Veta

Points of Interest: Fort Francisco Museum & Center for the Performing Arts, Scenic Highway of Legends, Goemmer Butte, La Veta Pass, Devils Stairstep, Cuchara Mountain Resort

Annual Events:

Snowfest	Early February	(719) 384-0004
4th of July Rodeo & Dance	Early July	(719) 742-3676
Country Cowboy Weekend	Early July	(719) 742-3676
Art in the Park	July	(719) 742-3676
Cuchara Hermosa Art Festival	July	(719) 742-3676
Cuchara Bluegrass Festival	Mid-July	(719) 742-3676
Cuchara Music Festival	Summer	(719) 389-0004
Huerfano County 4-H Fair	August	(719) 742-3676
Fort Francisco Day	Late August	(719) 742-3676
Antique Art Sale	Early October	(719) 742-3676
Oktoberfest	October	(719) 742-3676
Fort Francisco Christmas	December	(719) 742-3676
New Year's Torchlight Parade	Late December	(888) CUCHARA

Visitor Information

	Chamber of Commerce	132 W. Ryus Ave.	(719) 742-3676
Hospital	Huerfano Medical Center	23500 US Hwy. 160, Walsenburg	(719) 738-5100
Bus Line	Greyhound	111 W. 4th St., Walsenberg	(719) 738-1692
Airport	Cuchara Valley Airport, La Veta	3167 State Hwy. 12	(719) 742-9972
Post Office		117 E Ryus St.	(719)742-3733
Library	La Veta Public Library	310 S. Main St.	(719)742-3572
Museum	Fort Francisco Museum		(719) 742-3676
Public Golf Course	Grandote Peaks Golf Club	5540 Hwy. 12	(800) 457-9986
Ski Area	Cuchara Mountain Resort		(888) 282-4272
Police Department		204 S. Main St.	(719) 742-3344
Fire Department		202 W. 6th St., Walsenburg	(719) 742-3645
Newspapers	The Signature	120 W. Grand Ave.	(719) 742-5591
	Huerfano World		(719) 738-1720

La Veta, which means the vein in Spanish, got its name from the veins of yaso found in the area, a white mineral used to whitewash the town's adobe houses. The town is situated at the northern entrance to the Cuchara Valley and is an interesting and eclectic mix of ranchers, seniors, alternate lifestyle advocates, artists and Texas expatriates. Several artists who live in the area exhibit their work in the local art gallery. Aztec legend says that the valley was once a paradise on earth where no one suffered from pain or cold and happiness abounded. When the narrow-gauge railroad came to La Veta, it was, for many years, the highest railroad in the world. The old depot at the summit of La Veta Pass is listed on the National Register of Historical Places. The town and the valley have always relied principally on tourism and agriculture.

Leadville

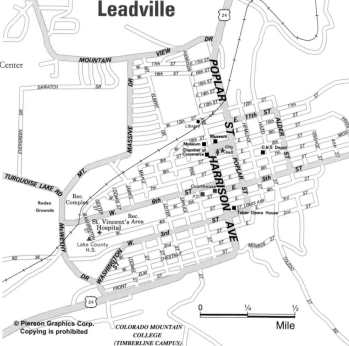

Points of Interest: Healy House and Dexter Cabin, Heritage Museum, Matchless Mine Cabin, Tabor Opera House, Tabor House, National Mining Hall of Fame, Old Church Arts & Humanities Center

Annual Events:

Leadville Crystal Carnival	Early March	(719) 486-3900
Turquoise Lake 20K Road & Trail Run	Mid-June	(719) 486-3581
Mosquito Marathon	Mid-July	(800) 933-3901
Leadville Boom Days	Early August	(800) 933-3901
International Pack Burro Race	Early August	(800) 933-3901
Tri-It High Triathlon	Mid-September	(800) 933-3901
St. Patrick's Day Practice Parade	Mid-September	(719) 486-3900
Victorian Home Tour	Early December	(800) 933-3901

Visitor Information

	Chamber of Commerce	809 Harrison Ave.	(719) 486-3900
Hospital	St. Vincent General Hosp.	822 W. 4th St.	(719) 486-0230
Airport	Leadville Airport	915 County Rd. 23	(719) 486-2627
Colleges	Colorado Mtn. College	901 S. US Hwy. 24	(719) 486-2015
Post Office		130 W. 5th St.	(719) 486-1667
Library	Lake County Library	1115 Harrison Ave.	(719) 486-0569
Museums	Healy House State Mus.	912 Harrison Ave.	(719) 486-0487
	Heritage Museum	102 E. 9th St.	(719) 486-1878
	Tabor Home	116 E. 5th St.	(719) 486-0551
	National Mining Hall of Fame	120 W. 9th St.	(719) 486-1229
Public Golf Course	Mt. Massive Golf Course	259 County Rd. 5	(719) 486-2176
Ski Area	Ski Cooper	Hwy. 24 N.	(719) 486-2277
Police Department		800 Harrison Ave.	(719) 486-1365
Fire Department		816 Harrison Ave.	(719) 486-2990
Newspaper	Herald Democrat	717 Harrison Ave.	(719) 486-0641

Leadville is the highest incorporated town in the US, sitting in a valley at the base of Mount Elbert, Colorado's highest peak. Silver was discovered in the area in 1877. The population of Leadville ranged between 20,000 and 40,000 during the boom years, making it the second largest city in Colorado at the time. Leadville's most famous citizens, Horace and Baby Doe Tabor, have been the subjects of many biographies, a play and, even, an opera, The Ballad of Baby Doe. Many legendary performers made the long, arduous trek to Leadville to appear in the Tabor Opera House, two of the most famous being Harry Houdini and Oscar Wilde. During Prohibition, Leadville became the moonshine capital of the Rockies. Moonshiners set up their stills in the abandoned mine tunnels turning out Leadville Moonshine, considered by connoisseurs to be one of the best whiskeys in the West. Today, the silver played out, Leadville is a popular tourist destination.

Nederland

Points of Interest: Eldora Mountain Resort, Nederland Historical Museum, Eldora Historic Mining District and Hessie Ghost Town, Indian Peaks Wilderness, Boulder Canyon, Peak-to-Peak Scenic Byway.

Annual Events:

Eldora Nighthawks Cross Country Ski Races		
	January, February	(303) 440-8700
Eldora Snowshoe Festival	Mid-February	(303) 440-8700
Eldora Easter Egg Hunt	Early April	(303) 440-8700
Eldora Skiesta	April	(303) 440-8700
4th of July in Nederland	Early July	(303) 258-3678
Garden Tour	July	(303) 258-3678
Ol' Timers & Miners Days	Late July	(800) 221-0044
Neder-Nederland Run	Early September	(800) 221-0044
Fall Film Festival	October	(303) 258-3678

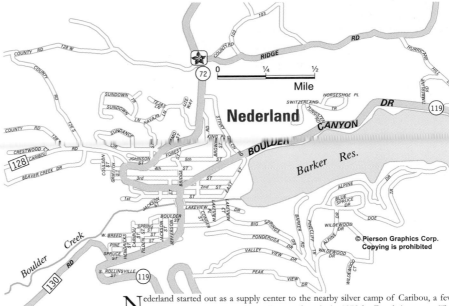

Visitor Information	Nederland Visitor Center	1st St. & Hwy. 119	(303) 258-3678
Hospital	Boulder Community Hospital	1100 Balsam Ave.,	
		Boulder	(303) 440-2273
Public Transportation	RTD		(303) 299-6000
Airport	Denver International Airport		(303) 270-1670
Ski Area	Eldora Mountain Resort		(888) 2ELDORA
Police Department			(303) 258-3250
Fire Department		750 State Hwy. 72	(303) 258-7992
Newspapers	The Mountain Ear	20 Lakeview Dr.	(303) 258-7075
	The Daily Camera	1048 Pearl St., Boulder	(303) 441-1202

Nederland started out as a supply center to the nearby silver camp of Caribou, a few miles to the west. The Caribou Mine was bought in 1873 by Dutch investors. The mine produced $3 million a year during its peak, but faltered in the 1893 silver bust. Caribou is now a ghost town but Nederland, named after the homeland of the mine owners, survived. During World War I, local tungsten deposits, necessary for hardening metal in gun barrels , helped bolster both the declining economy and population. Over $15 million worth was mined between 1913 and 1916. The most famous Nederland resident is Grandpa Bredo who is being kept in a storage shed packed in dry ice. The frozen body was discovered when grandson Trygue, who was tending the body, was deported. Nederland has since passed a law against such practices, but it does not cover Grandpa Bredo who still resides in his shed.

Ouray

Points of Interest: Ice climbing, hiking and four-wheel-driving in Box Canyon Falls & Park, Ouray County Museum, Wright's Opera House, Bachelor Syracuse Mine Tour, The San Juan Scenic Byway, The Million Dollar Highway, Ouray Hot Springs Pool.

Annual Events:

Arctic Wolf Ice Climbing Festival	January	(303) 258-7916
Family Fun Race	Mid-February	(970) 325-4469
Ouray Chamber Music Fest	June	(970) 325-4746
Old Fashioned 4th of July	Early July	(970) 325-7352
Quilt Show	July	(970) 325-4746
Artists Alpine Holiday	July	(970) 325-4746
Ouray High Graders Holiday	Mid-August	(970) 325-4576
Ouray County Fair & Rodeo (Ridgway)	Early September	(800) 228-1876
Imogene Pass Run	Early September	(970) 325-4746
Annual Jeep Jamboree	Mid September	(970) 333-4777
Octoberfest	Early October	(800) 228-1876
Yulenight	December	(800) 228-1876

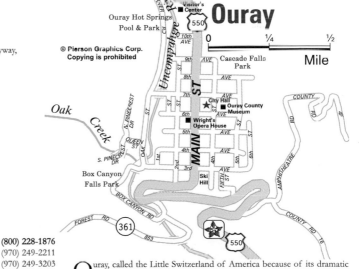

Visitor Information	Chamber & Resort Assn.	1222 Main St.	(800) 228-1876
Hospital	Montrose Memorial Hospital	800 3rd St., Montrose	(970) 249-2211
Airport	Montrose Regional Airport	2100 Airport Rd., Montrose	(970) 249-3203
Post Office		620 Main St.	(970) 325-4302
Library	Ouray Public Library	320 6th Ave.	(970) 325-4616
Museums	Ouray County Museum	420 6th Ave.	(970) 325-4576
	Bachelor Syracuse Mine Tour		(970) 325-0220
Golf Course	Fairway Pines Golf Club	117 Ponderosa Dr., Ridgway	(970) 626-5284
Hot Springs Pool		1220 Main St.	(970) 325-4638
Rotary Park Ice Skating Rink		US Hwy. 550, N. of town	(970) 325-4638
Ouray Ice Park	Uncompahgre Gorge		(970) 325-4925
Ironton Park Cross Country Ski Park		US Hwy. 550, S. of town	
Police Department		320 S. 6th Ave.	(970) 325-4225
Fire Department		320 6th Ave.	(970) 325-4047
Newspaper	Ouray County Plaindealer	333 6th Ave.	(970) 325-4412

Ouray, called the Little Switzerland of America because of its dramatic scenery, has been a tourist destination for over 100 years. The town sits in a narrow box canyon surrounded by 5,000 foot peaks in the rugged San Juan Mountains. Ouray was founded in 1876 after prospectors looking for, and finding, gold and silver settled in the valley. The region fell on hard times with the silver bust of 1893. In 1896, an Irish carpenter, Thomas F. Walsh discovered gold in an old silver mine, bought the rights to the mine and became an instant millionaire. By 1910, the mine had produced $26 million. Walsh used some of the profits to buy the Hope Diamond for his daughter Evalyn. Most of the town's buildings were erected between 1880 and 1900 and most of them are still standing. The entire town is listed on the National Register of Historic Districts. Ouray now depends on tourism, the famous hot springs and ranching for its livelihood.

Pagosa Springs

Pagosa Springs

© Pierson Graphics Corp.
Copying is prohibited

0 ¼ ½
Mile

Points of Interest: Fred Harmon Art Museum, Upper San Juan Historical Society Museum, Hot Springs, Pagosa Lake, Rocky Mtn. Wildlife Park

Annual Events:

Winterfest	Early February	(800) 252-2204
St. Patrick's Day Parade	Mid-March	(800) 252-2204
Spanish Fiesta & Mtn. Man Rendezvous	Late June	(800) 252-2204
4th of July Festival & Red Ryder Rodeo	July	(800) 252-2204
Archuleta County Fair	Early August	(800) 252-2204
Taste of Pagosa	Early August	(800) 252-2204
Four Corners Folk Festival	Labor Day Weekend	(800) 820-3385
Color Fest	Late September	(800) 252-2204
Turkey Trot	Early November	(800) 264-2209
Christmas in Pagosa	Early December	(800) 252-2204

Visitor Information	Chamber of Commerce	402 San Juan St.	(800) 252-2204
Public Transit	Archuleta County Transit	8th St.	(970) 264-2550
Airport	Stevensfield		(970) 731-3060
Post Office	Hot Springs Blvd.		(970) 264-5440
Library	Ruby S. Sisson Mem. Library		(970) 264-2209
Museums	Fred Harmon Art Museum	2560 W. Hwy. 160	(970) 731-5785
	Upper San Juan Historical Soc. Museum	1st St. & Hwy. 160	(970) 264-4424
Public Golf Course	Pagosa Springs Golf Club	1 Pines Club Pl.	(970) 731-4755
Ski Area	Wolf Creek		(970) 264-5639
Police Department		191 N. Pagosa Springs Blvd.	(970) 731-9700
Fire Department		191 N. Pagosa Springs Blvd.	(970) 731-4193
Newspapers	Pagosa Springs Sun	466 Pagosa St.	(970) 264-2101

Pagosa Springs takes its name from a Ute word meaning healing waters. In 1866, the Utes and the Navajos disputed the ownership of the hot springs. The Utes chose Col. Albert H. Pfeiffer, a US Indian agent to represent them. The Navajo chose their largest and bravest warrior. They fought a duel with Bowie knives for possession of the springs. Col. Pfeiffer won the fight and the Navajos accepted the outcome. In 1880, the US Government decided to ignore the rights of the Utes, claimed the springs and laid out a townsite. Though the town tried to promote itself as a hot springs resort, the idea never took off. Hot water from the springs are used for heating several buildings in the town. Besides soaking in the hot springs, summer activities include fishing, biking, jeep touring, and camping. Winter brings some of the best snow in Colorado to Wolf Creek Pass for down-hill and cross-country skiing.

Salida

Salida

© Pierson Graphics Corp.
Copying is prohibited

0 ¼ ½
Mile

Salida, Spanish for gateway, was originally called South Arkansas after the river, which flows past the east side of town. In the fall of 1878 engineers for the Atchison, Topeka & Santa Fe, anticipating the construction of the railroad through the Great Canyon of the Arkansas, laid out a town, naming it Cleora. The town flourished and by 1880 had a population of 600. But Cleora was not to last. In April of 1880 engineers for the Denver & Rio Grande surveyed the site of a new town one mile to the south in hopes that many court battles for the rail route would be settled in their favor. When the dust settled, the Denver and Rio Grande had won. The residents of Cleora, learning that their town would not become the railhead, moved lock, stock and buildings to the new one. Today, Salida is a great place to go for river rafting. For winter sports, Monarch Ski Area is nearby.

Points of Interest: Tenderfoot Mountain, Monarch Aerial Tramway, Monarch Ski Area, Salida Hot Springs Aquatic Ctr.

Annual Events:

FIBArk Boat Races & Festival	Mid-June	(719) 539-2068
Art Walk	Late June	(719) 539-2068
Salida Fall Festival	Mid-September	(719) 539-2068
Christmas Mountain USA	Late November	(719) 539-2068

Visitor Information	Chamber of Commerce	406 W. Rainbow Blvd.	(719) 539-2068
Hospitals	Heart of Rockies Reg. Med. Ctr.	448 E. 1st St.	(719) 539-6661
Bus Stations	TNM & O Carriers(Greyhound)	731 Blake St.	(719) 539-7474
Airport	Salida-Harriet Alexander Field	9255 CR 140	(719) 539-1185
Colleges	Colorado Mtn. College	210 N. F St.	(719) 539-3905
Post Office		310 D St.	(719) 539-2548
Library	Salida Regional Library	405 E St.	(719) 539-4826
Museum	Salida Museum	406 W. Rainbow Blvd.	(719) 539-2068
Public Golf Courses	Salida Golf Club	411 Crestone Ave.	(719) 539-1060
Ski Areas	Monarch Ski Area	#1 Powder Pl.	(888) 996-7669
Police Department	217 E. 3rd St.		(719) 539-2814
Fire Department			(719) 539-2212
Newspapers	The Mountain Mail	125 E. 2nd	(719) 539-6691

Steamboat Springs

Population: 6,768 ❋ **Elevation: 6,695** ❋ **Area Code: 970** ❋ **See Map 2** ❋ **Routt Co., CO 80477**

Points of Interest: Fish Creek Falls, Strawberry Park Hot Springs, Mineral Springs, Howelsen Hill Sports Complex, Steamboat Ski Area, Tread of Pioneers Museum, Steamboat Lake, Rabbit Ears Pass

Annual Events:

Norwest Cowboy Downhill	January	(970) 879-0880
Winter Carnival	Early February	(970) 879-0880
St. Patrick's Day Torchlight Parade	Mid-March	(970) 879-0880
Strings in the Mountains Music Fest	Summer	(970) 879-5056
Yampa River Festival	Mid-June	(970) 879-0880
Steamboat Marathon, Half Marathon & 10K Race	Early June	(970) 879-0880
Cowboy Roundup Days & 4th of July Celebration	July	(970) 879-0880
Rainbow Weekend	Mid-July	(970) 879-0880
Ride of the Valkyries	Late August	(970) 871-0038
Classic Labor Day Celeb. & Concours d'Elegance	Labor Day Weekend	(970) 879-0880
Literary Sojourn Fest. of Authors	Early September	(970) 879-0240
Fall Foliage & Mtn. Brewfest	Late September	(970) 879-0880
Sprint Ski Town USA Nordic Comb. World Cup	Early December	(970) 879-0880
Community Holiday Party	Mid-December	(970) 879-4300

Visitor Information

	Chamber of Commerce	1201 Lincoln	(970) 879-0880
Hospital	Routt Memorial Hosp.	80 Park Ave.	(970) 879-1322
Bus Stations	Greyhound Bus Lines	30060 W. US Hwy. 40	(970) 879-0866
Public Transit	Steamboat Springs Transit	1463 13th St.	(970) 879-3717
Airport	Steamboat Springs Airport	3495 Airport Cir.	(970) 879-9042
College	Colorado Mtn. College	1330 Bob Adams Dr.	(970) 870-4444
Post Offices		300 Lincoln Ave.	(800) 275-8777
		Sundance Plaza	(970) 879-3556
Libraries	Bud Werner Memorial Library	1289 Lincoln Ave.	(970) 879-0240
Museum	Tread of Pioneers Museum	800 Oak St.	(970) 879-2214
Public Golf Courses			
	Haymaker Golf Club	32400 County Rd. 24	(970) 870-1846
	Steamboat Golf Club	West on US Hwy. 40	(970) 879-4295
Ski Area	Steamboat		(970) 879-6111
	Howelson Ski Area	845 Howelson Pkwy.	(970) 879-8499
Police Department		840 Yampa St.	(970) 879-1144
Fire Department		840 Yampa St.	(970) 879-4518
Newspapers	Steamboat Pilot	1041 Lincoln Ave.	(970) 879-1502

Steamboat Springs

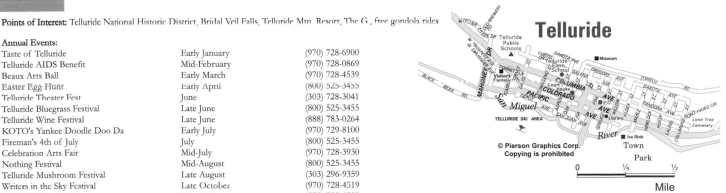

© Pierson Graphics Corp. Copying is prohibited

Steamboat Springs got its name from the sound made by one of the hot springs in the area. It was said to resemble a steamboat chugging upstream. The sound was lost when the bed for the railroad, which arrived in 1908, was cut. Now, only the name remains. The surrounding Yampa Valley, with its farms and ranches, keeps Steamboat Springs an agricultural center, though most people know it as a ski resort and home to Olympic skiing champions. Skiing and ski-jumping were introduced in 1913 by Norwegian Carl Howelson, a cross-country and ski jumping champion himself. He organized the first Winter Carnival in 1914 and the rest is history. Even though the town bills itself as Ski Town USA, the area abounds in year-round recreational activities.

Telluride

Population: 1,476 ❋ **Elevation: 8,745** ❋ **Area Code: 970** ❋ **See Map 28** ❋ **San Miguel Co., CO 81435**

Points of Interest: Telluride National Historic District, Bridal Veil Falls, Telluride Mtn. Resort, The G, free gondola rides

Annual Events:

Taste of Telluride	Early January	(970) 728-6900
Telluride AIDS Benefit	Mid-February	(970) 728-0869
Beaux Arts Ball	Early March	(970) 728-4539
Easter Egg Hunt	Early April	(800) 525-3455
Telluride Theater Fest	June	(303) 728-3041
Telluride Bluegrass Festival	Late June	(800) 525-3455
Telluride Wine Festival	Late June	(888) 783-0264
KOTO's Yankee Doodle Doo Da	Early July	(970) 729-8100
Fireman's 4th of July	July	(800) 525-3455
Celebration Arts Fair	Mid-July	(970) 728-3930
Nothing Festival	Mid-August	(800) 525-3455
Telluride Mushroom Festival	Late August	(303) 296-9359
Writers in the Sky Festival	Late October	(970) 728-4519
Black & White Affair	November	(970) 728-6900
New Year's Eve Torchlight Parade		(800) 525-3455

Visitor Information

	Telluride Central Reservations	666 W. Colorado Ave.	88-TELLU-RIDE
Hospital	Montrose Memorial Hospital	800 S. 3rd St., Montrose	(970) 249-2211
Public Transit	San Miguel Public Transit	370 Black Bear Rd.	(970) 728-5700
Airport	Telluride Regional Airport	1500 Last Dollar Rd.	(970) 728-5313
Post Office		101 E. Colorado Ave.	(970) 728-3900
Library	Wilkinson Public Library	134 S Spruce St.	(970) 728-4519
Museums	Telluride History Museum	220 E. Colorado Ave.	(970) 728-3344
	Telluride Nat'l. Historic Dist.		(970) 728-6639
Public Golf Course	Telluride Mtn. Village Golf Club	562 Mtn. Village Blvd.	(970) 728-6800
	Telluride Ski & Golf Club	136 Country Club Dr.	(970) 728-6157
Recreation Center	Telluride Community Center	450 W Galena Ave.	(970) 728-9943
Ski Area	Telluride		(800) 801-4832
Police Marshal		135 W. Columbia Ave.	(970) 728-3818
Fire Department		135 W. Columbia Ave.	(970) 728-3801
Newspapers	Telluride Daily Planet	283 1st St.	(970) 728-9788
	Telluride Times Journal	123 S. Spruce St.	(970) 728-4487

Telluride

© Pierson Graphics Corp. Copying is prohibited

First called Columbia, the town name was changed to Telluride in 1887 to avoid confusion with Columbia, California. Telluride is named for the rare gold-bearing ore called tellurium. Mining for silver and gold brought people to Telluride. The mines grew in size, employing hundreds. When the trees around the Gold King Mine were all cut to provide power for the mine, coal had to be transported in by horse and mule. The cost was prohibitive so the mine operator, L. L. Nunn, decided that electricity was the answer. In 1891, he hired engineers from Cornell University to build the world's first high-voltage, alternating-current water-generated power plant three miles away at the head of Bridal Veil Falls. By 1894, Telluride and most of the mines in the area were electrically powered. Other claims to fame include a bank robbery by Butch Cassidy, several music and film festivals and world-class skiing. Located in the end of a box canyon, Telluride is the eastern end of the 215-mile long Telluride-to-Moab mountain bike trail. Telluride has been designated a National Historic Landmark District.

Vail

Points of Interest: Camp Hale, Colorado Ski Museum, Gore Creek Schoolhouse, Beaver Creek Resort, Vail Mountain, Betty Ford Alpine Gardens, Vail Nature Center, Eagle-Bahn Gondola

Annual Events:

Easter Sunrise Service	Early April	(970) 476-1000
Jeep Whitewater Festival	Memorial Day Weekend	(800) 525-3875
Bravo Colorado Vail Valley Music Fest	June	(800) 525-3875
Vail Arts Festival	July	(800) 525-3875
Vail International Dance Fest	August	(800) 525-3875
Vail Invitational Soccer Tourn.	Mid-August	(970) 479-2280
Jerry Ford Invitational Golf Tournament	August	(970) 476-1000
Octoberfest Vail	Mid-September	(800) 525-3875
Minturn Jazz Fest	October, November	(970) 845-5720

Visitor Information			
Chamber of Commerce	Vail Tourism & Convention Bureau	100 E. Meadow Dr.	(970) 476-1000
Central Reservations		241 E. Meadow Dr.	(970) 949-5189
			(800) 525-3875
Hospital	Vail Valley Med. Ctr.	181 W. Meadow Dr.	(970) 476-2451
Bus Station	Greyhound Bus Lines	241 S. Frontage Rd. E.	(970) 476-5137
Public Transit	Bus Department		(970) 479-2358
Bus Schedule Information			(970) 328-8143
Airport	Eagle County Airport	215 Eldon Wilson Rd., Eagle	(970) 524-9490
College	Colorado Mtn. College	1310 Westhaven Dr.	(970) 476-4040
Post Office		1300 N. Frontage Rd. W.	(970) 476-5271
Library	Vail Public Library	292 W. Meadow Dr.	(970) 479-2184
Museums	Colorado Ski Museum/Hall of Fame	231 S. Frontage Rd. E.	(970) 476-1876
	Betty Ford Alpine Gardens	Ford Park	(970) 476-0103
Ski Area	Vail Resort		(800) 525-2287
Dobson Ice Arena		321 E. Lionshead Cir.	(970) 479-2271
Public Golf Courses	Vail Golf Club	1778 Vail Valley Dr.	(970) 479-2260
Police Department		75 S. Frontage Rd	(970) 476-2200
Fire Department		42 W. Meadow Dr.	(970) 479-2250
Newspapers	Vail Daily	143 E. Meadow Dr.	(970) 476-0555
	The Vail Trail	41184 US Hwy. 6 & 24	(970) 949-4004

Before World War II, the Vail Valley was predominantly settled by ranchers. The US Army brought outsiders to the area in 1942 when it began training the troops of the 10th Mountain Division in the mountains south of the Vail Valley. After the war, three of the soldiers who served in the 10th, Peter Seibert, Bob Parker and Bill Brown, came back to the valley and began developing a ski resort. The resort was scheduled to open in 1962, but there was one problem. No snow. Utes, who had been ousted from the valley earlier in the history of the area, were called in to perform a rain dance on the deck of the new lodge. Within a week a blizzard provided all the snow needed to open. A village developed around the resort and was incorporated in 1965. Vail rapidly became the place to look for the rich and famous from around the world who like to ski. Since the early 1980s, Vail has developed into a year-round resort offering such diverse activities as golf, tennis, camping, llama trekking, fishing, rafting and ballooning when the snow melts.

© Dann Coffey / Vail Resorts / Vail

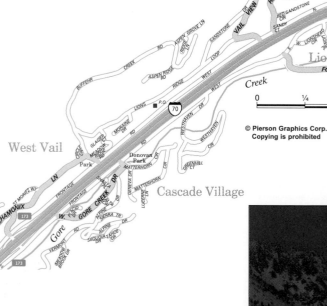

Vail

© Pierson Graphics Corp.
Copying is prohibited

© Dann Coffey / Vail Resorts / Vail

Fraser

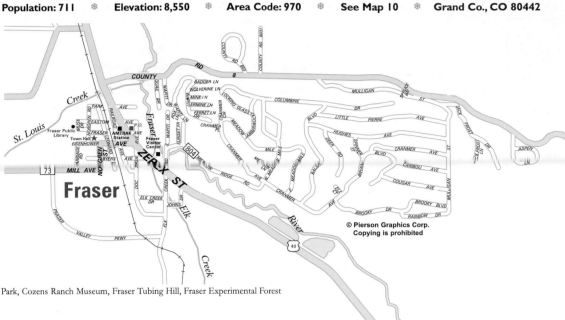

© Pierson Graphics Corp.
Copying is prohibited

The Fraser Valley was a favorite hunting ground for Utes and Arapahoes and was frequented by fur trappers and mountain men in the 1820s and 1830s. The first post office in the valley was established in 1850. The railroad arrived at the turn of the century. During World War II, the valley was the site of a German POW camp. Fraser was a favorite vacation destination of President Eisenhower. Fraser's national claim to fame is being the coldest spot in the nation. The temperature can drop to 50° F. below zero in the winter. Citizens of Fraser proudly call their town "the icebox of the nation."

Points of Interest: Walk Through History Park, Cozens Ranch Museum, Fraser Tubing Hill, Fraser Experimental Forest

Annual Events: See Winter Park

Visitor Information	Chamber of Commerce		(800) 903-7275
Visitor Center		120 Zerex	(970) 726-8312
Hospital	Kremmling Mem. Hospital	214 S. 4th, Kremmling	(970) 724-3442
Railroad	Amtrak	205 Fraser Ave.	(970) 726-8816
Library	Fraser Valley Library	421 Norgren Rd.	(970) 726-0338
Museum	Walk Through History Park	120 Zerex St.	(970) 726-8312
Golf Course	Pole Creek Golf Club	6827 County Rd. 51	(970) 726-8847
Cross Country Skiing/Winter Rec.		Devil's Thumb Ranch	(800) 933-4339
Fraser Tubing Hill		455 County Rd. 72	(970) 726-5954
Police Department			(970) 725-3343

Winter Park

Population: 601 ❄ **Elevation: 9,110** ❄ **Area Code: 970**
See Map 10 ❄ **Grand Co., CO 80482**

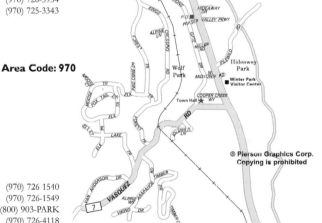

Winter Park

Cozens Ranch Museum

© Pierson Graphics Corp.
Copying is prohibited

0   ¼   ½
Mile

Points of Interest: Winter Park Resort, Berthoud Pass Ski Area, Cozens Ranch House Museum, The Ski Train, Moffat Tunnel

Annual Events:

Black Diamond Ball at Winter Park	February	(970) 726 1540
Ski for NSCD	Early April	(970) 726-1549
Pole Creek Golf Tournament	Mid-June	(800) 903-PARK
National Trail Days Celebration	Mid-June	(970) 726-4118
American Red Cross Fat Tire Classic	Late June	(303) 722-7474
Great Western Shootout	Late June	(970) 726-5514
Fraser Fireworks Festival	4th of July	(800) 903-PARK
Run/Walk for Independence	4th of July	(970) 726-4118
American Music Festival	Mid-July	(970) 726-4118
Winter Park Jazz Fest	Mid-July	(800) 903-PARK
Alpine Art Affair	Late July	(970) 726-5585
High Country Stampede Rodeo	July, August	(970) 726-4118
Rocky Mtn. Wine, Beer & Food Fest	Early August	(970) 726-1518
Fall Color Fest Month	September	(800) 903-PARK
Flamethrowers High Altitude Chili Cook-Off	Early September	(800) 903-PARK
National Sports Center for the Disabled Symposium	Early December	(970) 726-1540
Christmas Eve Torchlight Parade	Late December	(970) 726-1551

Visitor Information	Grand County Tourism Board	PO Box 208	(800) 247-2636
Chamber of Commerce		78841 US Hwy. 40	(970) 726-5656
Hospital	Kremmling Mem. Hospital	214 S. 4th, Kremmling	(970) 724-3442
Public Transit			
Bus Station	Greyhound	78841 US Hwy. 40	(970) 726-4118
Railroad	Ski Train	Base of Winter Park Ski Area	(303) 296-4754
Post Office		78490 US Hwy. 40	(970) 726-5488
Museum	Cozens Ranch House Museum	77849 US Hwy. 40	(970) 726-5488
Ski Areas	Winter Park Resort	677 Winter Park Dr.	(970) 726-5514
	Berthoud Pass Ski Area	US Hwy. 40	(303) 569-0100
Public Golf Course	Pole Creek Golf Course		(970) 726-8847
Sheriff's Department	Grand County Sheriff		(970) 725-3343
Fire Department		77601 US Hwy. 40	(970) 726-5824
Newspapers	Winter Park Manifest	Winter Park Dr.	(970) 726-5721

Winter Park was originally called West Portal because it was located at the western entrance to the Moffat Tunnel, which was completed in 1927. The Denver City Park System designated the location as a winter park when it opened up a ski area in 1940. Lift tickets were a dollar to ride the 800 foot rope tow. The name stuck, though it is a bit of a misnomer now. The summer months offer 600 miles of mountain bike trails, hiking, the American Music Festival and, even, a high altitude chili cook-off. Winter Park is proud to be the home of the National Sports Center for the Disabled, holding events throughout the year to allow disabled people to learn and to compete in sports such as skiing, mountain biking and white water rafting.

COLORADO SKI TOWNS

CROSS-COUNTRY SKIING

For additional information, contact National Forest ranger stations and the Colorado Cross-Country Ski Association
P.O. Box 8937, Keystone, Colorado 80435 (970) 668-5259
www.colorado-cross-country.org
The following is a select list of cross-country skiing opportunities:

Not all areas are shown on State Map section.

Name	Page	Grid	City	Phone	Surface	Length
Alfred A. Braun Huts	4	C-3	Aspen	(970) 925-5775	Ungroomed	100 km
Ashcroft Ski Touring Unlimited	4	C-3	Ashcroft	(970) 925-1971	Classic tracks, skating lanes, ungroomed	35 km
Aspen/Snowmass Nordic Trail System	4	C-3	Aspen	(970) 920-5120	Groomed	5 km
Barr Lake State Park	12	A-3	Brighton	(303) 659-6005	Ungroomed	.....
Beaver Creek Nordic Center	13	B-1	Avon	(970) 949-5750	Classic tracks, skating lanes	32 km
Breckenridge Nordic Ski Center	14	A-2	Breckenridge	(303) 659-6005	Classic tracks, skating lanes	22 km
C Lazy U Ranch	10	A-2	Granby	(970) 887-3344	Classic tracks, skating lanes	25 km
Chatfield State Park	15	C-2	Littleton	(303) 791-7275	Ungroomed	.....
Copper Mountain Cross-Country Center	13	C-2	Copper Mountain	(800) 458-8386	Classic tracks, skating lanes	25 km
Cordillera Nordic Center	13	A-1	Edwards	(970) 926-5100	Groomed	12 km
Crested Butte Nordic Center	22	C-2	Crested Butte	(970) 349-1707	Classic tracks, skating lanes	25 km
Devil's Thumb Ranch	10	B-3	Tabernash	(970) 726-8231	Classic tracks, skating lanes, ungroomed	105 km
Eldora Nordic Center	10	C-3	Nederland	(303) 440-8700	Classic tracks, skating lanes, ungroomed	45 km
Eleven Mile State Park	23	C-2	Lake George	(719) 748-3401	Ungroomed	.....
Fairplay Nordic Ski Center	14	A-4	Fairplay	(719) 836-2658	.....	.....
Frisco Nordic Center	13	C-2	Frisco	(970) 668-0866	Classic tracks, skating lanes	35 km
Gold Lake Mountain Resort	10	C-2	Ward	(303) 459-3544	Ungroomed	.....
Golden Gate Canyon State Park	11	A-3	Golden	(303) 582-3707	Ungroomed	.....
Grand Lake Touring Center	10	A-1	Grand Lake	(970) 627-8088	Classic tracks, skating lanes	30 km
Grand Mesa Lodge/Ski Trail System	21	C-2	Cedaredge	(800) 551-6372	Groomed	20 km
High Meadows Ranch	2	C-2	Steamboat Springs	(800) 457-4453	Groomed	15 km
Home Ranch Resort	2	C-1	Clark	(970) 879-1780	Classic tracks, skating lanes	40 km
Latigo Ranch	9	B-2	Kremmling	(970) 724-9008	Classic tracks, skating lanes	55 km
Monarch Mountain Guides	23	B-3	Salida	(719) 539-4680	Ungroomed	.....
Mountain Touring Association	22	A-2	Hotchkiss	(970) 835-3256	Classic tracks, skating lanes, ungroomed	20 km
Mueller State Park	24	A-2	Divide	(719) 687-2366	Ungroomed	.....
Never Summer Nordic Hut System	6	A-3	Fort Collins	(970) 482-9411	.....	.....
Phoenix Ridge Yurts	28	C-2	Creede	(800) 984-6275	Groomed	10 km
Piney Creek Nordic Center	13	C-4	Leadville	(719) 486-1750	Classic tracks, skating lanes	25 km
Redstone Inn Nordic Center	14	B-3	Redstone	(970) 963-2526	Ungroomed	.....
Rocky Mountain Adventures - Estes Park	6	C-4	Estes Park	(970) 586-6191	Ungroomed	.....
Rocky Mountain Adventures - Fort Collins	7	B-3	Fort Collins	(970) 493-4005	Ungroomed	.....
Rocky Mountain Adventures, Buena Vista	23	B-2	Buena Vista	(719) 395-8594	Ungroomed	.....
San Juan Guest Ranch	22	A-4	Ridgeway	(970) 626-5360	Classic tracks, skating lanes, ungroomed	10 km
Skyline Ranch	28	A-2	Telluride	(888) 754-1126	Groomed	30 km
Snow Mountain Ranch Nordic Center/YMCA	10	A-3	Granby	(970) 887-2152	Classic tracks, skating lanes	100 km
Trail Mountain Bed & Breakfast	10	A-2	Grandby	(970) 887-3944	Groomed	15 km
Vail Nordic Center	13	B-1	Vail	(970) 476-8366	Classic tracks, skating lanes	15 km
Vista Verde Ranch	2	C-1	Clark	(800) 526-7433	Classic tracks, skating lanes	30 km
Western Sports	4	B-3	Carbondale	(970) 963-3030	.....	.....
Whistling Elk Ranch	5	C-4	Rand	(970) 723-8311	Classic tracks, skating lanes	35 km
10th Mountain Division Trails	4	C-3	Aspen	(970) 925-5775	Ungroomed	500 km

COLORADO RECREATIONAL

STATE PARKS & RECREATION TABLE

Colorado State Parks and Wildlife Areas maintained by the Colorado Division of Parks and Recreation (303) 866-3437 and the Colorado Division of Wildlife (303) 297-1192. Call ahead to check on fees, licenses, reservations, etc.
For camping reservations, call (800) 678-CAMP/(303) 470-1144. To receive a Colorado State Parks Annual Pass, call (303) 866-3437.

Name & Phone Number	Page	Grid	Camp	Hike	Boat	Hunt	Fish	Cross-Country Ski	Ice Skate	Snowshoe	Snowmobile
Antero Res. State Wildlife Area (303) 297-1192	23	B-2	X				X[1]	X			X
Arkansas Headwaters State Park (719) 539-7289	23	B-3	X*[wc]		X	X	X				
Barbour Ponds State Park (970) 678-9402	11	C-2	X[wc]	X	X		X	X			
Barr Lake State Park (303) 659-6005	12	A-3		X	X	X		X		X	
Bonny State Park (970) 351-7306	20	C-2	X[m]	X	X	X	X				
Boyd Lake State Park (970) 669-1739	7	C-4	X*	X*	X	X	X[1]				
Castlewood Canyon State Park (303) 688-5242	16	A-3		X*							
Chatfield State Park (303) 791-7275	15	C-2	X*	X*	X		X*[1]	X	X	X	
Cherry Creek State Park (303) 699-3860	16	A-1	X*	X*	X		X*[1]	X	X	X	
Colorado River State Park - Connected Lakes, Corn Lake, Island Acres & Wild Life Area (970) 434-3388	21	B-1	X[wc]	X	X		X[1]	X	X		
Crawford State Park (970) 921-5721	22	A-3	X*	X*	X	X	X*[1]		X		X
Eldorado Canyon State Park (303) 494-3943	11	A-3		X		X	X		X		
Eleven Mile State Park (719) 748-3401	23	C-2	X*[wc]	X	X	X	X[1]	X	X		
Flagler State Wildlife Area (719) 765-4422	20	A-3	X		X						
Golden Gate Canyon State Park (303) 582-3707	11	A-3	X*[wc]	X*		X	X*	X	X	X	X
Harvey Gap State Park (970) 625-1607	4	A-2			X	X	X				
Highline State Park (970) 858-7208	21	A-1	X*	X	X	X	X*				
Island Acres State Park (970) 434-3388	21	B-1	X	X							
Jackson Lake State Park (970) 645-2551	17	B-2	X*[wc]	X	X	X	X*[1]		X		
Lake Hasty Rec. Area (719)336-3476	32	A-1	X	X	X						
Lathrop State Park (719) 738-2376	30	B-2	X*	X	X	X	X	X			
Lory State Park (970) 493-1623	7	B-3	X[wc]	X	X	X	X	X		X	
Mancos State Park (970) 883-2208	27	B-3	X*[wc]	X	X		X[1]	X		X	X
Miramonte State Wildlife Area (970) 297-1192	27	B-1	X*	X	X						
Mueller Ranch State Park (719) 687-2366 (No Pets)	24	A-2	X*[wc]	X		X		X	X	X	
Navajo State Park (970) 883-2208	28	B-4	X	X	X	X		X		X	X
North Sterling State Park (970) 522-3657	18	A-1	X	X	X	X	X[1]				
Paonia State Park (970) 921-5721	22	B-2	X		X			X			
Pearl Lake State Park (970) 879-3922	2	C-1	X*		X	X	X[1]			X	X
Picnic Rock State Park (970) 493-1623	7	B-2			X						
Pueblo State Park (719) 561-9320	24	B-4	X*[wc]	X*	X	X	X*[1]	X			
Ramah State Wildlife Area (303) 297-1192	24	C-1	X		X						
Ridgway State Park (970) 626-5822	22	A-4	X*[wc]	X*	X	X*	X[1]	X	X		
Rifle Falls State Park (970) 625-1607	4	A-2	X*	X			X	X			
Rifle Gap State Park (970) 625-1607	4	A-2	X[wc]	X	X	X	X[1]	X	X		X
Roxborough State Park (303) 973-3959 (No Pets)	15	C-2	X*	X			X	X	X		
San Luis Lake State Park (719) 378-2020	29	C-2	X*	X	X	X	X*[1]	X	X	X	X
Spinney Mountain State Park (719) 748-3401	23	C-2			X	X	X				
Stagecoach State Park (970) 736-2436	2	C-3	X*	X*	X		X[1]		X	X	
State Forest State Park (970) 723-8366	6	A-3	X	X	X	X	X				
Steamboat Lake State Park (970) 879-3922	2	B-1	X*	X	X	X	X	X		X	X
Sweitzer Lake State Park (970) 874-4258	21	C-2		X	X		X	X	X		
Sylvan Lake State Park (970) 625-1607	4	C-2	X*[wc]	X			X[1]	X		X	
Tarryall State Wildlife Area (303) 297-1192	14	B-4	X	X	X						
Trinidad State Park (719) 846-6951	30	C-4	X*[wc]	X*	X	X	X[1]	X		X	
Vega State Park (970) 487-3407	4	A-3	X[wc]	X	X	X	X	X			X
Yampa River/Elkhead Res. Legacy Project (970) 824-9473 (Yampa opening Summer, 2000)	2	B-2		X	X	X	X				

* Denotes some designated ADA accessible facilities are available. [1] Denotes ice fishing. [wc] Denotes winter camping.

MOUNTAIN PASSES

Name	Elev.	Page	Grid	Name	Elev.	Page	Grid	Name	Elev.	Page	Grid
Baxter Pass	8,422	3	A-2			34	B-2	Raton Pass	7,834	30	C-4
Berthoud Pass	11,315	10	B-4	Independence Pass	12,095	13	A-4	Red Hill Pass	10,051	14	A-3
Boreas Pass	11,481	14	A-3	Jones Pass	12,451	10	A-4	Red Mountain Pass	11,008	28	A-2
Buffalo Pass	10,180	5	A-3	Kebler Pass	9,980	22	B-2	Ripple Creek Pass	10,343	2	B-3
Cameron Pass	10,276	6	A-3	Kenosha Pass	10,001	14	B-3	Rollins Pass	11,671	10	B-3
		34	A-1	La Poudre Pass	10,200	34	A-1	Schofield Pass	10,707	22	B-2
Coal Bank Pass		28	A-2	La Veta Pass	9,382	30	A-2	Shrine Pass	11,089	13	C-2
				Lizard Head Pass		27	C-2	Slumgullion Pass	11,361	28	B-1
Cochetopa Pass	10,032	29	A-1	Loveland Pass	11,990	14	A-1	Spring Creek Pass	10,901	28	B-1
Columbine Pass	9,120	21	B-3	Los Pinos Pass	10,500	28	C-1	Squaw Pass	9,807	14	C-1
Cordova Pass	11,005	30	B-3	Marshall Pass	10,842	23	B-3	Taylor Pass		4	C-4
Cottonwood Pass	12,126	23	A-2	McClure Pass	8,755	4	B-3	Tennessee Pass	10,404	13	B-3
Crooked Creek Pass	10,002	4	C-2	Milner Pass	10,758	6	B-4	Tincup Pass	12,121	23	A-2
Cucharas Pass	9,941	30	A-3			34	A-2	Troublesome Pass		9	C-1
Cumberland Pass	12,200	23	A-2	Molas Pass	10,910	28	A-2	Trout Creek Pass	9,346	23	B-2
Cumbres Pass	10,022	29	A-4	Monarch Pass	11,312	23	A-3	Ute Pass	9,524	9	C-4
								Ute Pass	9,165	24	A-2
Douglas Pass	8,266	3	A-2	Mosca Pass	9,750	30	A-2	Vail Pass	10,666	13	C-2
Fall River Pass	11,796	6	B-4	Mosquito Pass	13,188	13	C-3	Wauneta Pass	10,280	23	A-3
		34	B-2	Muddy Pass	8,772	5	A-4	Webster Pass	12,096	14	B-2
Fremont Pass	11,318	13	C-3	North Pass	10,149	29	A-1	Weston Pass	11,900	13	C-4
Georgia Pass	11,585	14	A-2	North La Veta Pass	9,413	30	A-2	Wilkerson Pass	9,507	23	C-1
Guanella Pass	11,669	14	B-2	Ohio Pass	10,033	22	B-2	Willow Creek Pass	9,621	5	C-4
Gypsum Gap	6,100	27	A-1	Owl Creek Pass	10,115	22	A-4	Wind River Pass	9,160	34	C-3
Hagerman Pass	11,980	13	B-3	Pass Creek Pass	9,400	30	A-2	Wolf Creek Pass	10,850	28	C-3
Hoosier Pass	11,541	14	A-3	Poncha Pass	9,101	23	B-3	Yellowjacket Pass	7,544	2	A-3
Iceberg Pass	11,827	6	B-4	Rabbit Ears Pass	9,426	5	A-4	* Elevations are approximate			

Colorado Trail Information : The Colorado Trail, at elevations from 5,500 to 13,300 feet, and 469 miles in length offers hikers access to a day hike or an extended backpack through the Rocky Mountains. Maps and guide books are available at Maps Unlimited.

FISHING • HUNTING • WILDLIFE

CALL A COLORADO DIVISION OF WILDLIFE CUSTOMER SERVICE CENTER OR REGIONAL OFFICE FOR GENERAL INFORMATION AND REGIONAL FISHING AND HUNTING INFORMATION:

DENVER SERVICE CENTER
& NORTHEAST REGION OFFICE
6060 Broadway
Denver, CO 80216
(303) 291-7227

COLORADO SPRINGS SERVICE CENTER
& SOUTHEAST REGION OFFICE
2126 N. Weber St.
Colorado Springs, CO 80907
(719) 473-2945

US Fish and Wildlife Service
134 Union Blvd.
Lakewood, CO 80228
(303) 236-7905
www.fws.gov

For fishing seasons, conditions and stocking information, call:

Fishing seasons • (303) 291-7533
Fishing conditions • (303) 291-7534
Fish stocking info • (303) 291-7531

NORTHWEST REGION SERVICE CENTER
711 Independent Ave.
Grand Junction, CO 81505
(970) 255-6100

FORT COLLINS SERVICE CENTER
317 W. Prospect Ave.
Ft. Collins, CO 80526
(970) 484-2836

SOUTHWEST REGION SERVICE CENTER
2300 S. Townsend Ave.
Montrose, CO 81401
(970) 249-3431

Check the web site for additional information: www.dnr.state.co.us/wildlife

FISHING

Licensing and regulation are controlled by the Colorado Division of Wildlife. Other restrictions may apply on Indian or federal reservations or on private property. Fishing licenses can be purchased at most sporting good stores.

GOLD MEDAL WATERS & WILD TROUT WATERS:

Gold Medal Waters are designated lakes and streams offering trophy trout fishing. Wild Trout Waters are populated with self-sustaining fish populations. Check with the Colorado Division of Wildlife for locations. Portions of these streams may be on private land. Maps can be obtained from the National Forest Service or the Bureau of Land Management. Also see Lakes and Reservoirs and State Wildlife Areas.

US FOREST SERVICE
PO Box 25127
Lakewood, CO 80225
(303) 275-5350
www.fs.fed.us

BUREAU OF LAND MANAGEMENT
2850 Youngfield Rd.
Lakewood, CO 80215
(303) 239-3600
www.co.blm.gov

HUNTING

Hunting season information, hunting statistics, forecasts, and licenses for big and small game hunting are obtained through the Colorado Division of Wildlife. Hunter education cards are required for persons born after Jan. 1, 1949. Always ask permission to use private property.

Call the following numbers for information on hunting seasons and hunter education:

Big game • (303) 291-7529
Small game • (303) 291-7546
Upland game • (303) 291-7547
Waterfowl • (303) 291-7548
Hunter education • (303) 291-7530

Visit one of our stores for detailed maps and guides for hunting and fishing areas:

Maps Unlimited
800 Lincoln St.
Denver, CO 80203
(303) 623-4299 or
(800) 456-8703

Maps Unlimited
9955 E. Hampden Ave., Unit 7
Denver, CO 80231
(303) 755-6277

Call or write for a catalog. For online shopping, check our web site at: www.coloradomaps.com

WILDLIFE

The Colorado Division of Wildlife manages over 250 State Wildlife Areas and State Fishing Units to provide havens for wildlife and controlled environments for wildlife research projects. Most properties are open for wildlife observation, hunting, fishing, and trapping. Some also offer opportunities for boating, hiking, camping, and other recreation. State Wildlife Areas (SWA) are marked in this atlas.

COLORADO RECREATIONAL

National Forests and Grasslands are found all over the state, encompassing many different ecological systems. These areas are available for many types of recreational use and to sustain the ecosystem. Most of the areas have public campgrounds.

Forest Service Rocky Mountain Regional Office
Denver (303) 275-5350

For National Forest or Grasslands maps, contact one of our two stores:

Maps Unlimited
800 Lincoln St.
Denver, CO 80203
(303) 623-4299 or
(800) 456-8703

Maps Unlimited
9955 E. Hampden Ave.
Denver, CO 80231
(303) 755-6277

Or check our web site at www.coloradomaps.com

RANGER DISTRICTS & OFFICES
For information about a specific forest, grassland or wilderness area, call the district office in that area.

ARAPAHOE/ ROOSEVELT NATIONAL FORESTS & PAWNEE NATIONAL GRASSLANDS
Supervisor's Office
240 W. Prospect Rd
Fort Collins, CO 80526-2098
(970) 498-2770
TDD (970) 498-2707

Cache la Poudre Wilderness
Comanche Peak Wilderness
Eagles Nest Wilderness
Fraser Experimental Forest
Indian Peaks Wilderness
Mt. Evans Wilderness
Never Summer Wilderness
Rawah Wilderness

Boulder Ranger District
2995 Baseline Rd, Room 110
Boulder, CO 80303
(303) 444-6600

Clear Creek Ranger District
& Visitor Information Center
101 Chicago Creek
PO Box 3307
Idaho Springs, CO 80452
(303) 567-2901
(800) 769-3048
TTY (303) 567-3009

Estes-Poudre Ranger District &
Red Feather Ranger District
1311 S. College Ave
Ft. Collins, CO 80526
(970) 498-2775
TTY (970) 498-1375

Estes Park Office
161 2nd St
Estes Park, CO 80517
(970) 586-3440

Pawnee Ranger District
660 O St
Greeley, CO 80631
(970) 353-5004
(970) 346-5015

Sulphur Ranger District Visitor &
Information Center
62429 US Hwy 40
PO Box 10
Granby, CO 80446
(970) 887-4100
TTY (970) 887-4101

GRAND MESA/UNCOMPAHGRE & GUNNISON NATIONAL FORESTS
Supervisor's Office
2250 Hwy. 50
Delta, CO 81416-8723
(970) 847-7691
TDD (970) 874-6600

Collegiate Peaks Wilderness
La Garita Wilderness
Lizard Head Wilderness
Maroon Bells-Snowmass Wilderness
Mt. Sneffels Wilderness
Raggeds Wilderness
Uncompahgre Wilderness
West Elk Wilderness

Collbran Ranger District
PO Box 330
218 High St
Collbran, CO 81624
(970) 487-3534

Grand Junction Ranger District
764 Horizon Dr
Grand Junction, CO 81506
(970) 242-8211

Grand Mesa Visitor Center
Highway 65 & Forest Rd 121
(970) 244-3300

Norwood Ranger District
1760 E. Grand
PO Box 388
Norwood, CO 81401
(970) 327-4261

Ouray Ranger District
2505 S. Townsend
Montrose, CO 81401
(970) 240-5300

Paonia Ranger District
North Rio Grande Ave
PO Box 1030
Paonia, CO 81428
(970) 527-4131

Taylor River &
Cebolla Ranger Districts
216 N. Colorado
Gunnison, CO 81230
(970) 641-0471
TDD (970) 641-6817

PIKE/SAN ISABEL NATIONAL FORESTS & COMANCHE/CIMARRON NATIONAL GRASSLANDS
Supervisor's Office
1920 Valley Dr.
Pueblo, CO 81008
(719) 545-8737

Collegiate Peaks Wilderness
Holy Cross Wilderness
Lost Creek Wilderness
Mt. Evans Wilderness
Mt. Massive Wilderness

Comanche Grasslands Ranger District
27162 Hwy 287
PO Box 127
Springfield, CO 81073
(719) 523-6591

Comanche National Grassland Office
1420 E. 3rd
La Junta, CO 81050
(719) 545-8737

Leadville Ranger District
2015 N. Poplar
Leadville, CO 80461
(719) 486-0749

Pikes Peak Ranger District
601 S. Weber St
Colorado Springs, CO 80903
(719) 636-1602

Salida Ranger District
325 W. Rainbow Blvd
Salida, CO 81201
(719) 539-3591

San Carlos Ranger District
3170 E. Main
Canon City, CO 81212
(719) 269-8500

South Park Ranger District
PO Box 219
Fairplay, CO 80440
(719) 836-2031

South Platte Ranger District
19316 Goddard Ranch Ct
Morrison, CO 80465
(303) 275-5610

ROUTT NATIONAL FOREST
Supervisor's Office
2468 Jackson St
Laramie WY 82070
(307) 745-3400
(307) 745-2307

Flat Tops Wilderness
Mount Zirkel Wilderness
Neota Wilderness
Platte River Wilderness

Medicine Bow - Routt Annex
29587 W. US 40, Ste. 20
Steamboat Springs, CO 80487
(970) 879-1870

Hahns Peak/Bears Ears Ranger District
57 10th St
Box 771212
Steamboat Springs, CO 80477
(970) 879-1870

Parks Ranger District Kremmling Office
210 S. 6th
Kremmling, CO 80459
(970) 724-9004

Parks Ranger District Walden Office
612 5th St
PO Box 158
Walden, CO 80480
(970) 723-8204

COLORADO RECREATIONAL

Yampa Ranger District
300 Roselawn Ave
Box 7
Yampa, CO 80483
(970) 638-4516

SAN JUAN/ RIO GRANDE NATIONAL FORESTS
Supervisor's Office
1803 W. Hwy. 160
Monte Vista, CO 81144
(719) 852-5941

  La Garita Wilderness
  Lizard Head Wilderness
  South San Juan Wilderness
  Weminuche Wilderness

San Juan/Rio Grande Annex
701 Camino Del Rio
Room 301
Durango, CO 81301
(970) 247-4874

Columbine Ranger District East
367 S. Pearl St
PO Box 439
Bayfield, CO 81122
(970) 884-2512

Columbine Ranger District West
110 W. 11th St
Durango, CO 81301
(970) 385-1283

Conejos Peak Ranger District
15571 County Road T-5
PO Box 420
La Jara, CO 81140
(719) 274-8971

Creede Ranger District
3rd and Creede Ave.
PO Box 270
Creede, CO 81130
(719) 658-2556
TDD (719) 658-0217

Del Norte Ranger District
13308 W. Highway 160
Del Norte, CO 81132
(719) 657-3321

Dolores Ranger District
100 N. 6th
Dolores, CO 81323
(970) 882-7296

Mancos Ranger District
41595 E. Hwy 160
Box 330
Mancos, CO 81328
(970) 882-7130

Pagosa Ranger District
2nd and Pagosa
PO Box 310
Pagosa Springs, CO 81147
(970) 264-2268

Saguache Ranger District
46525 State Highway 114
PO Box 67
Saguache, CO 81149
(719) 655-2547

WHITE RIVER NATIONAL FOREST
Supervisor's Office
9th & Grand
PO Box 948
Glenwood Springs, CO 81602
(970) 945-2521
TDD (970) 945-3255

  Collegiate Peaks Wilderness
  Eagles Nest Wilderness
  Flat Tops Wilderness
  Holy Cross Wilderness
  Hunter Fryingpan Wilderness
  Maroon Bells-Snowmass Wilderness
  Raggeds Wilderness

Aspen Ranger District
806 W. Hallam
Aspen, CO 81611
(970) 925-3445

Blanco Ranger District
317 E. Market
Meeker, CO 81641
(970) 878-4039

Dillon Ranger District
680 Blue River Pkwy
PO Box 620
Silverthorne, CO 80498
(970) 468-5400

Eagle Ranger District
125 W. 5th St
PO Box 720
Eagle, CO 81631
(970) 328-6388

Holy Cross Ranger District
24747 US Hwy. 24
PO Box 190
Minturn, CO 81645
(970) 827-5715

Rifle Ranger District
0094 County Rd 244
Rifle, CO 81650
(970) 625-2371

Sopris District
620 Main St
PO Box 309
Carbondale, CO 81623
(970) 963-2266

L A K E S & R E S E R V O I R S

Name	County	Page	Grid
Abyss Lake	Clear Creek	14	B-2
Adams Lake	Garfield	2	B-4
Adams Lake	Grand	34	B-4
Addison Res	Jackson	5	D-3
Adobe Creek Res	Kiowa/Bent	32	A-1
Lake Agnes	Grand	5	A-4
		34	A-1
Lake Agnes	Jackson	6	A-4
Lake Albert	Jackson	5	A-3
Albert Res	Grand	9	A-1
Alberta Park Res	Mineral	28	C-3
Aldrich Lakes	Rio Blanco	2	A-3
Allen Basin Res	Rio Blanco	2	B-3
Allens Lake	Boulder	11	B-2
Antelope Res	Weld	8	A-3
Antero Res	Park	23	B-2
Aqua Fria Lake	Jackson	5	A-3
Arapahoe Lake	Gilpin	10	B-3
Arrowhead Lake	Larimer	6	B-4
		34	B-2
Aurora Rampart Res	Douglas	15	C-2
Aurora Res	Arapahoe	16	A-1
Lake Avery	Rio Blanco	2	A-4
Azure Lake	Larimer	34	B-2
Bacon Lake	Larimer	11	C-1
Bailey Res	Delta	4	A-4
Baker Lake	Park	14	B-3
Banner Lakes	Weld	12	B-2
Barker Res	Boulder	10	C-3
Barnes Meadow Res	Larimer	6	B-3
Baron Lake	Delta	3	C-4
Barr Lake	Adams	12	A-3
Base Line Res	Boulder	11	B-3
Basin Res	Grand	9	A-1
Bauer Lake	Montezuma	27	B-3
Bear Creek Res	Jefferson	15	B-1
Bear Lake	Jackson	5	A-2

Name	County	Page	Grid
Bear Lake	Lake	13	B-3
Bear Lake	Larimer	10	B-1
		34	B-3
Beartrack Lakes	Park	14	C-2
Beaver Creek Res	Rio Grande	29	A-2
Beaver Creek Res	Rio Grande	28	C-2
Beaver Lake	Eagle	13	A-2
Beaver Lake	Gunnison	4	B-3
Beaver Lake	Jackson	5	B-4
Beaver Lake	Routt	5	A-2
Beaver Res	Boulder	10	C-2
Beaver Res	Gunnison	22	A-2
Beckwith Res	Pueblo	30	B-1
Bee Lake	Larimer	7	C-2
Belmear Lake	Dolores	27	B-2
Bellaire Lake	Larimer	6	C-2
Bergen Res	Jefferson	15	B-1
Big Creek Lakes	Jackson	5	A-1
Big Creek Lakes	Jackson	2	C-1
Big Johnson Res	El Paso	24	B-2
Big Lake	Conejos	29	A-3
Big Lake	Eagle	13	A-2
Big Meadows Res	Mineral	28	C-3
Big Spruce Lake	Eagle	13	A-2
Bighorn Lake	Jackson	5	A-2
Binco Res	Grand	9	A-1
Black Hollow Res	Weld	7	C-3
Black Lake	Summit	9	C-4
Blodgett Lake	Eagle	13	A-3
Blue Lake	Boulder	10	C-2
Blue Lake	Conejos	29	A-3
Blue Lake	Garfield	4	B-2
Blue Lake	Jackson	5	A-2
Blue Lake	Lake	13	A-4
Blue Lake	Larimer	6	A-3
Blue Lake	San Miguel	28	A-2
Blue Lake	Summit	9	C-4

Name	County	Page	Grid
		13	C-3
Blue Mesa Res	Gunnison	22	B-3
Bluebird Lake	Boulder	10	D-1
		34	B-4
Boedecker Lake	Larimer	7	B-4
Boettcher Lake	Jackson	5	B-2
Bolts Lake	Eagle	13	B-2
Bonham Res	Mesa	3	C-3
Bonny Res	Yuma	20	C-2
Boot Lake Res	Adams	12	B-3
Boulder Res	Summit	13	C-1
Boulder Res	Boulder	11	B-2
Bowen Lake	Grand	10	A-1
Bowl of Tears	Eagle	13	B-2
Boxelder Res	Larimer	7	C-2
Boyd Lake	Larimer	7	C-4
Bracher Lake	Gilpin	10	C-3
Brainard Lake	Boulder	10	C-2
Brown Lakes	Hinsdale	28	B-2
Browns Lake	Larimer	6	B-3
Brush Creek Lakes	Custer	23	C-4
Brush Hollow Res	Fremont	24	A-3
Bubble Lake	Summit	9	B-4
Bubbles Lake	Larimer	7	C-2
Buckeye Res	Montrose	21	A-3
Burchfield Res	Baca	32	C-3
Button Rock Res	Boulder	11	A-1
Cabin Creek Res	Clear Creek	14	B-1
Canyon Res	Montezuma	27	B-3
Capote Lake	Archuleta	28	B-4
Carter Lake	Larimer	11	B-1
Case Res	Jackson	5	B-3
Casto Res	Mesa	21	B-2
Lake Catamount	Routt	2	C-3
Chambers Lake	Larimer	6	B-3
Chapman Lake	La Plata	27	C-3
Chapman Lake	Pitkin	13	A-3

NAME	COUNTY	PAGE	GRID
Missouri Lakes	Eagle	13	A-3
Mitchell Lake	Boulder	10	C-2
Model Res.	Las Animas	30	C-3
Mohawk Lake	Summit	13	C-3
Molas Lake	San Juan	28	A-2
Monarch Lake	Grand	10	B-2
Montgomery Res.	Park	13	C-3
Monument Lake	Garfield	4	B-2
Monument Lake	Las Animas	30	B-4
Moore Lake	Clear Creek	10	B-4
Morman Lake	Pitkin	13	A-3
Mormon Res.	La Plata	27	C-4
Morrow Point Res.	Montrose/Gunnison	22	A-3
Morton Lake	Lake	13	B-3
Mountain Home Res.	Costilla	30	A-3
Mountain Lake	Lake	13	C-3
Mt. Elbert Forebay	Lake	13	B-4
Mt. Massive Lakes	Lake	13	B-4
Mulligan Res.	Weld	11	C-1
Mystic Island Lake	Eagle	13	A-2
Lake Nanita	Grand	10	B-1
		34	B-3
Narraguinnep Res.	Montezuma	27	A-3
Naylor Lake	Clear Creek	14	B-1
Navajo Res.	Archuleta	28	B-4
Neegronda Res.	Kiowa	26	B-3
Neenoshe Res.	Kiowa	26	B-3
Neeshah Res.	Kiowa	26	B-3
Neesopah Res.	Kiowa	26	B-3
Neff Lake	Weld	8	A-4
Nelson Res.	Larimer	7	C-4
New York Lake	Eagle	13	A-2
Newell Lake	Weld	11	C-1
Newman Lake	Weld	8	A-4
Lake Nokoni	Grand	10	B-1
		34	B-3
North Catamount Res.	Teller	24	A-2
North Lake	Las Animas	30	B-4
North Michigan Lake	Jackson	6	A-3
North Poudre Res.	Larimer	7	B-2
North Poudre Res. No. 6	Larimer	7	C-2
North Poudre Reservoirs	Larimer	7	C-2
Odessa Lake	Larimer	34	B-3
Orlando Res.	Huerfano	30	B-2
Overland Res.	Delta	4	A-3
Ovo Res.	Moffat	2	A-1
Owl Creek Res.	Weld	8	B-3
Pagoda Lake	Rio Blanco	2	B-3
Palmer Lake	El Paso	15	C-4
Panama Res. No. 1	Boulder	11	B-2
Panhandle Res.	Larimer	6	B-1
Paonia Res.	Gunnison	22	B-2
Park Creek Res.	Larimer	7	B-2
Park Res.	Delta	3	C-4
Parvin Lake	Larimer	6	C-2
Pastorius Res.	La Plata	28	A-4
Patterson Reservoirs	Delta	4	A-4
Peanut Lake	Gunnison	4	B-4
Pear Res.	Boulder	10	C-2
Pearl Lake	Routt	2	C-1
Peggy Lake	Jackson	5	A-2
Peterson Lake	Boulder	10	C-3
Peterson Lake	Larimer	6	B-3
Pettingell Lake	Grand	34	B-3
Pinewood Lake	Larimer	7	B-4
Piney Lake	Eagle	13	B-1
Pipit Lake	Boulder	10	B-1
		34	B-4
Pitkin Lake	Eagle	13	B-1
Platoro Res.	Conejos	29	A-3
Pole Mtn. Lake	Jackson	5	B-3
Poudre Lake	Larimer	34	A-2
Powderhorn Lakes	Hinsdale	22	B-4
Lake Powell	Grand	10	B-1
		34	B-3
Prewitt Res.	Washington	17	C-2
Pristine Lake	Routt	5	A-2
Prospect Res.	Weld	12	B-2
Ptarmigan Lake	Grand	10	B-1
		34	B-3
Ptarmigan Lake	Routt	5	A-2
Pueblo Res.	Pueblo	24	B-4
Puett Res.	Montezuma	27	B-3
Lower Queens Res.	Kiowa	26	B-3
Upper Queens Res.	Kiowa	26	B-3
Quincy Res.	Arapahoe	16	A-1
Rainbow Lake	Custer	23	C-4
Rainbow Lake	Jackson	2	C-2
Rainbow Lake	Jackson	5	A-3
Rainbow Lake	Larimer	34	B-2
Ralph White Res.	Moffat	2	A-2
Ralston Res.	Jefferson	11	B-4
Rampart Res.	El Paso	24	B-2
		33	
Red Canyon Res.	Jackson	5	A-2
Red Deer Lake	Boulder	10	C-2
Red Dirt Res.	Grand	9	A-1
Res. No. 2	Teller	33	
Ridgway Res.	Ouray	22	A-4
Ridings Res.	Jackson	5	B-3
Rifle Gap Res.	Garfield	4	A-2
Rio Blanco Res.	Rio Blanco	1	C-3
Rio Grande Res.	Hinsdale	28	B-2
Riverside Res.	Weld	12	C-1
Road Canyon Res. #1	Hinsdale	28	B-2
Robinson Lake	Eagle	13	C-3
Rock Lake	Hinsdale	28	A-2
Rocky Ridge Lake	Larimer	7	B-3
Round Lake	Jackson	5	A-4
Roxy Ann Lake	Jackson	5	A-2
Ruby Jewel Lake	Jackson	6	A-3
Ruedi Res.	Pitkin	4	C-3
Russell Lakes	Saguache	29	B-1
Ryan Gulch Lake	Larimer	7	B-4
Sage Creek Res.	Routt	2	B-2
Saliba Lake	Huerfano	30	B-2
Salmon Lake	Summit	13	C-1
Lake San Cristobal	Hinsdale	28	B-1
Lake San Isabel	Custer	30	A-1
San Luis Res.	Alamosa	29	C-2
Sanchez Res.	Costilla	30	A-4
Sandbeach Lake	Boulder	10	C-1
Santa Maria Res.	Mineral	28	B-2
Savage Lakes	Pitkin	13	A-3
Sawmill Lake	Jackson	5	A-3
Schraeder Res.	Mesa	21	A-2
Seaman Res.	Larimer	7	B-2
Seeley Lake	Weld	8	A-4
Sellar Lake	Pitkin	13	A-3
Seven Lakes	Jackson	5	A-1
Seven Lakes Res.	Las Animas	30	C-3
Seymour Lake	Jackson	5	B-4
Shadow Mtn. Lake	Grand	34	A-3
Shadow Mtn. Res.	Grand	10	B-1
Shawver Res.	Jackson	5	C-3
Shelf Lake	Clear Creek	14	B-2
Shepherd Lake	Garfield	2	B-4
Sheriff Res.	Rio Blanco	2	B-3
Sherman Lake	Rio Grande	29	B-3
Silver Dollar Lake	Clear Creek	14	B-1
Silver Jack Res.	Gunnison	22	A-4
Silver Lake	Boulder	10	C-2
Skaguay Res.	Teller	24	A-2
Skinny Fish Lake	Garfield	2	B-3
Sky Pond	Larimer	10	B-1
		34	B-3
Skyscraper Res.	Boulder	10	B-3
Slackweiss Res.	Jackson	5	B-4
Slate Lake	Summit	9	C-4
Slide Lake	Jackson	5	A-3
Slide Lake	Lake	13	B-3
Slough Grass Res.	Eagle	9	B-3
Smith Res.	Costilla	29	C-3
Snow Lake	Jackson	6	A-4
		34	A-1
Snowline Lake	Gilpin	10	C-3
Snowmass Lake	Pitkin	4	B-3
Soda Lakes	Jefferson	15	B-1
Spectacle Lakes	Larimer	6	B-4
		34	B-1
Spence Res.	Archuleta	28	C-4
Spinney Mountain Reservoir	Park	23	C-2
Spirit Lake	Grand	10	B-1
		34	B-4
Sprague Lake	Larimer	34	C-3
Spring Creek Res.	Gunnison	4	C-4
Spring Park Res.	Eagle	4	B-2
St. Charles Res.	Pueblo	24	B-4
St. Louis Lake	Grand	10	A-4
St. Mary's Lake	Clear Creek	10	C-4
Stagecoach Res.	Routt	2	C-3
Stalker Lake	Yuma	18	C-3
Standley Lake	Jefferson	11	B-3
Steamboat Lake	Routt	2	C-1
Sterling Res.	Logan	18	A-1
Stillwater Res.	Garfield	2	B-3
Strawberry Lake	Grand	10	B-1
Strontia Springs Res.	Douglas/Jeff	15	B-3
Sullenburger Res.	Archuleta	28	B-3
Summit Lake	Clear Creek	14	B-1
Summit Lake	Montezuma	27	B-3
Sunnyslope Res.	Larimer	11	C-1
Sweetwater Lake	Garfield	2	B-4
Sweitzer Lake	Delta	21	C-2
Sylvan Lake	Eagle	4	C-2
Sylvan Lake	Lake	13	B-3
Sylvan Res.	Grand	9	C-3
Tarryall Res.	Park	14	C-2
Taylor Lake	Gunnison	4	C-3
Taylor Park Res.	Gunnison	23	A-2
Teller Res.	Pueblo	24	B-3
Temple Res. #1	Routt	2	B-2
Terrace Res.	Conejos	29	B-3
Terry Lake	Boulder	11	B-1
Terry Lake	Larimer	7	C-3
The Loch	Larimer	34	A-2
Lake Thomas	Eagle	13	A-2
Lake Thomas	Weld	11	C-1
Thompson Reservoirs	Mesa	3	A-4
Thompson Reservoirs	Mesa	21	A-2
Thorn Lake	Gilpin	10	C-3
Three Island Lake	Routt	5	A-2
Three Island Lake	Routt	2	C-2
Thunder Lake	Boulder	10	B-1
		34	B-4
Thurston Res.	Prowers	26	B-4
Tibbits Lake	Larimer	7	B-2
Timber Lake	Grand	34	A-2
Timberline Lake	Lake	13	B-3
Timnath Res.	Larimer	7	C-3
Totten Res.	Montezuma	27	B-3
Trap Lake	Larimer	6	B-3
Trappers Lake	Garfield	2	B-3
Trinidad Lake	Las Animas	30	C-4
Triple Lakes	Boulder	10	C-2
Trout Lake	San Miguel	27	C-2
Trujillo Meadows Res.	Conejos	29	A-4
Tucker Lake	Jefferson	11	B-4
Tuhare Lakes	Eagle	13	B-2
Turquoise Lake	Lake	13	B-3
Turquoise Lakes	Eagle	13	A-2
Twin Crater Lakes	Larimer	6	A-3
Twin Lake	Jackson	5	A-2
Twin Lakes	Conejos	29	C-4
Twin Lakes	Garfield	2	B-4
Twin Lakes	Larimer	6	B-3
Twin Lakes Res.	Lake	23	A-1
Twin Lakes Res.	Larimer	6	C-3
Two Buttes Res.	Baca	32	B-2
Two Ledge Res.	Jackson	5	B-4
Uneva Lake	Summit	13	C-2
Union Res.	Weld	11	C-2
Upper Camp Lake	Larimer	6	A-2
Upper Cataract Lake	Summit	9	B-4
Upper Coney Lake	Boulder	10	C-2
Upper Homestake Lake	Pitkin	13	B-3
Upper Long Lake	Jefferson	11	B-4
Upper Queens Res.	Kiowa	26	B-3
Upper Slate Lake	Summit	9	C-4
Ute Lake	Jackson	5	A-2
Vallecito Res.	La Plata	28	A-3
Valmont Res.	Boulder	11	B-2
Van Springs Res.	Eagle	4	B-2
Vaughn Lake	Rio Blanco	2	B-3
Vega Res.	Mesa	4	A-3
Lake Verna	Grand	34	B-3
Victoria Lake	Conejos	29	A-4
Walden Res.	Jackson	5	B-2
Wall Lake	Garfield	2	B-4
Walsenburg Res.	Huerfano	30	B-2
Walters Lake	Eagle	9	B-3
Warren Lake	Larimer	7	C-3
Warren Lakes	Pitkin	4	C-3
Welch Res.	Larimer	11	B-1
Wellington Lake	Jefferson	15	A-3
West Arapaho Res.	Jackson	5	B-4
West Lake	Larimer	6	C-2
West Tennessee Lakes	Lake	13	B-3
Whale Lake	Jackson	5	A-3
Wheeler Lake	Park	13	C-3
Whiteley Peak Res.	Grand	9	B-1
Wildcat Res.	Pitkin	4	C-3
Williams Creek Res.	Hinsdale	28	B-3
Williams Fork Res.	Grand	9	C-2
Willow Creek Res.	Grand	10	A-2
Willow Lake	Eagle	2	B-4
Willow Lake	Summit	13	C-1
Windsor Lake	Lake	13	B-4
Windsor Lake	Weld	7	C-3
Windsor Res.	Larimer	7	C-3
Wolford Mtn. Res.	Grand	9	B-2
Wolverine Lake	Routt	5	A-2
Woods Lake	Eagle	4	C-2
Woods Lake	Eagle	13	A-2
Woods Lake	Weld	8	A-3
Wyman Res.	Routt	2	B-3
Ypsilon Lake	Larimer	34	B-1

COLORADO RECREATIONAL

C O L O R A D O   R E C R E A T I O N A L

Name	Zip	Pop.	Elev.	Page	Grid	Name	Zip	Pop.	Elev.	Page	Grid
Abarr			4,230	20	B-2	Brandon	81026		3,930	26	C-3
Agate	80101		5,430	19	B-3	Branson	81027	64	6,298	31	B-4
Aguilar	81020	514	6,400	30	B-3	Breckenridge	80424	1,654	9,603	14	A-2
Akron	80720	1,481	4,662	18	A-3	Breen			7,500	27	C-4
Alamosa	81101	7,739	7,544	29	C-3	Briggsdale	80611		4,840	8	C-3
Alice	80452			10	B-4	Brighton	80601	16,116	4,982	12	A-3
Allenspark	80510			10	C-1					67	....
				34	C-4	Bristol	81028		3,550	32	C-1
Allison			6,250	28	A-4	Broadmoor	80906			24	B-2
Alma	80420	199	10,355	14	A-3					69	....
Almont	81210		8,010	22	C-3	Brook Forest	80439			15	A-2
Alpine (Chaffee)				23	A-2	Brookvale	80439			15	A-1
Alpine (Rio Grande)				29	A-2	Broomfield	80020	31,743	5,420	11	B-2
Alvin				18	C-3					67	....
Americus				23	B-2	Broughton				21	B-2
Ames				27	C-2	Brush	80723	4,723	4,231	17	C-3
Amherst	80721		3,680	18	C-2	Buckeye (Larimer)				7	B-2
Antero Junction			9,220	23	B-2	Buckeye (Baca)				32	C-3
Anton	80801		4,870	20	A-2	Buckingham			4,940	17	B-2
Antonito	81120	871	7,888	29	B-4	Buckskin Joe				24	A-3
Apex				10	C-3	Buena Vista	81211	1,873	7,954	23	B-2
Arapahoe	80802		4,050	26	C-2	Buffalo Creek	80425		6,750	15	B-3
Arboles	81121		6,260	28	B-4	Buford			7,100	2	A-4
Arikaree				20	A-2	Burlington	80807	3,006	4,163	20	C-3
Arlington	81021		4,240	25	C-3	Burns	80426		6,600	4	C-1
Aroya			4,600	26	A-2	Burnt Mill				24	B-4
Arriba	80804	221	5,228	20	A-3	Byers	80103		5,200	16	C-1
Arriola			6,400	27	A-3						
Arvada	m 80002	96,340	5,337	11	B-4	Caddoa				32	A-1
				67	....	Cahone	81320		6,600	27	A-2
Ashcroft				4	C-4	Calhan	80808	646	6,507	24	C-1
Aspen	81611	5,245	7,908	4	C-3	Cameo			4,820	21	B-1
Aspen Park	80433			15	B-2	Camp Bird			9,750	28	A-1
Atwood	80722		3,990	18	A-2	Camp Hale				13	B-2
Ault	80610	1,300	4,940	8	A-3	Campion	80537		5,120	11	B-1
Aurora	m 80010	252,341	5,342	16	A-1	Campo	81029	115	4,339	32	B-4
				67	....	Canfield	80026			11	C-2
Austin	81410			21	C-2	Canon City	81212	14,804	5,332	24	A-3
Avon	81620	2,437	7,430	13	A-1	Capulin	81124		7,810	29	B-3
Avondale	81022		4,550	24	C-4	Carbondale	81623	4,181	6,181	4	B-3
						Caribou	80466			10	C-3
Badito				30	B-2	Carlton			3,530	32	C-1
Bailey	80421		7,750	14	C-3	Carr	80612		5,700	7	C-1
Bakerville				14	B-1	Cascade	80809		7,370	24	B-2
Baldwin				22	B-2					69	....
Balltown				23	B-1	Castle Rock	80104	12,868	6,202	16	A-3
Barela				31	A-4	Cathedral				28	B-1
Barnesville			4,650	8	B-4	Cedar Creek				22	A-3
Barr Lake	80601			12	A-3	Cedar Crest				30	C-2
				67	....	Cedar Point				19	B-3
Bartlett			3,870	32	C-3	Cedaredge	81413	1,742	6,100	21	C-2
Basalt	81621	1,770	6,624	4	B-3	Cedarwood			5,600	30	C-1
Basin				27	B-1	Center	81125	2,378	7,645	29	B-2
Bartlement Mesa				3	C-2	Centerville				23	B-2
Baxter			4,610	24	C-4	Central City	80427	357	8,496	10	C-4
Bayfield	81122	1,576	6,900	28	A-3	Chacra				4	A-2
Bedrock	81411		4,970	21	A-4	Chama	81126		6,420	30	A-4
Beecher Island				20	C-2	Cheney Corner			3,570	32	C-2
Bellevue	80512		5,120	7	B-3	Cheraw	81030	283	4,130	31	C-1
Bennett	80102	1,931	5,483	12	C-4	Cherry Hills Village	80110	6,332	5,380	15	C-1
Bergen Park	80439			15	A-1					37	....
Berthoud	80513	3,904	5,030	11	B-1	Cheyenne Wells	80810	1,067	4,296	26	C-2
Beshoar			5,910	30	C-4	Chimney Rock	81127		6,540	28	B-3
Beulah	81023		6,200	24	B-4	Chipita Park			7,560	24	B-2
Beverly Hills	80104			15	C-2	Chivington	81031		3,890	26	B-3
Black Forest	80908		7,730	24	B-2	Chromo	81128		7,280	28	C-4
				69	....	Cimarron	81220		6,900	22	A-3
Black Hawk	80422	248	8,042	10	C-4	Clark	80428		7,260	2	C-1
Blanca	81123	309	7,746	29	C-3	Clarkville			4,050	18	B-2
Blue Mountain			5,820	1	A-3	Clifford				25	C-1
Blue River	80424	597	10,000	14	A-2	Clifton	81520		4,710	21	B-1
Bonanza		21	9,400	23	B-4	Climax	80429		11,320	13	C-3
Boncarbo	81024		6,870	30	B-4	Coal Creek	81221	179	5,600	24	A-3
Bond	80423		6,710	9	A-3	Coaldale	81222		6,480	23	C-3
Boone	81025	438	4,500	24	C-4	Coalmont	80430		8,200	5	B-3
Boulder	m 80302	90,928	5,363	11	B-2	Cokedale	81032	120	6,200	30	C-4
				67	....	Collbran	81624	272	5,987	21	C-1
Bovina				19	C-3	Colorado City	81019		5,800	30	B-1
Bow Mar	80123	914	5,500	15	C-1	Colorado Springs	m 80903	345,127	6,012	24	B-2
				67	....					69	....
Bowie			5,850	22	A-2	Columbine			8,680	2	C-1
Box Prairie				7	A-3	Columbine Valley	80123	1,200	5,280	15	C-2
Boyero	80806		4,730	26	A-2	Commerce City	80022	17,540	5,150	11	C-4
Bracewell				8	A-4					67	....

COLORADO RECREATIONAL

Name	Zip	Pop.	Elev.	Page	Grid
Como	80432		9,800	14	A-3
Conejos	81129		7,800	29	B-4
Conifer	80433		8,270	15	B-2
Cooper				17	C-3
Cope	80812		4,400	20	A-2
Cornish			6,670	8	C-3
Cortez	81321	8,781	6,200	27	B-3
				33	
Cotopaxi	81223		6,380	23	C-3
Cottonwood				29	C-1
Cowdrey	80434		7,910	5	B-1
Craig	81625	8,504	6,185	2	A-2
Crawford	81415	257	6,800	22	A-2
Creede	81130	432	8,852	28	C-2
Crested Butte	81224	1,079	8,885	22	C-2
Crestone	81131	65	7,863	29	C-1
Cripple Creek	80813	780	9,494	24	A-2
Critchell	80127			15	B-2
Crook	80726	145	3,711	18	B-1
Crowley	81033	261	4,275	25	B-4
Crystola				24	A-2
Cuchara	81055		8,470	30	A-3
Cuchara Junction				30	B-2
Cumbres				29	A-4
Dacono	80514	2,572	5,017	11	C-2
Dailey			4,130	18	B-2
DeBeque	81630	275	4,935	21	B-1
Dearfield				12	C-1
Deckers	80135		6,400	15	B-4
Deer Trail	80105	536	5,183	19	B-3
Deermont	80127			15	B-2
Del Norte	81132	1,725	7,874	29	A-2
Delcarbon				30	B-2
Delhi			5,040	31	B-2
Delta	81416	4,235	4,961	21	C-2
Denver	m 80202	497,840	5,280	11	C-4
				67	
Devine			4,570	24	C-4
Dillon	80435	641	9,156	14	A-1
Dinosaur	81610	354	5,900	1	A-3
Divide	80814		9,160	24	A-2
Dolores	81323	1,038	6,936	27	B-3
Dominguez				21	B-2
Dotsero			6,160	4	B-2
Dove Creek	81324	718	6,843	27	A-2
Dowd			7,750	13	B-1
Doyleville			8,070	23	A-3
Drake	80515		6,160	7	A-4
Dumont	80436		7,950	10	C-4
Dunton			8,840	27	C-2
Durango	81301	13,923	6,512	27	C-3
Eads	81036	729	4,213	26	B-3
Eagle	81631	2,241	6,600	4	C-2
Earl				31	A-3
East Portal			9,200	10	B-3
Eastlake	80614		5,270	11	C-3
				67	
Eastonville				24	B-1
Eaton	80615	2,305	4,839	8	A-3
Eckley	80727	218	3,894	18	B-3
Edgewater	80214	4,598	5,355	11	C-4
				67	
Edwards	81632		7,220	13	A-1
Eggers				6	C-2
Egnar	81325		7,330	27	A-1
El Moro			5,770	30	C-4
El Rancho	80401		7,670	15	A-1
Elba				20	A-2
Elbert	80106		6,720	16	B-4
Eldora	80466		8,700	10	C-3
Eldorado Springs	80025		5,750	11	B-3
Eldredge				22	A-4
Elizabeth	80107	1,175	6,448	16	B-3
Elk Springs	81633		6,370	1	B-3
Ellicott			6,010	24	C-2
Empire	80438	431	8,601	10	B-4
Englewood	m 80110	31,575	5,306	15	C-1
				67	
Erie	80516	1,672	5,038	11	C-2
Escalante				21	B-2
Estes Park	80517	3,989	7,522	6	C-4
				77	C-2
Estrella				29	C-3
Evans	80620	7,160	4,651	8	A-4
*Evergreen	80439	u 6,376	7,040	15	A-1
Fairplay	80440	528	9,953	14	A-4
Farisita	81037		6,960	30	A-2
Fairview				30	A-1
Falcon			6,830	24	B-2
Farmers				8	A-4
Federal Heights	80221	10,572	5,535	11	C-3
				67	
Fenders	80465			15	B-2
Firestone	80520	1,558	4,970	11	C-2
Firstview			4,580	26	B-2
Flagler	80815	562	4,931	20	A-3
Fleming	80728	344	4,240	18	B-2
Florence	81226	3,538	5,187	24	A-3
Florissant	80816		8,170	24	A-2
Ft. Collins	m 80521	104,196	4,984	7	B-3
Ft. Garland	81133		7,936	30	A-3
Ft. Lewis			7,610	27	C-4
Ft. Lupton	80621	5,697	4,914	12	A-2
Ft. Lyon	81038		3,870	32	A-1
Ft. Morgan	80701	10,102	4,330	17	C-3
Fosston			4,900	8	C-3
Fountain	80817	11,823	5,546	24	B-2
Fowler	81039	1,172	4,341	31	B-1
Foxfield	80016			16	A-2
Fox Creek				29	B-4
Foxton	80441		6,460	15	B-3
Franktown	80116		6,120	16	A-3
Fraser	80442	711	8,550	10	A-2
Frederick	80530	1442	4,982	11	C-2
Frisco	80443	2,176	9,097	13	C-2
Fruita	81521	4,285	4,498	21	A-1
Galatea			4,380	26	A-3
Galeton	80622		4,760	8	B-3
Garcia	81134		7,693	29	C-4
Gardner	81040		7,000	30	A-2
Garo			9,180	14	A-4
Gary				17	C-3
Gateview				22	B-4
Gateway	81522		4,590	21	A-3
Gem Village			6,850	28	A-4
Genoa	80818	174	5,602	19	C-3
Georgetown	80444	944	8,519	14	B-1
Gilcrest	80623	1,169	4,754	12	A-1
Gill	80624		4,670	8	B-4
Gillett				24	A-2
Gilman	81634		8,970	13	B-2
Gilpin	80403			10	C-3
Glade Park	81523		6,750	21	A-2
Gladstone			10,600	28	A-2
Glen Haven	80532		7,100	6	C-4
Glendale	80222	2,989	5,350	15	C-1
				67	
Glendevy				6	A-2
Glenisle	80421			14	C-3
Glenwood Springs	81601	7,625	5,746	4	B-2
Glentivar				23	C-1
Gold Hill	80302			11	A-2
Gold Park				13	B-3
Golden	80401	15,021	5,675	11	B-4
				67	
Goodrich			4,380	17	B-3
Gothic				22	C-2
Gould			8,910	6	A-3
Granada	81041	537	3,484	32	C-1
Granby	80446	1,100	7,935	10	A-2
Grand Junction	m 81502	34,540	4,586	21	B-1
Grand Lake	80447	276	8,369	10	B-1
				77	A-3
Grand Mesa				21	C-1
Granite	81228		8,920	23	B-1
Grant	80448		8,580	14	B-2
Great Divide			6,850	1	C-1
Greeley	m 80632	68,593	4,663	8	A-4
Green Mountain Falls	80819	708	7,000	24	A-2
Greenhorn				30	B-2
Greenland	80118			16	A-4
Greenwood Village	80121	12,749	5,422	15	C-1
				67	
Grover	80729	141	5,071	8	C-1

Name	Zip	Pop.	Elev.	Page	Grid
Guadalupe				29	B-4
Guffey	80820		8,660	23	C-2
Gulnare	81042		6,800	30	B-3
Gunnison	81230	5,129	7,703	22	C-3
Gypsum	81637	2,348	6,334	4	C-2
Hahns Peak			8,120	2	C-1
Hale	80730		3,600	20	C-2
Hall				18	A-2
Hamilton	81638		6,240	2	A-2
Hanna				29	A-2
Hanover				24	C-3
Happy Canyon	80101			16	A-3
Harris Park				14	C-2
Hartman	81043	113	3,600	32	C-1
Hartsel	80449		8,860	23	C-1
Hasty	81044		3,870	32	A-1
Haswell	81045	61	4,538	26	A-3
Hawley			3,930	31	C-1
Haxtun	80731	966	4,028	18	B-2
Hayden	81639	1,459	6,336	2	B-2
Hays				31	C-1
Heartstrong			4,050	18	B-4
Heeney			7,870	9	B-3
Henderson	80640		5,020	11	C-3
				67	
Henson				28	B-1
Hereford	80732		5,260	8	C-1
Hermosa			6,640	27	C-3
Hesperus	81326		8,110	27	C-3
Hiawatha			7,200	1	B-1
Higbee				31	C-2
Highlands Ranch	80126			15	C-2
Hillrose	80733	183	4,165	17	C-3
Hillside				23	C-4
Hoehne	81046		5,700	30	C-3
Holly	81047	880	3,397	32	C-1
Holyoke	80734	2,015	3,746	18	C-2
Homelake	81135		7,620	29	B-3
Hooper	81136	121	7,553	29	C-2
Hot Sulphur Springs	80451	388	7,670	9	C-2
Hotchkiss	81419	918	5,351	22	A-2
Houghton				31	B-2
Howard	81233		6,720	23	C-3
Hoyt	80641		4,760	17	B-4
Hudson	80642	1,081	5,024	12	B-2
Hugo	80821	672	5,046	19	C-4
Hygiene	80533		5,090	11	B-1
Idaho Springs	80452	1,996	7,540	10	C-4
Idalia	80735		3,960	20	C-2
Idledale	80453		6,460	15	B-1
				67	
Idywilde				6	B-2
Ignacio	81137	791	6,432	28	A-4
Iliff	80736	185	3,833	18	A-1
Indian Hills	80454		6,840	15	B-1
Irwin				22	B-2
Jamestown	80455	274	6,920	11	A-2
Jansen			6,070	30	C-4
Jaroso	81138		7,568	29	C-4
Jasper				29	A-3
Jefferson	80456		9,500	14	B-3
Joes	80822		4,270	20	B-2
Johnson Village			7,850	23	B-2
Johnstown	80534	2,049	4,820	11	C-1
Julesburg	80737	1,236	3,477	18	C-1
Juniper Hot Springs				1	C-2
Karval	80823		5,070	25	C-2
Keenesburg	80643	669	4,958	12	B-2
Kellytown	80125			15	C-2
Ken Caryl Ranch	80127			15	B-2
				67	
Keota			4,961	17	B-2
Kersey	80644	1,108	4,617	8	B-4
Keystone	80435		9,250	14	A-1
Kim	81049	84	5,690	31	C-3
King Center				25	B-4
Kings Canyon				5	C-1
Kiowa	80117	323	6,347	16	B-3
Kirk	80824		4,220	20	B-2
Kit Carson	80825	301	4,285	26	B-2
Kittredge	80457		6,810	15	B-1
Kline			6,950	27	C-4
Kornman			3,680	32	B-1
Kremmling	80459	1,322	7,364	9	B-2
Kuner				8	B-4
Kutch			5,670	25	B-2
La Garita			7,840	29	B-2
La Jara	81140	734	7,602	29	B-3
La Junta	81050	7,998	4,066	31	C-1
La Plata			9,200	27	C-3
La Salle	80645	1,895	4,676	12	A-1
La Veta	81055	782	7,013	30	B-3
Lafayette	80026	18,784	5,237	11	B-3
				67	
Laird	80739		3,400	18	C-3
Lake City	81235	324	8,671	28	B-1
Lake George	80827		7,980	24	A-2
Lakewood	m 80226	134,999	5,440	15	C-1
				67	
Lamar	81052	8,473	3,622	32	B-1
Laporte	80535		5,060	7	B-3
Larkspur	80118	450	6,680	15	C-4
Las Animas	81054	2,822	3,901	32	A-1
Last Chance			4,780	19	C-2
Lawson	80436		8,120	10	C-4
Lay			6,170	2	A-2
Lazear	81420		5,440	22	A-2
Leadville	80461	2,609	10,152	13	B-3
Leadville Jct				13	B-3
Lebanon			6,672	27	B-3
Lenado				4	C-3
Lewis	81327		6,650	27	A-3
Leyden	80403			11	B-3
Lime				24	B-4
Limon	80828	1,906	5,366	19	C-3
Lindon	80740		4,890	19	C-2
Littleton	m 80120	39,504	5,362	15	C-1
				67	
Livermore	80536		5,800	7	B-2
Lochbuie	80601	1,353	4,980	12	A-3
Log Cabin				6	C-2
Log Lane Village		767	4,330	17	B-3
Logan				17	C-2
Loma	81524		4,510	21	A-1
Lonetree			7,030	28	B-4
Lone Tree(Douglas)	80124			15	2-C
Longmont	80501	58,318	4,979	11	B-2
Los Cerritos				29	C-4
Louisville	80027	17,780	5,350	11	B-3
				67	
Louviers	80135		5,680	15	C-2
Loveland	80537	44,923	4,982	7	C-4
Lucerne	80646		4,750	8	A-4
Ludlow				30	C-3
Lyons	80540	1,435	5,374	11	B-1
Mack	81525		4,520	21	A-1
Madrid				30	C-4
Maher	81421		6,700	22	A-3
Malachite				30	A-2
Malta			9,560	13	B-4
Manassa	81141	1,081	7,683	29	B-4
Mancos	81328	1,020	6,993	27	B-3
Mancos River Trading Post				27	A-4
Manitou Springs	80829	4,835	6,412	24	B-2
				69	
Manzanola	81058	444	4,252	31	B-1
Marble		77	7,950	4	B-3
Marcott				18	B-1
Marigold				24	A-3
Marshall	80303		5,480	11	B-3
Marshdale	80439			15	A-2
Marvel	81329		6,720	27	C-4
Masonville	80541		5,380	7	B-4
Masters			4,490	12	C-1
Matheson	80541		5,780	19	B-4
May Valley			3,710	32	B-1
Maybell	81640		5,920	1	C-2
Mayday			8,080	27	C-3
Maysville				23	B-3
McClave	81057		3,860	32	B-1
McCoy	80463		6,690	9	A-3
McKenzie Junction				30	A-1

Name	Zip	Pop.	Elev.	Page	Grid
Mead	80542	754	5,140	11	C-1
Medina Plaza				30	B-4
Meeker	81641	2,146	6,249	3	C-1
Meeker Park	80510		8,480	10	C-1
Meredith				4	C-3
Merino	80741	238	4,035	17	C-2
Mesa	81643		5,650	21	C-1
Mesita	81142		7,600	29	C-4
Messex				17	C-2
Midland				24	A-2
Midway				32	C-4
Milliken	80543	1,795	4,760	12	A-1
Milner	80477		6,350	2	B-2
Mineral Hot Springs			7,740	23	B-4
Minturn	81645	1,137	7,817	13	B-2
Mishawaka				7	A-2
Mitchell				13	B-3
Model	81059		5,610	31	A-3
Moffat	81143	133	7,561	29	C-1
Molina	81646			21	C-1
Monarch				23	A-3
Monson				30	B-3
Monte Vista	81144	4,487	7,663	29	B-2
Montrose	81401	11,003	5,794	21	C-3
Monument	80132	1,125	6,960	24	B-1
Monument Park			8,523	30	B-4
Morley				30	C-4
Morrison	80465	466	5,800	15	B-1
Mosca	81146		7,550	29	C-2
Mt. Crested Butte	81225	371	8,945	22	C-2
Mt. Princeton Hot Springs			8,100	23	B-2
Mountain View	80212	546		11	C-4
				67	.....
Nast				4	C-3
Nathrop	81236		7,690	23	B-2
Naturita	81422	491	5,431	21	B-4
Nederland	80466	1,247	8,236	10	C-3
Nepesta				24	C-4
New Castle	81647	1,285	5,550	4	A-2
Nine Mile Corner				17	C-3
Niwot	80544		5,090	11	B-2
North Avondale	81022		4,510	24	C-4
North Delta	81416			21	C-2
North La Junta	81050			31	C-1
Northdale				27	A-2
Northglenn	m 80233	29,214	5,460	11	C-3
				67	.....
Norwood	81423	433	7,014	27	B-1
Nucla	81424	715	5,862	21	B-4
Nunn	80648	369	5,185	8	A-2
Nyburg				24	C-4
Oak Creek	80467	665	7,414	2	C-3
Oak Grove				21	C-3
Ohio	81237		8,560	23	A-3
Olathe	81425	1,483	5,346	21	C-3
Olney Springs	81062	360	4,391	25	B-4
Ophir	81426	66	9,280	28	A-2
Orchard	80649		4,400	17	B-3
Orchard City		2,731	5,800	21	C-2
Orchard Mesa	81503			21	B-1
Ordway	81063	1,010	4,312	25	B-4
Otis	80743	450	4,335	18	A-3
Ouray	81427	808	7,706	28	A-1
Ovid	80744	357	3,521	18	C-1
Owl Canyon				7	B-2
Oxford			6,590	28	A-4
Oxyoke	80135			15	B-3
Padroni	80745		4,000	18	A-1
Pagoda			6,570	2	B-3
Pagosa Junction			6,260	28	B-4
Pagosa Springs	81147	1,684	7,079	28	B-3
Palisade	81526	1,979	4,727	21	B-1
Palmer Lake	80133	1,480	7,225	15	C-4
Paoli	80746	30	3,898	18	B-2
Paonia	81428	1,603	5,674	22	A-2
Parachute	81645	707	5,095	3	C-2
Paradox	81429		5,300	21	A-3
Parkdale			5,760	24	A-3
Parker	80134	11,802	5,870	16	A-2
Parlin	81239		7,930	22	C-3
Parma				29	B-3

Name	Zip	Pop.	Elev.	Page	Grid
Parshall	80468		7,560	9	C-2
Peaceful Valley	80540			10	C-2
Peckham			4,720	12	A-1
Peconic				20	C-3
Peetz	80747	188	4,432	18	A-1
Penrose	81240		5,330	24	A-3
Perry Park	80135			15	C-4
Peyton	80831		6,780	24	C-1
Phillipsburg	80127			15	B-2
Phippsburg	80469		7,420	2	C-3
Pierce	80650	917	5,035	8	A-3
Pine	80470		6,770	15	A-3
Pine Junction	80421			15	A-2
Pine Nook	80135			15	C-3
Pinecliffe	80471		8,000	11	A-3
Pinery, The	80134			16	A-2
Pines, The				29	C-1
Pinewood Springs			6,500	11	A-1
Pinneo				17	C-3
Pinon				24	B-3
Pitkin	81241	217	9,241	23	A-3
Placerville	81430		7,300	27	C-1
Platner				18	A-3
Platoro			9,750	29	A-3
Platteville	80651	1,809	4,820	12	A-1
Pleasant View	81331		6,900	27	A-2
Poncha Springs	81242	264	7,469	23	B-3
Portland				24	A-3
Poudre Park			5,676	7	B-2
Powars	80621			12	A-2
Powder Wash			6,700	1	B-1
Powderhorn	81243		8,080	22	B-4
Pritchett	81064	148	4,827	32	B-3
Proctor			3,770	18	A-1
Prospect Valley			4,840	12	C-2
Prowers				32	B-1
Pueblo	m 81002	99,406	4,695	24	B-4
Pueblo West	81007		4,960	24	B-4
Punkin Center			5,360	25	C-2
Purcell			5,010	8	B-3
Querida				30	A-1
Radium			6,910	9	A-3
Ramah	80832	102	6,094	24	C-1
Rand	80473		8,620	5	C-4
Range				4	C-1
Rangely	81648	2,455	5,224	1	A-3
Raymer	80742	109	4,773	17	B-2
Raymond	80540		7,800	10	C-2
Red Cliff	81649	306	8,750	13	B-2
Red Feather Lakes	80545		8,200	6	C-2
Red Mesa			6,550	27	C-4
Red Wing	81066		7,750	30	A-2
Redlands				21	B-1
Redstone			7,180	4	B-3
Redvale	81431		6,470	21	B-4
Rico	81332	119	8,827	27	C-2
Ridgway	81432	588	6,985	22	A-4
Rifle	81650	5,411	5,345	4	A-2
Rio Blanco			7,250	3	C-1
Riverside	80540			11	A-2
Rockport			5,700	8	A-1
Rockvale	81244	346	5,350	24	A-3
Rockwood			7,350	28	A-3
Rocky Ford	81067	4,201	4,178	31	B-1
Roggen	80652		4,700	12	C-2
Rollinsville	80474		8,420	10	C-3
Romeo	81148	379	7,750	29	B-4
Rosita			8,810	30	A-1
Roubideau				21	C-2
Roxborough	80125			15	C-2
Rulison				3	C-2
Rush	80833		6,010	25	B-2
Rustic			7,160	6	C-2
Rye	81069	215	6,900	30	B-1
Saguache	81149	687	7,697	29	B-1
St. Elmo			10,000	23	A-2
Salida	81201	5,029	7,036	23	B-3
Salt Creek				24	B-4
San Acacio	81150		7,820	29	C-4
San Antonio				29	B-4
San Francisco			9,200	30	A-4

Name	Zip	Pop.	Elev.	Page	Grid
San Isabel				30	B-1
San Luis	81152	895	7,965	30	A-4
San Pablo			8,100	30	A-4
Sanford	81151	749	7,560	29	C-3
Sapinero	81247		7,600	22	B-3
Sargents	81248		7,920	23	A-3
Sawpit		63	7,554	27	C-1
*Security	80911	u 18,768	5,730	24	B-2
Sedalia	80135		5,860	15	C-2
Sedgwick	80749	173	3,500	18	B-1
Segundo	81070		6,480	30	B-4
Seibert	80834	180	4,710	20	A-3
Sevenmile Plaza				29	B-2
Severance	80546	227	4,890	8	A-3
Shamballah Ashrama	80135			15	C-3
Sharpsdale				30	A-2
Shawnee	80475		8,150	14	C-3
Sheridan	80110	5,492	5,307	15	C-1
				67	
Sheridan Lake	81071	98	4,283	26	C-3
Sherman				28	B-2
Silt	81652	1,309	5,423	4	A-2
Siloam				24	B-4
Silver Cliff	81249	465	7,982	30	A-1
Silver Plume	80476	152	9,118	14	B-1
Silverthorne	80498	3,031	8,790	13	C-1
Silverton	81433	540	9,318	28	A-2
Simla	80835	571	6,029	19	B-4
Skyway			9,800	21	C-1
Slater	81653		6,540	2	B-1
Slick Rock	81333		5,510	27	A-1
Snowmass	81654		6,880	4	C-3
Snowmass Village	81615	1,441	8,575	4	C-3
Snyder	80750		4,180	17	C-3
Somerset	81434		6,040	22	A-2
South Fork	81154	395	8,180	29	A-2
South Platte	80135			15	B-3
Southern Ute Agency				28	A-4
Spar City			9,440	28	C-2
Spicer				5	B-4
Springfield	81073	1,423	4,365	32	B-3
Sprucedale	80439			15	A-2
Starkville	81074	112	6,360	30	C-4
State Bridge			6,740	9	A-3
Steamboat Springs	80477	6,768	6,695	2	C-2
Stem Beach				24	B-4
Sterling	80751	10,535	3,935	18	A-2
Stoneham	80754		4,600	17	C-2
Stoner			7,480	27	B-2
Stonewall			7,800	30	B-4
Stonington	81075		3,940	32	C-3
Stove Prairie				7	A-3
Strasburg	80136		5,380	12	C-4
Stratton (Kit Carson)	80836	650	4,414	20	B-3
Stratton (Teller)				24	A-2
Sugar City	81076	287	4,308	25	C-4
Sugarloaf	80302			11	A-2
Summitville			11,250	29	A-3
Sunbeam			5,880	1	C-2
Superior	80027	3,377	5,512	11	B-3
				67	
Swink	81077	510	4,118	31	C-1
Tabernash	80478		8,320	10	B-3
Tarryall				23	C-1
Ted's Place			5,240	7	B-3
Telluride	81435	1,476	8,745	28	A-1
Tercio				30	B-4
Texas Creek	81250		6,230	23	C-3
Thatcher			5,420	31	B-3
Thornton	m 80229	67,217	5,433	11	C-3
				67	
Three Bridges				30	B-3
Timnath	80547	220	4,877	7	C-3
Tincup			10,160	23	A-2
Tiny Town	80465		6,480	15	B-1
Tobe			5,850	31	C-4
Tolland				10	C-3
Toonerville			4,170	32	A-2
Toponas	80479		8,280	2	C-3
Torres				29	B-2
Towaoc	81334		5,800	27	A-4
Towner	81080		3,920	26	C-3
Trails End				6	C-1
Trinchera	81081		5,800	31	B-4
Trinidad	81082	8,831	6,025	30	C-4
Truckton				24	C-2
Tungsten	80302			11	A-3
Twin Cedars	80135			15	B-3
Twin Forks	80465			15	B-2
Twin Lakes	81251		9,210	23	A-1
Two Buttes		62	4,125	32	C-3
Tyrone			5,520	31	A-3
Uncompahgre				21	C-3
Uravan	81436		4,990	21	A-3
Utleyville			5,150	32	A-3
Vail	81657	3,925	8,150	13	B-1
Valdez			6,470	30	B-4
Valley View				24	B-4
Valley View Hot Springs				23	C-4
Vanadium				27	C-1
Vancorum			5,340	21	B-4
Vernon	80755		3,930	18	C-4
Vicksburg				23	A-2
Victor	80860	321	9,693	24	A-2
Vigil				30	B-4
Vilas	81087	106	4,158	32	C-3
Villa Grove	81155		7,980	23	B-4
Villegreen	81088		5,500	31	C-3
Vineland			4,640	24	C-4
Virginia Dale	80548		6,970	7	A-1
Vollmar	80621			12	A-2
Vona	80861	103	4,504	20	B-3
Vroman				31	B-1
Wagon Wheel Gap			8,390	28	C-2
Walden	80480	837	8,099	5	C-2
Walsenburg	81089	3,500	6,185	30	B-2
Walsh	81090	689	3,956	32	C-3
Walts Corner				31	B-4
Ward	80481	158	9,253	10	C-2
Waterton (Kassler)	80127		5,500	15	B-2
Watkins	80137		5,530	12	B-4
Wattenberg	80621			12	A-2
Wauneta				18	C-3
Wauneta Hot Springs			8,940	23	A-3
Waverly				7	C-2
Weber				27	B-3
Webster				14	B-2
Weldona	80653		4,340	17	B-3
Wellington	80549	1,362	5,201	7	C-2
West Glenwood				4	B-2
Westcliffe	81252	438	7,888	29	C-1
Westcreek	80135		7,520	15	B-4
Westminster	m 80030	93,115	5,280	11	C-3
				67	
Weston	81091		7,000	30	B-4
Wetmore	81253		5,990	24	A-4
Wheat Ridge	m 80033	29,922	5,445	11	C-4
				67	
White Pine				23	A-3
Whitewater	81527		4,660	21	B-2
Widefield	80911		5,730	24	B-2
Wiggins	80654	637	4,540	17	B-3
Wild Horse (Pueblo)	80862		4,470	24	B-4
Wild Horse (Cheyenne)				26	A-2
Wiley	81092	421	3,731	32	B-1
Willard			4,340	17	C-2
Williamsburg		297	5,380	24	A-3
Windsor	80550	6,818	4,800	7	C-4
Winfield				23	A-2
Winter Park	80482	601	9,110	10	B-3
Wolcott	81655		6,960	13	A-1
Wondervu	80403			11	A-3
Woodland Park	80863	6,179	8,465	24	A-2
Woodrow	80757		4,480	19	C-1
Woody Creek	81656		7,400	4	C-3
Wray	80758	2,053	3,516	18	C-3
Yampa	80483	312	7,892	2	C-3
Yarmony				9	A-3
Yellow Jacket	81335		6,900	27	A-3
Yoder	80864		6,020	24	C-2
Yuma	80759	2,864	4,132	18	B-3

u - denotes an unicorporated area
m - denotes multiple zip codes

COLORADO RECREATIONAL

USEFUL WEB SITES
Pierson Graphics, Corp./ Maps Unlimited
Web site: www.coloradomaps.com

Colorado Travel & Tourism Authority
Phone: (800) COLORADO (265-6736)
Web site: www.colorado.com

Vacation Information for Colorado
Web site: www.coloradoadventure.net

ROAD CONDITIONS
Colorado Department of Transportation
   State Patrol
Phone: (303) 639-1111 (within 2 hours
   from Denver)
(303) 639-1234 (statewide)
Web site: www.cotrip.org/road/road.html

Bridgestone Winter Driving School
PO Box 774167
Steamboat Springs, CO 80477
Phone: (800) 949-7543
Web site: www.winterdrive.com

WEATHER REPORTS & AVALANCHE CONDITIONS
National Weather Service
Phone: (303) 398-3964

Colorado Avalanche Hotline
Phone: (303) 275-5360

Colorado Avalanche Information Center
10230 Smith Road
Denver, CO 80239
Phone: (303) 371-1080
Web site: www.caic.state.co.us

Colorado Dept. of Transportation
Current road and weather conditions
Web site: www.dot.state.co.us

National Weather Service
Web site:
   www.crh.noaa.gov/den/links.html

The Weather Channel
Web site: www.weather.com

AVALANCHE TRAINING
Colorado Mountain Club
710 10th St.
Golden, CO 80401
Phone: (303) 279-3080
Web site: www.cmc.org/cmc

Colorado Outward Bound School
945 Pennsylvania St.
Denver, CO 80203
Phone: (303) 837-0880
Web site: www.cobs.org

Forest Service National Avalanche Center
Web site: www.avalanche.org

International Alpine School
PO Box 3037
Eldorado Springs, CO 80025
Web site: www.nsp.org

National Avalanche School
133 S Van Gordon Street, Suite 100
Lakewood, CO 80228
Phone: (303) 988-1111

National Ski Patrol, Rocky Mountain Division
Web site: www.nsprmd.org

Silverton Avalanche School
San Juan Search & Rescue
Silverton, CO 81433
Phone: (970) 387-5531

ACCOMMODATIONS
American Youth Hostels
Phone: (303) 442-1166
Web site: www.hiayh.org

Bed & Breakfast Innkeepers of Colorado
Phone: (800) 265-7696
Web site: www.innsofcolorado.org

Colorado Dude & Guest Ranch Association
Phone: (970) 887-9248
Web site: www.coloradoranch.com

Colorado Hotel & Lodging Association
Phone: (303) 297-8335
Web site: www.coloradolodging.com

Colorado Hotels on the Web
Web site: www.hotelsontheweb.com/co/co_a.htm

Distinctive Inns of Colorado
Phone: (970) 586-8683

Historic Hotels of the Rockies
Phone: (303) 546-9040
Timeshares By Owner
Phone: (888) 545-SOLD (7653)

10th Mountain Division Hut Association
Phone: (970) 925-5775

GUIDES & OUTFITTERS
Colorado Outfitters Association
Phone: (970) 878-4043
Web site: www.colorado-outfitters.com

RESTAURANTS
Colorado Restaurant Association
Phone: (303) 830-2973
Web site: www.coloradorestaurant.com

SKIING
Colorado Ski Country USA
Phone: (303) 837-0793
Web site: www.skicolorado.org

SKI CONDITIONS
Web site: www.goski.com

Colorado Cross Country Ski Association
Web site: www.colorado-xc.org

Backcountry Skiers Alliance
P.O. Box 134
Boulder, CO 80306
Phone: (303) 443-7839

SNOWMOBILING
Colorado Snowmobile Association
Phone: (800) 235-4480

ROCK & ICE CLIMBING

Name	Page	Grid	City	Phone
Boulder Rock School	11	B-2	Boulder	(303) 447-2804
Colorado Mountian School	6	C-4	Estes park	(303) 586-5758
Front Range Mountian Guides	11	B-2	Boulder	(303) 666-5523
International Alpine School	22	A-4	Ridgway	(970) 626-5722
Ouray Ice Park	28	A-1	Ouray	(970) 325-4925
Southwest Adventures	27	C-3	Durango	(800) 642-5389

HOT SPRINGS

Name	Page	Grid	City	Phone
Box Canyon Hot Springs	28	A-1	Ouray	(970) 325-4981
Cement Creek Ranch	22	C-2	Crested Butte	(970) 349-6512
Cottonwood Hot Springs	23	B-2	Buena Vista	(719) 395-6434
Desert Reef Beach Club	24	A-3	Florence	(719) 784-6134
Dunton Hot Springs	28	A-1	Telluride	(970) 728-4840
Eldorado Springs	11	B-3	Eldorado Springs	(303) 499-1316
Glenwood Springs Hot Springs	4	B-2	Glenwood Springs	(970) 945-6571
Hot Sulphur Springs	9	C-2	Hot Sulpher Springs	(970) 725-3306
Indian Springs Resort	10	C-4	Idaho Springs	(303) 623-2050
Iron Springs Spa	4	B-2	Glenwood Springs	(970) 945-8464
Mount Princeton Hot Springs	23	B-2	Nathrop	(719) 395-2361
Orvis Hot Springs	22	A-4	Ridgway	(970) 626-5324
Ouray Hot Springs Pool	28	A-1	Ouray	(970) 325-4638
Salida Hot Springs Aquatic Center	23	B-3	Salida	(719) 539-6738
Srawberry Hot Springs	2	C-2	Steamboat Springs	(970) 879-0342
Steamboat Springs Health & Recreation Association	2	C-2	Steamboat Springs	(970) 879-1828
The Spa Motel	28	B-3	Pagosa Springs	(970) 264-5910
The Springs at Springs Inn	28	B-3	Pagosa Springs	(970) 264-4168
The Well at Brush Creek	24	A-3	Penrose	(719) 372-9250
The Wiesbaden Hot Springs Spa	28	A-1	Ouray	(970) 325-4347
Trimble Hot Springs	27	C-3	Durango	(970) 247-0111
Valley View Hot Springs	23	B-4	Villa Grove	(719) 256-4315
Waunita Hot Springs Ranch	22	C-3	Gunnison	(970) 641-1266
Yampah Spa	4	B-2	Glenwood Springs	(970) 945-0667

Thank you for selecting this
Pierson Guide

Comments, suggestions, and corrections can now be sent to Pierson Graphics Corp.
via the World Wide Web at: www.coloradomaps.com or Email to: research@coloradomaps.com
800 Lincoln St. • Denver, Colorado • 80203 • Phone (303) 623-4299 • 1-800-456-8703 • Fax (303) 623-7428

Please help us improve the
Pierson Guides.

We value your comments, suggestions and corrections!

Our goal at Pierson Graphics Corp. is to provide you with the most accurate and up-to-date information. After investing many hours of research, cartography and editing to this edition of the *Pierson Guide*, we have provided you with the most comprehensive and accurate recreation road atlas available. However, we acknowledge the potential for errors and omissions that occur when mapping and indexing a large and everchanging geographic location.

Please help us improve future editions of the *Pierson Guides* by sending us any errors or omissions that you may discover.

1. **Which *Pierson Guide* are you using?**
   ❑ Colorado Recreational Road Atlas
   ❑ Denver Regional
   ❑ Metropolitan Denver
   ❑ Boulder/Longmont
   ❑ Northern Colorado Front Range Cities
   ❑ Colorado Springs/Pueblo
   ❑ Colorado Ski Atlas

2. **What page number and grid is the correction on?**
   Page # _____   Grid _____
   Page # _____   Grid _____

3. **Enter corrections here.**
   _____
   _____
   _____
   _____
   _____
   _____
   _____
   _____
   _____

4. **May we contact you about your corrections or suggestions?**
   ❑ Yes
   ❑ No

We would appreciate you taking a few moments to complete this survey. This information will help us serve you better in the future.

1. **Tell us about yourself.**
   Your Name: _____
   Company Name:_____
   Address:_____
   City, State, Zip:_____
   Telephone Number: (   ) _____
   Email Address:_____

2. **Tell us about your *Pierson Guide* purchase.**
   Month/Day/Year:_____
   Place of Purchase:_____
   Edition of *Pierson Guide*: _____

3. **Why did you purchase this *Pierson Guide*?**
   _____
   _____
   _____
   _____

4. **What is your *Pierson Guide* used for?**
   ❑ Personal   ❑ Both
   ❑ Business

5. **What changes or improvements would you like to see in future editions of the *Pierson Guides*?**
   _____
   _____
   _____
   _____
   _____

6. **Are there any products you would like to see Pierson Graphics Corp. publish that would benefit you or your organization?**
   _____
   _____
   _____
   _____

COLORADO RECREATIONAL

BUSINESS REPLY MAIL
FIRST-CLASS MAIL PERMIT NO.183 DENVER, CO

POSTAGE WILL BE PAID BY ADDRESSEE

**PIERSON GRAPHICS CORP
800 LINCOLN ST
DENVER CO 80203-9942**